THE BEST OF TREVOR LYNCH

by

TREVOR LYNCH

EDITED BY GREG JOHNSON

Counter-Currents Publishing Ltd.
San Francisco
2025

Copyright © 2025 by Greg Johnson
All rights reserved

Cover design by
Kevin I. Slaughter

Published in the United States by
COUNTER-CURRENTS PUBLISHING LTD.
http://www.counter-currents.com/

Hardcover ISBN: 978-1-64264-053-3
Paperback ISBN: 978-1-64264-054-0
E-book ISBN: 978-1-64264-055-7

Contents

Preface ❖ iii

1. *Blue Velvet* ❖ 1
2. *The Bridge on the River Kwai* ❖ 17
3. *The Dark Knight Trilogy* ❖ 23
4. *Doctor Zhivago* ❖ 52
5. *Fight Club* ❖ 61
6. *La Dolce Vita* ❖ 71
7. *Lawrence of Arabia* ❖ 81
8. *The Leopard* ❖ 95
9. *The Man Who Shot Liberty Valance* ❖ 107
10. *Mishima: A Life in Four Chapters* ❖ 117
11. *Network* ❖ 130
12. *Once Upon a Time in the West* ❖ 145
13. *Pulp Fiction* ❖ 156
14. *Rashomon &* Realism ❖ 183
15. *The Searchers* ❖ 194
16. *Watchmen* ❖ 203

Index ❖ 219
About the Author ❖ 236

Preface

I have been reviewing films and television series since December of 2001. I began publishing reviews at the *Vanguard News Network*. Since then, I have published at *The Occidental Quarterly Online*, *The Occidental Observer*, *Counter-Currents*, and *The Unz Review*. The reprints of my reviews now fill five volumes spanning about 1,000 pages.[1] A sixth volume is half-way done, and if I complete it, I will begin work on a seventh.

My reviews fall into three categories. First, there are reviews of new movies, which tend to be brief and avoid summarizing too many plot points. Second, there are medium-length reviews, which usually focus on older films that I like a great deal. Third, there are longer-form essays, which generally focus on older films that I particularly like and which contain important political and philosophical messages. These essays contain full plot summaries and deep analyses.

I am proud of all my reviews. Even when I heap scorn on something terrible, I try to have fun with it. But the longer, deeper essays are my best work. I have collected sixteen such essays here, covering eighteen films. If you read these essays carefully, you will discover my entire worldview.

The essays in this volume were first published at *Counter-Currents* and *The Unz Review*. My essays on *Network* and *Once Upon a Time in the West* were originally written

---

[1] *Trevor Lynch's White Nationalist Guide to the Movies* (2012), *Son of Trevor Lynch's White Nationalist Guide to the Movies* (2015), *Return of the Son of Trevor Lynch's CENSORED Guide to the Movies* (2019), *Trevor Lynch: Part Four of the Trilogy* (2020), and *Trevor Lynch's Classics of Right-Wing Cinema* (2022).

in connection with Frodi Midjord's Decameron Film Festival. Thus I wish to thank both Ron and Frodi.

Beyond that, I wish to thank two publishers, one in France the other in Italy, who prompted this collection by expressing an interest in translating some of my film essays.

Moreover, I wish to thank John Morgan, David Zsutty, James J. O'Meara, Collin Cleary, Michael Polignano, Kevin Deanna, the original Trevor, the other Greg, Matthew Peters, Raven Gatto, Tim Belk, Petronius, Alex Graham, Sally Hull, Millennial Woes, and many other friends who can't be named, for their contributions to my work as a reviewer.

Once again, I am grateful to Kevin Slaughter for his superb cover design. I am also grateful to Derek Hawthorne, Kevin MacDonald, Morgoth, F. Roger Devlin, and James J. O'Meara for their promotional quotes. Finally, I wish to thank the readers, writers, commenters, donors, and back office of *Counter-Currents*, who make all my work possible.

This book is dedicated to James O'Meara, one of my favorite film critics.

December 17, 2024

"NOW IT'S DARK"
BLUE VELVET

JEFFREY: I'm seeing something that was always hidden. I'm involved in a mystery. And it's all secret.

SANDY: You like mysteries that much?

JEFFREY: Yeah. You're a mystery. I like you. Very much.

Blue Velvet (1986) is the quintessential David Lynch film, filled with quirky humor and shocking violence. It features one of the most terrifying villains in all of film: Frank Booth, brilliantly portrayed by Dennis Hopper. *Blue Velvet* is a "mystery" story. But it is more than just a crime drama. Sometimes it is described as neo-*noir*. But it is a much darker shade of *noir*.

Blue Velvet is about the great mysteries of life. It is a coming-of-age tale about callow college-boy Jeffrey Beaumont (Kyle MacLaughlin) becoming a man. It is also an initiation tale, with sexual, spiritual, and political dimensions. A good mystery can be engaging but superficial. *Blue Velvet* is powerful and moving because its archetypal, religious, and philosophical themes stir deeper parts of the soul.

Jeffrey's initiation into the mysteries is a descent into the underworld: both a literal, criminal underworld as well as the "deep river" of the unconscious, including obsessive and sadomasochistic sexuality. But Lynch also hints that the unconscious is not merely human, but a portal through which essentially demonic powers enter our world.

Jeffrey conquers and controls these forces, returning

to the sunlit world not only as a man but as a guardian of the social and the family order. In his journey, he has encountered the libidinal, criminal, and demonic forces that can tear society apart, and he has learned about the artifices of civilization that keep chaos at bay. Politically speaking, this is a profoundly conservative vision.

After the nocturnal opening titles, with their elegant script, shimmering blue-velvet backdrop, and lush, Italianate theme music by Angelo Badalamenti, the famous opening sequence sets up the whole story. To Bobby Vinton's oldie "Blue Velvet," we see a clear blue sky, then our eyes descend to red roses in front of the archetypal white picket fence. An old-fashioned firetruck drives by, complete with a Dalmatian and a fireman benevolently waving from the running board, a gesture that subtly puts the viewer in the position of a child. Then we see yellow tulips. A crossing guard carefully shepherds little girls across the street.

It is a vision of childlike wholesomeness and safety. Indeed, all the adults are people charged with keeping the public safe. The guardians of public safety are an important theme in *Blue Velvet* and *Twin Peaks*.

Then we see the modest Beaumont house. Mr. Beaumont is watering the yard. Mrs. Beaumont is watching a crime drama on TV—the first hint of darkness—although the gun on the screen usually elicits a laugh, and it is all tidily contained on the tube. Then we hear an amplified gurgling and see Mr. Beaumont's hose snagged and kinked on a branch. As he yanks the hose, he is suddenly stricken and falls to the ground, water geysering everywhere. Then we see him on his back, a baby in diapers watching as a terrier seems to attack the water squirting from the hose. The film slows, giving the dog both maniacal and mechanical qualities. Then we dive into the well-watered lawn, down to the roots, where in the darkness we find a writhing mass of beetles and other insects fighting and devouring one another.

Next we hear a corny radio jingle, which welcomes us to Lumberton, an idyllic North Carolina logging town, the model for the titular town in *Twin Peaks*, Lynch's next project.

Young Jeffrey Beaumont has been called home from college to visit his stricken father and help run the family hardware store. On the way home from the hospital, Jeffrey discovers a severed human ear in a field. It has greenish splotches of decay on it, and it is crawling with bugs. Bugs, again, are associated with evil.

Jeffrey puts the ear in a paper bag and takes it to Detective Williams (George Dickerson) at the Lumberton Police Department. Detective Williams immediately begins an investigation. He and Jeffrey first take the ear to the morgue, where the medical examiner observes that it had been cut off with scissors. Then they go to the field to search for evidence.

Cut to later that evening. A door opens, and light descends into a darkened stairwell. Jeffrey descends into the darkness as well. His journey into the underworld has begun. He tells his mother (Priscilla Pointer) and fretful aunt Barbara (Frances Bay) that he is going out walking. "You're not going down by Lincoln, are you?" asks aunt Barbara fearfully. Jeffrey says no. It seems a silly prejudice, but later we realize that it was well-founded. Bad things happen down by Lincoln. (Odd that Lynch chose that name, associated with a president unpopular in North Carolina.)

As Jeffrey walks the neighborhood, we cut to a closeup of the ear in the morgue. There is a loud humming as we enter the ear, then everything fades to black. This too is a descent into mystery, into the underworld.

Cut to Jeffrey knocking at the door of the Williams house. Jeffrey wants to know more about the ear, but Detective Williams can't tell him, and asks him not to disclose anything he already knows, until the case is concluded. Detective Williams is stern but warm, a surrogate for Jeffrey's stricken father. He tells Jeffrey that he understands his curiosity. It is what got him into police work in the first place. "It must be great," Jeffrey volunteers. "It's horrible too," he replies. But Jeffrey seems undaunted. He is on a path that may lead him to becoming a guardian of public order, someone who exposes himself to evil, risking his life to serve the common good.

When Jeffrey leaves the Williams house, he hears a voice: "Are you the one that found the ear?" He looks into the darkness. Detective Williams' daughter Sandy (Laura Dern) emerges from the night, a pink-clad blonde vision of loveliness. She is coy and mysterious, teasing Jeffrey with her knowledge of the case.

As they walk together, she tells him that she overheard her father talking. The ear may somehow be connected to the case of Dorothy Vallens (Isabella Rossellini), a singer who lives nearby. Sandy leads Jeffrey to Dorothy's apartment building. With a slightly comic/ominous music cue, the camera pans up to the sign: Lincoln St.

The next afternoon, Jeffrey picks Sandy up after school. They go to Arlene's, a diner that is the prototype of the RR in *Twin Peaks*, right down to the passing logging truck. Jeffrey then tries to involve Sandy in a scheme. He wants to look around Dorothy Vallens' apartment. He will pretend that he is the pest control man, there to spray for bugs (which are of course already associated with darkness and evil). Sandy will pretend to be a Jehovah's witness, with copies of *Awake!* magazine, who will draw Dorothy away, allowing Jeffrey to open one of the windows for a later visit. (There is an interesting Manichean polarity in their covers, mirrored in Jeffrey's near black and Sandy's golden blonde hair.)

How Jeffrey plans to get in a seventh-floor window is

not explained, but he hasn't really thought it out. He doesn't even know Dorothy's name or apartment number without Sandy's help. When we arrive, we see that Dorothy lives in the Deep River Apartments, a nomen that may also be an omen of Jeffrey getting in way over his head. (Betty Elms, in Lynch's *Mulholland Drive*, hails from Deep River, Ontario.)

Dorothy's apartment is pure Lynch: retro, slightly dingy, with dusky pink walls and carpets, dark red draperies (shades of *Twin Peaks*), lavender sofas, magenta cushions, and putrid green accents in the form of pots with spiky "mother in law's tongue" plants. The warm colors have a womblike feel, but the overall effect is seedy and sluttish, not maternal. Jeffrey does not manage to find a window, and before Sandy can knock, Dorothy is visited by a glowering man in a bright yellow sport jacket. But he does manage to pocket an extra pair of keys, hoping they will unlock the apartment.

That evening, Jeffrey takes Sandy to dinner at The Slow Club to watch Dorothy Vallens sing. She doesn't have much of a voice, but she still makes a captivating spectacle, with her huge retro microphone and blue-lit band against dark red draperies, more foreshadowing of *Twin Peaks*. Then Jeffrey and Sandy return to Dorothy's apartment. When Sandy says goodbye, she tells him, "I don't know if you're a detective or a pervert." Jeffrey sneaks inside. When Dorothy comes home suddenly, Jeffrey hides in the closet. Peering through the slats, he watches her undress. It turns out he's both a detective and a pervert.

Dorothy hears a rustling in her closet and confronts Jeffrey with a knife, jabbing him in the cheek when he does not answer one of her questions. She thinks he is a voyeur. But instead of calling the police, she orders him to undress. Then she kneels, with a worshipful look on her face, and pulls down his boxer shorts. She kisses and caresses him but also threatens to kill him, demanding that he neither look at nor touch her. Then she asks if he likes that kind of talk. He doesn't. She tells him to lie down on a couch, following him knife held high like a stage actress. Then she gets on top of him, knife poised, and kisses him.

Terrified by a loud pounding on the door, Dorothy hustles Jeffrey into the closet and orders him to stay silent. Jeffrey is the voyeur again, poised to witness one of the weirdest and sickest scenes in all of cinema. Enter Frank Booth, a middle-aged man in a leather jacket and rockabilly shirt, seething with unfocused rage. Frank and Dorothy then role-play a sexual scenario not unlike the one that has just transpired with Jeffrey, although this time Frank is in control.

Frank's scenario is very specific. Dorothy has to wear a blue velvet robe, provide him with a glass of bourbon, dim the lights and light a candle ("Now it's dark," he says), and sit on a particular chair. He demands that Dorothy not look at him and punches her savagely when she does. (She looks at least three times.) Loosening his inhibitions by swigging the bourbon, then huffing some sort of gas from a cylinder under his jacket, he refers to her as "mommy" and himself as "baby" and "daddy."

He begins by viewing her vagina, then pinching her breasts, then, red-faced and maniacal, he hurls her to the floor, threatens her with a pair of scissors, then pantomimes intercourse, yelling "Daddy's coming home, daddy's coming home."

He has a fetishistic attachment to her blue velvet bathrobe. She stuffs it in his mouth, he stuffs it in her mouth, and he even carries around a piece of it that he has cut from the hem, perhaps with the scissors he uses to threaten her. When it is all over, he blows out the candle. "Now it's dark," he repeats.

As Jeffrey later says, "Frank is a very sick and dangerous

man." A drug dealer, he has kidnapped Dorothy's husband Don and their small boy, Donny, holding them hostage to force Dorothy into sexual bondage. It is Don's ear that Jeffrey found, cut off as a threat to Dorothy, perhaps with the same scissors with which he menaced her. Frank has removed Dorothy's real baby and daddy so he can have "mommy" all to himself.

But Dorothy's own disturbing behavior makes it hard to view her as simply a victim. When Frank screams "Don't you fucking look at me" and punches Dorothy, her head lolls back with an ecstatic smile on her face. When she looks at him again and again, is she asking for it? She herself has forced Jeffrey to strip at knife point, ordering him not to look at or touch her while she looks at and touches him. One way to make someone into an object is to forbid him to be a subject.

When Frank leaves, Jeffrey creeps out of the closet to comfort Dorothy, who first claims she is all right. Then she asks Jeffrey to hold her, referring to him as her husband Don. Either she is delirious or simply playing a role. The latter seems more likely. For without missing a beat, she begins to seduce Jeffrey, asking him to look at her, then touch her . . . then hit her. Now she's *literally* asking for it.

A feminist would automatically claim that Dorothy has been so traumatized by Frank that she is simply reenacting her trauma with Jeffrey. But another possibility suggests itself. Dorothy is very much in control with Jeffrey. She is not so worried about Frank or her husband and son that she cannot start an affair with a new man.

It is interesting that when Jeffrey tells Dorothy that he knows what has happened to her husband and son, she is impassive. She only reacts when he suggests telling the police, and she uses her reaction to finally goad Jeffrey into hitting her.

This awakens something in both of them, represented

by a burst of flames bringing to mind similar effects in Lynch's next movie, *Wild at Heart*, as well as slowing down the film and replacing the sound of their lovemaking by distorted animal shrieks and growls. This is Jeffrey's baptism in the deep river of repressed animal sexuality. Jeffrey is in way over his head, but Dorothy is in firm control.

Did Frank undergo a similar initiation? Was the kidnapping his way of seeking somehow to regain a semblance of control in the throes of an obsession?

Now it's *really* dark.

There are a number of clues that point to Frank's deep sexual abjection. As the "baby" he can pinch Dorothy's breasts. But as "daddy" he merely pantomimes intercourse. Frank may actually be impotent. At least he is with Dorothy.

When Jeffrey returns to The Slow Club, he sees Frank in the audience, fondling his blue velvet fetish, deeply moved by Dorothy's performance, almost at the edge of tears.

The night Dorothy goads Jeffrey into hitting her, he bumps into Frank and his gang as he leaves her apartment. Frank flies into a jealous rage, forcing Jeffrey and Dorothy to go on a "joy ride." At their first stop, Frank says: "This. Is. It." And sure enough, a red neon sign reads: "This Is It."

But it is hard to say what "it" is. It seems like a retirement home for old fat whores. The interior color scheme is very much like Dorothy's apartment. It is littered with beer and prescription bottles and presided over by a flamboyant aging homosexual named Ben, hilariously played by Dean Stockwell, all pursed lips and rolling eyes. Ben is involved with Frank's drug trade and is holding Dorothy's husband and son hostage.

Frank goes on and on about how "suave" Ben is, with his smoking jacket, ruffled shirt, and long cigarette holder.

Every other word is "fuck." When Ben proposes a toast to Frank's health, he hilariously rejects it, suggesting "Here's to your fuck" instead. After transacting some drug business, Frank asks Ben to lip-sync to Roy Orbison's "In Dreams," which Frank childishly refers to as "candy-colored clown," a phrase in the first line of the song.

Ben switches on an inspection light, which he uses as a fake microphone, giving his powdered face a ghastly pallor. One gets the feeling that Ben has done this kind of thing before in a thousand drag shows. When we get to the words, "In dreams you're mine, all the time," Frank's face becomes agitated, and Ben fearfully cuts short the mime. Frank shuts off the tape, Ben shuts off the light, and Frank says, "Now it's dark." Then they make to leave, Frank's departing words: "Let's fuck. I'll fuck anything that moves!"

Next stop is a sawmill near Meadow Lane. Frank begins huffing his gas, then tells Jeffrey, "You're like me." Thanks to Dorothy, that's now truer than Jeffrey would like to think. Then Frank begins to pinch Dorothy's breasts, hurting her. Jeffrey tells Frank "Leave her alone," then punches him in the face. He's already slapped Dorothy around that evening. He's getting comfortable with this.

Frank flies into absolute fury. His henchmen drag Jeffrey out of the car and hold him. There's an ominous industrial thrumming and thumping in the background, as in *Eraserhead*. Frank puts on Dorothy's lipstick then kisses Jeffrey all over his face, saying "pretty, pretty," huffing more fumes, and threatening to kill him if he sees Dorothy again.

While "In Dreams" plays in the car and one of Ben's vacant whores dances on the roof, Frank repeats the words "In dreams, I walk with you. In dreams, I talk to you. In dreams you're mine, all the time. We're together in dreams, in dreams," adding the words "forever in dreams." He places a hand to Jeffrey's ear and "lip-syncs" the words like it is a sock puppet. One thing is for sure: Frank is going to haunt Jeffrey's dreams for the rest of his life. Frank is putting his disease in him.

Frank caresses Jeffrey's face with his blue velvet fetish, wiping off the lipstick. Flexing his biceps, he tells Jeffrey to feel them. "You like that? You like that?" Then Frank begins beating Jeffrey senseless while Dorothy screams. Cut to a guttering candle. And now it's dark.

Frank's constant talk of fucking, as well as merely pantomiming the act with Dorothy, suggest he is impotent. The song "In Dreams" is also about unrequited love for someone who can be possessed only in dreams, itself very close to sexual impotence. Frank's repeated compliments to Ben, as well as the lipstick, kisses, and "feel my muscles" routine with Jeffrey, strongly suggest latent homosexuality.

The guy is a mess.

Jeffrey recovers consciousness in the morning. In addition to the pain of the beating, he feels pangs of guilt as well, for he too has tasted the pleasures of sadism. In some ways, he really is like Frank.

Jeffrey resolves to go to Detective Williams at the police station but discovers that Williams' partner, Detective Gordon, is the "yellow man," one of Frank's partners in crime. That evening, we see Jeffrey emerge from the dark carrying an envelope, suggesting his return from the underworld. He shares his findings with Detective Williams, who begins plotting to take down Frank and his gang.

A couple days pass. It is Friday. Jeffrey waters the lawn, visits his dad, then picks up Sandy to go to a party. They are now officially dating. After the party, they are followed by a menacing car. They think it is Frank, but when the car pulls alongside, Sandy sees that it is her jealous ex-boyfriend Mike. When they pull up to the Beaumont house, Mike threatens to beat up Jeffrey, but then Dorothy Vallens staggers out of the dark, beaten and bloody. Mike stammers out an apology, and Jeffrey and Sandy take Dorothy to the Williams house to call an ambulance.

Sandy cringes in horror as Dorothy calls Jeffrey her "secret lover" and repeats, "He put his disease in me." In truth, Dorothy is the one who put her sadomasochistic disease in Jeffrey.

After Dorothy is taken to the hospital, Jeffrey goes to her apartment and finds evidence of Frank's fury. Dorothy's husband Don is dead, his brains blown out, Frank's strip of blue velvet stuffed in his mouth. The yellow man is standing in the middle of the room in shock, a huge hole blown in the side of his head, brain matter visible. Over the yellow man's police radio, Jeffrey hears that the raid on Frank's apartment has commenced. As Jeffrey leaves, however, he sees Frank approaching the apartment. He rushes back inside, calls for help on the police radio, grabs the yellow man's gun, and hides in the closet.

Frank, who has heard the call on his police radio, bursts into the apartment. Yanking his swatch of blue velvet from Don's mouth and draping it over the silencer of his pistol, then huffing his mysterious fumes, he searches for Jeffrey in the bedrooms, calling out "Here pretty, pretty" like he is summoning a dog. Returning to the living room, he silences the TV and topples the yellow man with bullets, then realizes Jeffrey is in the closet. Huffing more fumes, he ecstatically closes in for the kill, but Jeffrey sees him coming through the slats and shoots him in the head. The voyeur has become an actor.

The slow-motion headshot is accompanied by a terrifying simian shrieking. The bulbs in the floor lamp then surge with electricity and burn out, as if Frank's life force is fleeing through the wiring. In the visual code established in *Eraserhead,* this signifies the presence of the supernatural, especially the demonic. Frank is somehow both more and less than human.

There is a strong spiritual-religious element to *Blue Velvet,* as with all of Lynch's work. Although Lynch himself is a practitioner of Transcendental Meditation, which makes him a Hindu of sorts, the spiritual imagery of his movies tends to be Western, primarily Christian but also Gnostic. I read *Eraserhead,* for instance, as a Gnostic anti-sex film.[1] Like *Eraserhead, Blue Velvet* treats sex as a form of bondage to subhuman powers, both animal and demonic. But *Blue Velvet* is far less nihilistic than *Eraserhead.* The demonic forces are balanced out by angelic ones, represented by robins and light from above, as opposed to electric light, which for Lynch has demonic connotations.

The night after his first terrifying encounter with Frank, Jeffrey tells Sandy what he has seen. Sandy picks him up in her car, an odd role reversal putting her in the driver's seat. She parks near a church with colorful stained-glass windows, brightly lit from inside. Organ music plays in the background.

Jeffrey prefaces the story of Frank and Dorothy with the words, "It's a strange world," which becomes something of a *Leitmotif* in the film. After telling Sandy who Frank is and what he has done, Jeffrey asks "Why are there people like Frank? Why is there so much trouble in this world?" His face is anguished and childlike, for he is just discovering the darkness of the adult world. Jeffrey's question is not merely psychological. Given the backdrop of church and organ music, it is also theological. It is *the* problem of evil: If God is perfect in his power and goodness, why are there people like Frank? Why is there so

---

[1] See my "*Eraserhead*: A Gnostic Anti-Sex Film," in *Return of the Son of Trevor Lynch's CENSORED Guide to the Movies.*

much trouble in this world?

Sandy says she doesn't know the answer. But she does in a way. For she tells Jeffrey of the dream she had the night they met:

> In the dream, there was our world, and the world was dark, because there weren't any robins. And the robins represented love. And for the longest time, there was just this darkness. And all of a sudden, thousands of robins were set free, and they flew down and brought this blinding light of love. And it seemed like that love would be the only thing that would make any difference. And it did. So I guess it means, there is trouble till the robins come.

As Sandy speaks of the blinding light of love, one realizes the organ music is not coming from the church. It is part of the score, underscoring the essentially religious nature of her dream. Love, light from above, and robins are the forces that will beat back hate, darkness, and bugs. Evil is only temporary, until the robins come. Sandy has essentially delivered a religious sermon, sitting in the driver's seat.

After Jeffrey's first encounter with Frank and Dorothy, we see him on the sidewalk. He emerges from darkness. Then he freezes as a light comes from above. Is this the light of judgment? Then we see distorted images of Jeffrey's father in the hospital, then Frank raving, then the guttering candle, then Dorothy saying "Hit me." We then see Frank punch at the camera. Is he hitting Dorothy or Jeffrey at this point? Jeffrey then awakens from a nightmare.

After Jeffrey kills Frank, Sandy, her father, and a legion of police and paramedics arrive on the scene. Even though Jeffrey has rescued himself, we only really breathe again when we see the flashing lights and guardians of order. In the middle of the bustling crime scene, Jeffrey and Sandy embrace and kiss, bathed in white light from above. There is trouble till the robins come.

Cut to an extreme closeup of an ear. Near the beginning of the story, we were drawn into the mystery by entering the dead ear to ominous industrial noise. Now we are at the end of the story, the mystery solved, emerging from a pink and living ear to Julee Cruise's ethereal "Mysteries of Love" (yet another foreshadowing of *Twin Peaks*).

As the camera pulls back, we see that the ear belongs to Jeffrey, sleeping in the sunshine. He opens his eyes and sees a robin perched in a tree. Sandy calls out, "Jeffrey, lunch is ready." Mr. Beaumont is out of the hospital, up on his feet, working on something in the yard with Detective Williams. Jeffrey's mother and Mrs. Williams are chatting together in the living room. The families have come together. It is a sign that Jeffrey and Sandy have a serious relationship. Perhaps marriage is in the future.

Aunt Barbara and Sandy are preparing lunch in the kitchen when the robin appears on the windowsill with a bug squirming in its beak. The forces of good have quelled the forces of evil. "Maybe the robins are here," says Jeffrey.

"I don't see how they could do that. I could never eat a bug" volunteers aunt Barbara, before stuffing something that looks vaguely bug-like in her mouth. Aunt Barbara is a robin without even knowing it. Thus *Blue Velvet* vindicates all guardians of public order, even the silliest and least self-conscious form, namely *prejudice*: "You're not going down by Lincoln, are you?"

"It's a strange world, isn't it?" observes Sandy.

Then we see the yellow tulips, the friendly fireman, and the red roses. But before we return to the blue sky, we see Dorothy Vallens and her little boy in a park. She picks him up and holds him, smiling, although her face then takes on a sad and haunted look.

It is the happiest ending possible after such a hellish journey.

What is the political philosophy of *Blue Velvet*? I read Lynch as fundamentally conservative. The typical sneering Leftist take on Lynch's opening is that the idyllic surface of Lumberton is fake and kitschy, whereas the truth about Lumberton is the bloody struggle of vermin in the dark. But Lynch's own view is far more nuanced.

Lynch knows that civilization is artificial, a construct, a triumph over nature. But Lynch is not a liberal or a Leftist because he does not think that nature is good. Thus he does not conclude that the conventions that constrain nature are bad. Lynch thinks that nature is profoundly dangerous, especially sex and sadism, which for him have a supernatural, demonic quality. Lynch does not believe in the "natural goodness" of man. He believes in the natural—and supernatural—badness of man. Which means that human nature needs to be constrained by human conventions.

Frank Booth is Lynch's portrait of what you get when nature is liberated by the breakdown of social repressions. The French Revolution ended with the Terror. The Sixties ethic of sex, drugs, and rock-and-roll didn't lead us back to the Garden of Eden. It gave us the Tate-LaBianca murders, the Weathermen, and Frank Booth.

Frank is not just a sex maniac. He is a drug dealer. His partner in crime, Ben, sells both sex and drugs. Frank uses alcohol and also his mysterious gas to break down his inhibitions and release his sadism. Moreover, Frank always has his Roy Orbison soundtrack tape handy. Finally, to channel F. Roger Devlin for a moment, Dorothy Vallens can also be seen as an example of the havoc created by female narcissism, masochism, and hypergamy when social conventions break down.[2]

Sade knew human nature better than Rousseau.

Many viewers note that the robin at the end is clearly fake, some sort of puppet. It might simply have been the best effect that Lynch could create with the available budget. But it could very well have been intentional. The bugs represent hate and evil whereas the robins represent love and goodness. The bugs are darkness; the robins are light. If the bugs represent nature, then the robins have to represent something other than nature. In Sandy's dream, they clearly have a supernatural aspect.

But another opposite of nature is convention, in which case it makes sense to have an obviously artificial robin. The robin represents the conventions that hold the savagery of nature in check, including the guardians of public order: the police, firemen, paramedics, even the crossing guards. These conventions also include moral principles, manners, and even aunt Barbara's prejudices.

Although *Blue Velvet* was Lynch's fourth feature film, it was really the first where he had both creative control and an adequate budget. (Well, maybe not for the robin.) *The Elephant Man* (1980) and *Dune* (1984) gave Lynch adequate funding but no creative control. *Eraserhead* (1977) was entirely Lynch's baby, but he created it over a period of years on a shoestring budget. It is a measure of Lynch's genius that the very first time he had the financial and creative freedom to fully realize his vision, he created what is arguably his greatest film. Certainly it is his most Lynchian.

The Unz Review, July 26, 2019

---

[2] See F. Roger Devlin's *Sexual Utopia in Power* (San Francisco: Counter-Currents, 2015).

THE BRIDGE ON THE RIVER KWAI

David Lean's *The Bridge on the River Kwai* (1957) is not just a great film, it is a nearly perfect one. Even better, it was recognized as such from the start by virtually everyone. The critics lionized it and continue to include it on their "best" lists. The movie business showered it with prizes. *Bridge* won seven Oscars, including best picture and best director. Audiences made it the biggest film of 1957 and a perennial favorite ever since.

Bridge was Lean's twelfth film and his first "epic," which cast the die for the rest of his career. It was followed by *Lawrence of Arabia* (1962) and *Doctor Zhivago* (1965), also classics. Then Lean ended his career with *Ryan's Daughter* (1970) and *A Passage to India* (1984), which fail as films in part because their slighter stories were overwhelmed by Lean's epic style of treatment, which had hardened into mannerisms.

Bridge might have shared the same fate because of its source material. Lean's film adapts Pierre Boulle's best-selling 1952 novel *Le Pont de la rivière Kwaï*. (Boulle is also famous for another novel that made it to the screen as *Planet of the Apes*.) The novel is set in Japanese-occupied Thailand during the Second World War. The Japanese are building a railroad to connect Bangkok with Rangoon using forced labor, both native civilians and British prisoners of war.

The British prisoners in a particular camp are tasked with building a bridge over the river Kwai. The main conflict is between the Japanese camp Commander Saito and British Lt. Colonel Nicholson. Saito demands that officers do manual labor. This being contrary to the military code, Nicholson refuses, and he and his officers are punished. Naturally, the construction project is plagued by sabotage.

Saito eventually relents because he needs the cooperation of the British officers to finish the bridge on schedule.

Nicholson then marshals his men in order to build a better bridge than the Japanese could have done. Nicholson appeals to legalism, *esprit de corps*, and British chauvinism—but they all fall short of a case for enthusiastic collaborationism. The core of the novel is the absurdity of a man who collaborates with the enemy out of a misplaced sense of duty. It is not clear if Nicholson is supposed to be an imbecile or a madman, but he's definitely something of a buffoon: a snob, a bore, a martinet, and ultimately a traitor.

Most Brits who read the novel found it to be offensive and rather tasteless: offensive, because it comes off as a crude Gallic lampoon of the British national character, especially the British military; tasteless, because approximately 13,000 prisoners of war died during the construction of the railway, plus up to 100,000 of the local civilians. It is just not something to be treated lightly.

Lean followed Boulle's plot fairly faithfully. The main departure—the destruction of the bridge at the end of the film—was approved by Boulle. Where Lean departed from Boulle is his treatment of the character of Nicholson. Lean turned Nicholson from a buffoon into a tragic hero worthy of Sophocles or Shakespeare. In Lean's eyes, Nicholson stands for genuine virtues: patriotism, loyalty, duty, and pride in one's work, as well as obedience to law, authority, and moral principles. He wouldn't be a tragic hero unless he had genuine virtues.

Nicholson's "tragic flaw" is that he does not see that his virtues only really make sense when practiced among his own people, for their benefit. In the prison camp, however, these virtues are being exploited by a ruthless enemy who aims to destroy the empire that Nicholson so loyally fought to preserve. There's a lesson in this for white people today, since our openness to strangers, altruism, and moral idealism are being exploited by a system that is destroying us as well.

The Bridge on the River Kwai is masterful at exploring the fundamental distinction between the aristocratic ethos that prizes honor above all else and the bourgeois ethos that prizes comfort, security, long life, and pleasure above all else.

G. W. F. Hegel famously claims that history begins with a battle to the death over honor, in which two men are willing to risk their lives for an idea. Prehistory is governed by the necessities of life. History is governed by ideas. If both men prize honor above life, and one is defeated, he will choose death before dishonor. But if the defeated party chooses life at the price of honor, he is revealed to be a very different kind of man who is reduced to the status of a slave, to toil for the victor.

This is exactly how Japanese Commander Saito (played by Sessue Hayakawa) sees the matter. By surrendering, the British have lost their honor and have been reduced to slaves, including the officers, thus all must work. Saito will not spare the officers from the full measure of their disgrace because of a mere legalism that forbids imprisoned officers from doing manual labor, as if they were still gentlemen. To him, the Geneva Convention is nothing compared to the Japanese warrior code of *bushido*. The Japanese military felt superior to the British because the Japanese still committed suicide to avoid the dishonor of defeat, whereas the British, being a Christian nation, rejected suicide and used legalisms to preserve their honor even in defeat.

The dispute between Saito and Nicholson—brilliantly portrayed by Alec Guinness—becomes another struggle to the death over honor. Saito puts Nicholson in a metal box in the blazing sun to break his will, but he refuses to relent and do manual labor, even if it kills him. Unfortunately for Saito, the bridge is behind schedule, the Japanese engineer is incompetent, and the prisoners are at best sullen workers, at worst prone to malingering and sabotage.

If the bridge is not completed on schedule, Saito will be expected to commit suicide, a fate that he wishes to avoid. Thus Saito uses the anniversary of the Japanese victory over Russia as the occasion for a face-saving amnesty. Nicholson and his officers will not have to labor but will organize their men to complete the bridge on time. The roles have been reversed. Nicholson has chosen death over dishonor, and Saito has flinched, choosing dishonor over death. It is Nicholson's high point. After that, his fall begins.

Nicholson's quest to build a better bridge than the Japanese also makes sense in terms of Hegel's master-slave dialectic. Nicholson has beaten Saito on an essential point of honor. But he is still a prisoner, and his men are still slaves. However, Hegel describes a pathway by which the slave can restore his self-respect and humanity. The master rules over men, including slaves. The slave, however, can make himself a master over nature, which is what Nicholson and his men do by building the bridge, and doing it better than the Japanese could. Saito is shamed by this, and even though the bridge is completed on time, he still plans to kill himself.

But in a deeper sense, the Japanese have still won, because they got their bridge, which is an important strategic asset in their war against the British. Next stop: India.

Since both Saito and Nicholson are master types, albeit at times "temporarily embarrassed" master types, the film needs a well-developed slave type as a contrast. The American studio wanted a big American star to appeal to American ticket buyers. Enter William Holden as the American Commander Shears. (In the novel, Shears is British.) The Americans also wanted a love interest to appeal to chicks. Lean groaned, because war stories are guy stories. (Lean got his way on his next film, *Lawrence of*

Arabia, in which there are no speaking roles for women.)

Lean gave in to the studio but turned defeat into victory, because the character of Commander Shears is a brilliant encapsulation of the slave type: cowardly, dishonest, and cynical about honor. Shears' character is brought into sharper focus by making him an American, since America is a thoroughly bourgeois society that took pride in throwing off European aristocratic civilization, although vestiges of its ethos survived among the military and Southern planters. Making Shears a womanizer to boot perfected the character. But don't fear: Shears has a redemption arc and chooses death over dishonor in the end. There is still hope for the Yanks.

By making an American the voice of cynicism, cowardice, and dishonesty, Lean also perfects another trait of the film. Inverting Boulle's Gallic snark, Lean's *Bridge* valorizes the British character and especially the British military. Lean's politics are a bit complicated. He was conservative, patriotic, and despised communism. He was a tax exile for years because he also despised the British Labour Party.

But Lean was also drawn to such anti-colonial, anti-imperialistic figures as T. E. Lawrence and Gandhi. (Lean wanted to make a movie about Gandhi and actually met Nehru to discuss the project.) Yet in films like *Bridge* and *Lawrence of Arabia*, Lean presents the British Empire in a highly flattering light.

A Passage to India is anti-Imperialist, but these sentiments are primarily expressed by two repulsive liberal females, whose desire to mix with the natives creates chaos for all involved. So in the end, it subtly affirms the wisdom of the colonial regime remaining aloof from the natives.

Like every Lean film, *The Bridge on the River Kwai* is a first-class production. The cast is excellent, with particularly distinguished performances by Alec Guinness (who won the Oscar for best actor), William Holden, and Jack Hawkins. The musical score by Malcolm Arnold is one of his best and was duly rewarded with an Oscar. The striking locations in Ceylon were captured by cinematographer Jack Hildyard, who also received an Oscar, as did editor Peter Taylor.

The script of *Bridge*, which also won the Oscar for best adaptation, is a masterpiece. Originally, the script was credited to Boulle, who didn't even speak English. Boulle's name was there in place of two blacklisted writers, Carl Foreman and Michael Wilson. But everything that makes the script deep and powerful is the work of David Lean.

I have talked about the central themes of *Bridge*, but I have left out a great deal of the story, because I want you to enjoy discovering it for yourself. But I should warn you that, although *The Bridge on the River Kwai* is a beautiful and entertaining spectacle, it is also gut-wrenchingly tragic. This makes the film's popularity all the more remarkable. It is proof that even "the masses" are not satisfied by mere entertainment. They hunger for deep feelings, even painful ones, if they are stirred by an encounter with deep truths about the human condition.

The Unz Review, June 18, 2021

THE DARK KNIGHT TRILOGY

Batman Begins

In *Batman Begins* (2005), director Christopher Nolan breaks with the campy style of earlier Batman films, focusing instead on character development and motivations. This makes the film psychologically dark and intellectually and emotionally compelling.

Nolan's cast is superb. I was disappointed to learn that David Boreanaz—the perfect look, in my opinion—had been cast as Batman right up until the part was given to Christian Bale. But it is hard to fault Bale's Batman. He may be too pretty. But he has the intelligence, emotional complexity, and heroic physique needed to bring Batman to life. (Past Batmans Adam West, Michael Keaton, and George Clooney were jokes, but Val Kilmer was an intriguing choice.)

Batman Begins also stars Michael Caine, Gary Oldman, Liam Neeson, Cillian Murphy, Ken Watanabe, Rutger Hauer, and Morgan Freeman as one of those brilliant black inventors and mentors for confused whites so common in science fiction.

Batman Begins falls into three parts. In the first part we cut between Bruce Wayne in China and flashbacks of the course that brought him there. I despise the cliché that passes for psychology in popular culture today, namely that a warped psyche can be traced back to a primal trauma. So I was annoyed to learn that young Bruce Wayne became obsessed with bats when he fell down a well and was swarmed by them, and that he became a crime-fighter because his wealthy parents were gunned down in front of him by a mugger. Haunted by these traumas, billionaire Bruce Wayne ended up dropping out of Princeton to immerse himself in the criminal underworld, eventually ending up in a brutal prison somewhere in the Himalayas.

Wayne is released by the mysterious Mr. Ducard—played by the imposing and charismatic Liam Neeson—who oversees his training in a mysterious fortress run by "The League of Shadows," an ancient order of warrior-ascetics led by Ra's al Ghul (Ken Watanabe). The League follows the Traditional teaching that history moves in cycles, beginning with a Golden Age and declining into a Dark Age, which then collapses and gives place to a new Golden Age. The mission of the League of Shadows is to appear when a civilization has reached the nadir of decadence and is about to fall—and then give it a push. (Needless to say, they do not have a website or a Facebook page. Nor can one join them by sending in a check.)

The League's training is both physical and spiritual. The core of the spiritual path is to confront and overcome one's deepest fears using a hallucinogen derived from a Himalayan flower. In a powerful and poetic scene of triumph, Bruce Wayne stands unafraid in the midst of a vast swarm of bats. The first time I watched this, I missed the significance of this transformation, which is an implicit critique of "trauma" psychology, for traumas are shown to be ultimately superficial compared with the heroic strength to stand in the face of the storm. It is, moreover, perfectly consistent with the conviction that nature is ultimately more powerful than nurture.

Bruce Wayne accepts the League's training but in the end rejects its mission. He thinks that decadence can be reversed. He believes in progress. He and Ducard fight. Ra's al Ghul is killed. The fortress explodes. Wayne escapes, saving Ducard's life. Then he calls for his private jet and returns to Gotham City.

In act two, Bruce Wayne becomes Batman. Interestingly enough, Batman is much closer to Nietzsche's idea of the "Superman" than the Superman character is. Superman isn't really a man to begin with. He just looks like us.

His powers are just "given." But a Nietzschean superman is a man who makes himself more than a mere man. Bruce Wayne conquers nature, both his own nature and the world around him. As a man, he makes himself more than a man.

But morally speaking, Batman is no *Übermensch*, for he remains enslaved by the sentimental notion that every human life has some sort of innate value. He does not see that this morality negates the worth of his own achievement. A Batman can only be suffered if he serves his inferiors. Universal human rights, equality, innate dignity, the sanctity of every sperm: these ideas license the subordination and ultimately the destruction of everything below—or above—humanity. They are more than just a death sentence for nature, as Pentti Linkola claims. They are a death sentence for human excellence, high culture, anything in man that points above man.

Of course Batman's humanistic ethic has limits, particularly when he makes a getaway in the Batmobile, crushing and crashing police cars, blasting through walls, tearing over rooftops. Does Bruce Wayne plan to reimburse the good citizens of Gotham, or is there a higher morality at work here after all?

In act two, Batman begins to clean up Gotham City and uncovers and unravels a complex plot. In act three, we learn who is behind it: the League of Shadows. We learn that Neeson's character Ducard is the real Ra's al Ghul, and he and the League have come to a Gotham City tottering on the brink of chaos—to send it over the edge. Of course Batman saves the day, and Gotham is allowed to limp on, sliding deeper into decadence as its people lift their eyes towards the shining mirages of hope and eternal progress that seduce and enthrall their champion as well.

Batman Begins is a dark and serious movie, livened with light humor. It is dazzling to the eye. The script was co-authored by Christopher Nolan and Jewish writer-director David Goyer. There are a few politically correct touches, such as Morgan Freeman (although I find it impossible to dislike Morgan Freeman) and the little fact that one of Wayne's ancestors was an abolitionist, but nothing that really stinks.

Batman Begins touches on many of the themes that I discerned in my reviews of Guillermo del Toro's *Hellboy* and *Hellboy II*.[1] Again, the villains seem to subscribe to the Traditionalist, cyclical view of history; they hold that the trajectory of history is decline; they believe that we inhabit a Dark Age and that a Golden Age will dawn only when the Dark Age is destroyed; and they wish to lend their shoulders to the wheel of time. That which is falling, should be pushed. The heroes, by contrast, believe in progress. Thus they hold that a better world can be attained by building on the present one.

This is a rather elegant and absolutely radical opposition, which can be exploited to create high stakes dramatic conflict. What fight can be more compelling than the people who want to destroy the world versus the people who want to save it?

This raises the obvious question: Who in Hollywood has been reading René Guénon and Julius Evola—or, in the case of *Hellboy*, Savitri Devi and Miguel Serrano? For somebody inside the beast clearly understands that a weaponized Traditionalism is the ultimate revolt against the modern world.

Counter-Currents, September 23, 2010

The Dark Knight

Batman Begins generates a dramatic conflict around the highest of stakes: the destruction of the modern world

---

[1] In Trevor Lynch's *White Nationalist Guide to the Movies*.

(epitomized by Gotham City) by the Traditionalist "League of Shadows" versus its preservation and "progressive" improvement by Batman.

Batman's transformation into a Nietzschean *Übermensch* was incomplete, for he still accepted the reigning egalitarian-humanistic ethics that devalued his superhuman striving and achievements even as he placed them in the service of the little people of Gotham.

This latent conflict between an aristocratic and an egalitarian ethic becomes explicit in Nolan's breath-taking sequel *The Dark Knight* (2008), which is surely the greatest supervillain movie ever. (The greatest superhero movie has to be Zack Snyder's *Watchmen* [2009], reviewed later in this volume.)

Philosophizing with Dynamite

The true star of *The Dark Knight* is Heath Ledger as the Joker. The Joker is a Nietzschean philosopher. In the opening scene, he borrows Nietzsche's aphorism, "Whatever doesn't kill me, makes me stronger," giving it a twist: "I believe whatever doesn't kill you, simply makes you . . . *stranger*." Following Nietzsche, who philosophized with a hammer, the Joker philosophizes with knives as well as "dynamite, gunpowder, and . . . gasoline!"

Yes, he is a criminal. A ruthless and casual mass murderer, in fact. But he believes that "Gotham deserves a better class of criminal, and I'm going to give it to them. . . . It's not about money. It's about sending a message. Everything burns." In this, the Joker is not unlike another Nietzschean philosopher, the Unabomber, who philosophized with explosives because he too wanted to send a message.

The Joker's message is the emptiness of the reigning values. His goal is the transvaluation of values. Although he initially wants to kill Batman, he comes to see him as a kindred spirit, an alter ego: a fellow superhuman, a fellow freak, who is still tragically tied to a humanistic morality. Consider this dialogue:

> **BATMAN**: Then why do you want to kill me?
>
> **THE JOKER**: I don't want to kill you! What would I do without you? Go back to ripping off mob dealers? No, no, NO! No. *You . . . you . . . complete me.*
>
> **BATMAN**: You're garbage who kills for money.
>
> **THE JOKER**: Don't talk like one of them. You're not! Even if you'd like to be. To them, you're just a freak, like me! They need you right now, but when they don't, they'll cast you out, like a leper! You see, their morals, their code, it's a bad joke. Dropped at the first sign of trouble. They're only as good as the world allows them to be. I'll show you. When the chips are down, these . . . these civilized people, they'll eat each other. See, I'm not a monster. I'm just ahead of the curve.

The Joker may want to free Batman, but he is a practitioner of tough love. His therapy involves killing random innocents, then targeting somebody Batman loves.

DEATH, AUTHENTICITY, & FREEDOM

The basis of the kinship the Joker perceives between himself and Batman is not merely a matter of eccentric garb. It is their relationship to death. The Joker is a bit of an existentialist when it comes to death: "in their last moments, people show you who they really are." Most people fear death more than anything. Thus they flee from it by picturing their death as somewhere "out there," in the future, waiting for them. But if you only have one death, and it is somewhere in the future, then right now, one is immortal. And immortal beings can afford to live foolishly and inauthentically. People only become real when they face death, and they usually put that off to the very last minute.

The Joker realizes that there is something scarier than death, and that is a life without freedom or authenticity.

The Joker realizes that mortality is not something waiting for him *out there* in the future. It is something that he carries around *inside him* at all times. He does not need a *memento mori*. He feels his own heart beating.

Because he knows he can die at any moment, he *lives* every moment.

He is *ready* to die at any moment. He accepts Harvey Dent's proposal to kill him based on a coin toss. He indicates he is willing to blow himself up to deter the black gangster Gambol—and everybody believes him. He challenges Batman to run him down just to teach him a lesson.

In his mind, the Joker's readiness to die at any moment may be his license to kill at any moment.

The Joker can face his mortality, because he has learned not to fear it. Indeed, he has come to love it, for it is the basis of his inner freedom. When Batman tries to beat information out of the Joker, he simply laughs: "You have nothing, nothing to threaten me with. Nothing to do with all your strength." Batman is powerless against him, because the Joker is prepared to die.

The Joker senses, perhaps mistakenly, that Batman could attain a similar freedom.

What might be holding Batman back? Could it be his conviction of the sanctity of life? In *Batman Begins*, Bruce Wayne breaks with the League of Shadows because he refuses the final initiation: taking another man's life. Later in the movie, he refuses to kill Ra's al Ghul (although he hypocritically lets him die). In *The Dark Knight*, Batman refuses to kill the Joker. If that is Batman's hang-up, the Joker will teach him that one can only live a more-than-human life if one replaces the love of mere life with the love of liberating death.

LESSONS IN TRANSVALUATION

Many of the Joker's crimes can be understood as moral experiments and lessons.

1. When the Joker breaks a pool cue and tosses it to Gambol's three surviving henchmen, telling them that he is having "tryouts" and that only one of them (meaning the survivor) can "join our team," he is opposing their moral scruples to their survival instincts. The one with the fewest scruples or the strongest will to survive has the advantage.

2. The Joker rigs two boats to explode, one filled with criminals and the other with the good little people of Gotham. He gives each boat the detonator switch to the other one, and tells them that unless one group chooses to blow up the other by midnight, he will blow up both boats. Again, he is opposing moral scruples to survival instincts.

The results are disappointing. The good people cannot act without a vote, and when they vote to blow up the other ship, not one of them has the guts to follow through. They would rather die than take the lives of others, and it is clearly not because they have conquered their fear of death, but simply from a lack of sheer animal vitality, of will to power. Their morality has made them sick. They don't think they have the right to live at the expense of others. Or, worse still, they all live at the expense of others. This whole System is about eating one another. But none of them will own up to that fact in front of others.

Batman interprets this as a sign that people "are ready to believe in goodness," i.e., that the Joker was wrong to claim that, "When the chips are down, these . . . these civilized people, they'll eat each other." The Joker hoped to put oversocialized people back in touch with animal vitality, and he failed. From a biological point of view, eating one another is surely healthier than going passively to one's death *en masse*.

3. The Joker goes on a killing spree to force Batman to take off his mask and turn himself in. Thus Batman must choose between giving up his mission or carrying on at the cost of individual lives. If he chooses to continue, he has to regard the Joker's victims as necessary sacrifices to serve the greater good, which means that humans don't have absolute rights that trump their sacrifice for society.

4. The Joker forces Batman to choose between saving the life of Rachel Dawes, the woman he loves, or Harvey Dent, an idealistic public servant. If Batman's true aim is to serve the common good, then he should choose Dent. But he chooses Dawes because he loves her. But the joke is on him. The Joker told him that Dawes was at Dent's location, so Batman ends up saving Dent anyway. When Batman tells the Joker he has "one rule" (presumably not to kill) the Joker responds that he is going to have to break that one rule if he is going to save one of them, because he can save one only by letting the other die.

5. As Batman races towards the Joker on the Batcycle, the Joker taunts him: "Hit me, hit me, come on, I want you to hit me." The Joker is free and ready to die at that very moment. Batman, however, cannot bring himself to kill him. He veers off and crashes. The Joker is willing to die to teach Batman simply to kill out of healthy animal anger, without any cant about rights, due process, or other moralistic claptrap.

6. Later in the film, Batman saves the Joker from falling to his death. He could have just let him die, as he did Ra's al Ghul. The Joker says:

> Oh, you. You just couldn't let me go, could you? This is what happens when an unstoppable force

meets an immovable object. You are truly incorruptible, aren't you? . . . You won't kill me out of some misplaced sense of self-righteousness. And I won't kill you because you're just too much fun. I think you and I are destined to do this forever.

Again, one has the sense that the Joker would have been glad to die simply to shake Batman out of his "misplaced sense of self-righteousness."

At the risk of sounding like the Riddler:

Q: What do you call a man who is willing to die to make a philosophical point?

A: A philosopher.

Materialistic versus Aristocratic Morals

Modern materialistic society is based on two basic principles: that nothing is worse than death and nothing is better than wealth. Aristocratic society is based on the principles that there are things worse than death and better than wealth. Dishonor and slavery are worse than death. And honor and freedom are better than wealth.

We have already seen that the Joker fears death less than an inauthentic and unfree life. In one of the movie's most memorable scenes, he shows his view of wealth. The setting is the hold of a ship. A veritable mountain of money is piled up. The Joker has just recovered a trove of the mob's money—for which he will receive half. Tied up on top of the pile is Mr. Lau, the money launderer who tried to abscond with it.

One of the gangsters asks the Joker what he will do with all his money. He replies: "I'm a man of simple tastes. I like dynamite, and gunpowder, and . . . gasoline." At which point his henchmen douse the money with gasoline. The Joker continues: "And you know what they all have in common? They're cheap." He then lights the pyre and addresses the gangster: "All you care about is money. Gotham deserves a better class of criminal, and I'm going to give it to them."

Aristocratic morality makes a virtue of transforming wealth into something spiritual: into honor, prestige, or beautiful and useless things. Trading wealth for spiritual goods demonstrates one's freedom from material necessity. But the ultimate demonstration of one's freedom from material goods is the simple destruction of them.

The Indians of the Pacific Northwest practice a ceremony called the "Potlatch." In a Potlatch, tribal leaders gain prestige by giving away material wealth. However, when there was intense rivalry between individuals, they would vie for honor not by giving away wealth but by destroying it.

The Joker is practicing Potlatch. Perhaps the ultimate put-down, though, is when he mentions that he is only burning *his share* of the money.

THE MAN WITH THE PLAN

Gotham's District Attorney Harvey Dent (played by Nordic archetype Aaron Eckhart) is a genuinely noble man. He is also a man with a plan. He leaves nothing up to chance, although he pretends to. He makes decisions by flipping a coin, but the coin is rigged. It has two heads.

The Joker kidnaps Harvey Dent and Rachel Dawes and rigs them to blow up. He gives Batman the choice of saving one. He races off to save Dawes but finds Dent instead. Dawes is killed, and Dent is horribly burned. Half his face is disfigured, and one side of his coin (which was in Rachel's possession) is blackened as well. Harvey Dent has become "Two-Face."

The Joker, of course, is a man with a plan too. Truth be told, he is a criminal mastermind, the ultimate schemer. (Indeed, one of the few faults of this movie is that his elaborate schemes seem to spring up without any time for preparation.) When the Joker visits Dent in the hospital, however, he makes the following speech in answer to Dent's accusation that Rachel's death was part of the Joker's plan.

> Do I really look like a guy with a plan? You know what I am? I'm a dog chasing cars. I wouldn't know what to do with one if I caught it. You know, I just . . . *do* things.
>
> The mob has plans, the cops have plans. . . . You know, they're schemers. Schemers trying to control their little worlds. I'm not a schemer. I try to show the schemers how pathetic their attempts to control things really are. . . . It's the schemers that put you where you are. You were a schemer, you had plans, and look where that got you. I just did what I do best. I took your little plan and I turned it on itself. Look what I did to this city with a few drums of gas and a couple of bullets. Hmmm?
>
> You know . . . You know what I've noticed? Nobody panics when things go "according to plan." Even if the plan is horrifying! If, tomorrow, I tell the press that, like, a gang banger will get shot, or a truckload of soldiers will be blown up, nobody panics, because it's all "part of the plan." But when I say that one little old mayor will die, *well then everyone loses their minds!*
>
> Introduce a little anarchy. Upset the established order, and everything becomes chaos. I'm an agent of chaos. Oh, and you know the thing about chaos? It's fair!

The Joker's immediate agenda is to gaslight Harvey Dent, to turn Gotham's White Knight into a crazed killer. "Madness," he says, "is like gravity. All you need is a little push." This speech is his push, and what he says has to be interpreted with this specific aim in mind. For instance, the claim that chaos is "fair" is clearly *a propos* of Dent's use of a two-headed coin because he refuses to leave anything up to chance. (Chaos here is equivalent to chance.) Dent's reply is to propose to decide whether the Joker lives or dies based on a coin toss. The Joker agrees, and the coin comes up in the Joker's favor. We do not see what happens, but the Joker emerges unscathed and Harvey Dent is transformed into Two-Face.

THE CONTINGENCY PLAN

But the Joker's speech is not merely a lie to send Dent over the edge. In the end, the Joker really isn't a man with a plan, and the clearest proof of that is that *he stakes his life on a coin toss*. Yes, the Joker plans for all sorts of contingencies, but he knows that the best laid plans cannot eliminate contingency as such. But that's all right, for the Joker embraces contingency as he embraces death: it is a principle of freedom.

The Joker is in revolt not only against the morals of modernity, but also its metaphysics, the reigning interpretation of Being, namely that the world is ultimately transparent to reason and susceptible to planning and control. Heidegger called this interpretation of Being the *"Gestell,"* a term which connotes classification and arrangement to maximize availability, like a book in a well-ordered library, numbered and shelved so it can be located and retrieved at will. For modern man, "to be" is to be susceptible to being classified, labeled, shelved, and available in this fashion.

Heidegger regarded such a world as an inhuman hell, and the Joker agrees. When the Joker is arrested, we find that he has no DNA or fingerprints or dental records on file. He has no name, no address, no identification of any kind. His clothes are custom made, with no labels. As Commissioner Gordon says, there's "nothing in his pockets but knives and lint." Yes, the system has him, but has nothing on him. It knows nothing about him. When he escapes, they have no idea where to look. He is a book without a barcode: unclassified, unshelved, unavailable . . . free.

For Heidegger, the way to freedom is to meditate on the origins of the *Gestell*, which he claims are ultimately mysterious. Why did people start thinking that everything can be understood and controlled? Was the idea cooked up by a few individuals and then propagated according to a plan? Heidegger thinks not. The *Gestell* is a transformation of the *Zeitgeist* that cannot be traced back to individual thoughts and actions, but instead conditions and leads them. Its origins and power thus remain inscrutable. The *Gestell* is an *"Ereignis,"* an event, a contingency.

Heidegger suggests that etymologically *"Ereignis"* also has the sense of "taking hold" and "captivating." Some translators render it "appropriation" or "enown-ing." I like to render it "enthrallment": The modern interpretation of Being happened, we know not why. It is a dumb contingency. It just emerged. Now it enthralls us. We can't understand it. We can't control it. It controls us by shaping our understanding of everything else. How do we break free?

The spell is broken as soon as we realize that the idea of the *Gestell*—the idea that we can understand and control everything—cannot itself be understood or controlled. The origin of the idea that all things can be understood cannot be understood. The sway of the idea that all things can be planned and controlled cannot be planned or controlled. The reign of the idea that everything is necessary, that everything has a reason, came about as sheer, irrational contingency.

The Joker seeks to break the power of the *Gestell* not merely by *meditating* on contingency, but by *acting from it*, i.e., by *being* an irrational contingency, by being an agent of chaos.

He introduces chaos into his own life by acting on whim, by just "doing things" that don't make sense, like "a dog chasing cars": staking his life on a coin toss, playing chicken with Batman, etc. When Batman tries to beat information out of the Joker, he tells him that "The only sensible way to live in this world is without rules."

Alfred the butler understands the Joker's freedom: "Some men aren't looking for anything logical, like money. They can't be bought, bullied, reasoned, or negotiated with. Some men just want to watch the world burn."

The Joker introduces chaos into society by breaking the grip of the System and its plans.

He is capable of being an agent of chaos because of his relationship to death. He does not fear it. He embraces it as a permanent possibility. He is, therefore, free. His freedom raises him above the *Gestell*, allowing him to look down on it . . . and laugh. That's why they call him the Joker.

IN ALL SERIOUSNESS

I like the Joker's philosophy. I think he is right. "But wait," some of you might say, "the Joker is a monster! Heath Ledger claimed that the Joker was 'a psychopathic, mass murdering, schizophrenic clown with zero empathy.' Surely you don't like someone like that!"

But remember, we are dealing with Hollywood here. In a "free" society we can't suppress dangerous truths altogether. So we have to be immunized against them. That's why Hollywood lets dangerous truths appear on screen, *but only in the mouths of monsters:* Derek Vinyard in *American History X*, Travis Bickle in *Taxi Driver*, Bill the Butcher in *Gangs of New York*, Ra's al Ghul in *Batman Begins*, the Joker in *The Dark Knight*, etc.

We need to learn to separate the message from the messenger, and we need to teach the millions of people who have seen this movie (at this writing, the seventh biggest film of all time) to do so as well. Once we do that, the film ceases to reinforce the system's message and reinforces ours instead. That's what I do best. I take their propaganda and turn it on itself.

What lessons can we learn from *The Dark Knight*?

Batman Begins reveals a deep understanding of the fundamental opposition between the Traditional cyclical view of history and modern progressivism, envisioning a weaponized Traditionalism (The League of Shadows) as the ultimate enemy of Batman and the forces of progress.

The Dark Knight reveals a deep understanding of the moral and metaphysical antipodes of the modern world: the Nietzschean concept of master morality and critique of egalitarian slave morality, allied with the Heideggerian concept of the *Gestell* and the power of sheer irrational contingency to break it.

The Joker weaponizes these ideas, and he exploits Batman's latent moral conflict between Nietzschean self-overcoming and his devotion to human rights and equality.

In short, somebody in Hollywood understands who the System's most radical and fundamental enemy is. They know what ideas can destroy their world. It is time we learn them too.

Let's show these schemers how pathetic their attempts to control us really are.

Counter-Currents, September 27, 2010

THE DARK KNIGHT RISES

The Dark Knight Rises, the third and final film of Christopher Nolan's epic Batman trilogy, does not equal *The Dark Knight*—which was scarcely possible anyway—but it is a superb piece of filmmaking. It is a better film than *Batman Begins* and develops the characters and themes of both previous films into a tremendously satisfying and deeply moving conclusion.

Christian Bale, Gary Oldman, Michael Caine, Morgan Freeman, and Cillian Murphy reprise their roles from the earlier films. Michael Caine steals the film whenever he appears on screen. New cast members include ravishing minx Anne Hathaway as the Cat Woman, the hulking, charismatic Tom Hardy as Batman's nemesis Bane, Marion Cotillard as Miranda Tate/Talia, and Joseph Gordon-Leavitt (the least Jewish-looking Jew since William Shatner) as (Robin) John Blake.

Aside from Hans Zimmer's insipid and forgettable score, this is a superbly made film, artistically and technically. It would be a shame if people did not see *The Dark Knight Rises* in theaters because of a madman's shooting rampage on opening night in Aurora, Colorado. (Many of the audience members in Aurora demonstrated, by the way, that heroism is not just for the movies.) You need to see this film on the big screen. Lightning doesn't strike twice, right?

Although I will discuss isolated elements of the plot, including the epilogue, I will say only this about the plot as a whole: the League of Shadows returns to destroy Gotham, and Batman returns to stop them. What I wish to focus upon are the larger themes of the movie, particularly those that run through the whole trilogy. The continuities between *Batman Begins* and *The Dark Knight Rises* are easy to see, since the League of Shadows is Batman's opponent in both movies. The continuities between *The Dark Knight* and the rest of the series are not so obvious, but they are deep and important.

Traditionalism

In *Batman Begins*, the young Bruce Wayne is rescued

from a brutal prison in the Himalayas by Henri Ducard a.k.a. Ra's al Ghul (Arabic for "head of the demon," played by Liam Neeson), a member of the League of Shadows, a secret brotherhood of warrior-initiates whose headquarters is somewhere high in the Himalayas.

The League of Shadows believes in the Traditional view of history. History moves in cycles, and its trajectory is decline. A historical cycle begins with a Golden Age or Age of Truth (Satya Yuga) in which mankind lives in harmony with the cosmic order. As mankind falls away from truth, however, society declines through Silver and Bronze Ages to the fourth and final age: the Iron or Dark Age (Kali Yuga), which dissolves of its own corruptions, after which a new Golden Age will arise.

The purpose of the League of Shadows is to hasten the end of the Dark Age and the dawn of the next Golden Age. Thus when a civilization is falling, they appear to give it a final push into the void: Rome, Constantinople, and now Gotham. And in every case, these are not mere cities, but cities that stand for entire civilizations. Thus the League of Shadows is here to destroy nothing less than the whole modern world.

In *Batman Begins*, the League of Shadows trains Bruce Wayne as an initiate, but he rebels before his final test and flees back to Gotham, where he reinvents himself as Batman. The League, however, follows him to Gotham to destroy the city, which is rife with corruption and decadence. Batman defeats them and kills Ra's al Ghul, but in *The Dark Knight Rises*, the League of Shadows returns under new leadership to finish the job.

"DO YOU WANNA KNOW HOW I GOT THESE SCARS?"

When the League of Shadows finds Bruce Wayne, he is a young man almost at the end of the road to self-destruction. Wayne is destroying himself due to his inability to deal with the scars of his past. His primal traumas include seeing his parents murdered by a mugger, as well as an inordinate fear of bats.

In addition to rigorous physical training, the League of Shadows also involves spiritual initiation. One such exercise involves the use of a hallucinogen derived from a Himalayan flower to confront and overcome one's deepest fears.

Another exercise is to transcend the world's ruling morality—the egalitarian notion that all human beings have some sort of intrinsic value—by killing a man. We are told he is a murderer and deserving of death. But Wayne thinks that even a murderer has value and thus deserves more than mere summary justice. He has rights to due process. So Wayne balks at this test and ends up killing quite a few members of the League of Shadows in the process. But he has no trouble with that, because they are "bad" people who don't believe in due process and the American way.

When Bruce Wayne returns to Gotham, he is an incomplete initiate. He has overcome the traumas of his past, giving him superhuman courage. His training in martial arts has given him superhuman abilities. But he has not rejected egalitarian humanism. He still subjects himself to the conventional morality. He is, in short, a superhero: a superhuman being who lives to serve his inferiors out of a sentimental sense of humanity.

Now this might not be such a bad thing, if the people he served actually looked up to him and honored him as their superior. But they are egalitarians too, thus they resent their superiors, even if they are their benefactors.

In *The Dark Knight*, the Joker is a portrait of a fully achieved *Übermensch*. (Remember that Hollywood only allows superior men to appear as monsters, because to people today, they *are* monsters.) Like Batman, the Joker has overcome the scars of his past—literal scars, in the case of the Joker. When the Joker tells people how he got his scars, he spins a new story each time. As James O'Meara brilliantly suggested, this shows that the Joker has overcome his past.[2] He tells different stories because, to him, it does not matter how he got his scars. He has transcended them—and, as we shall see, everything else in his past.

Unlike Batman, however, the Joker has also gone beyond egalitarian humanism. He is psychologically free from his past and morally free from the yoke of serving his inferiors. As I argued in my essay on *The Dark Knight*, the Joker's crimes need to be seen as moral experiments to break down Batman's commitment to egalitarian humanism.

The Joker has all the traits of a fully realized initiate, but he doesn't exactly seem to be a team player. But of course we don't know how the Joker came to be the way he is, because that is part of the past he has transcended.

In *The Dark Knight Rises*, eight years have passed since the death of Harvey Dent/Two-Face. Batman's final act of self-sacrifice for the city of Gotham was to accept responsibility for Two-Face's crimes in order to preserve Harvey Dent as a symbol of incorruptible commitment to justice. Batman has disappeared, but Gotham's organized crime problem has been solved by the Dent Act, which provides for the indefinite detention of criminals.

The lie has, however, taken its toll on its architects: Bruce Wayne and Commissioner Gordon. Commissioner Gordon has lost his wife and family. Bruce Wayne has hung up his Batman costume and lives in seclusion in Wayne Manor, in mourning for Rachel Dawes, who he thought was waiting for him even though she had chosen to marry Harvey Dent. Wayne Enterprises is in a shambles, defaulting on its obligations to its shareholders and

---

[2] James J. O'Meara, "Andy Nowicki's *The Columbine Pilgrim*," Counter-Currents, March 23, 2011.

the public at large.

In short, Bruce Wayne has returned to his state at the beginning of *Batman Begins*: he is destroying himself because he cannot deal with the traumas of his past, and he is dragging everyone else down with him. Wayne is not just psychologically crippled; he is also physically crippled, walking with a cane.

When the League of Shadows returns, Wayne gets a leg brace, dusts off his Batman costume, and goes out to fight them. But Alfred warns him that despite his technological crutches, he is spiritually and physically incapable of beating Bane, who fights with the strength of belief, the strength of an initiate in the League of Shadows. And Bruce Wayne is no longer an initiate.

Alfred is right. When Bane and Batman finally clash, Bane trounces Batman, twisting his spine and then casting him into a vast pit in some god-forsaken place in Central Asia. The pit is a prison. It is open to the surface, which adds to the torment of the prisoners, who can see the world above but cannot reach it. Only one person has ever managed to climb out. Many others have died trying.

In the darkness, Wayne has to physically and spiritually rebuild himself. It is a recapitulation of his original initiation with the League of Shadows. It also recapitulates the initiation of one of his opponents, who was born in the pit and eventually climbed out as a child. Wayne masters his fear again and escapes, rising from darkness to light, the cave to the real world: perennial symbols of spiritual initiation. In this case, however, Wayne masters fear not by suppressing it but by using it. By dispensing with the safety of the rope, he reactivates his fear and uses it as motive power to make the final leap.

Having been effectively re-initiated by the League of Shadows, Wayne is now able to fight and defeat them. The message could not be clearer: technology cannot make us superhuman without the underlying spiritual preparation of initiation.

INITIATION & SUPERHUMANISM

What is the connection between Nietzschean superhumanism, which is emphasized in *The Dark Knight*, and Traditionalist initiation, which is emphasized in the other two films?

I understand Traditionalism ultimately in terms of the nondualistic interpretation of Vedanta: the height of initiation is the mystical experience of the individual soul's identity with Being, the active principle of the universe. In our ordinary human consciousness, we experience ourselves as finite beings conditioned by other finite beings, including our traumas; these are our scars. When we experience our identity with Being, however, our finite bodies are infused with the active, creative, infinite power: the source of all things. This gives the initiate the power to overcome his merely finite, conditioned self, as well as other finite beings. Thus Traditionalists have their own supermen: the yogic adepts who attain magical powers (*siddhis*) through consciously experiencing their identity with Being.

Being is one, thus it is beyond all dualities, including the duality of good and evil. Thus the initiate who achieves mystical unity with Being rises beyond good and evil. He also rises beyond egalitarianism, since there is a fundamental difference between the initiated and the uninitiated. Finally, he rises above humanism, since he realizes that individual humans have no intrinsic worth or being. We are merely roles that Being plays for a while, masks that Being assumes and then discards. And if the initiate's role in the cosmic play is to negate millions of these nullities, what's the harm in that? Being itself cannot die, and its creative power is infinite, so there's always more where they came from.

In sum, on the nondualist Vedantic model, the culmination of initiation in a mystical experience of the identity of the self with Being leads to: (1) the infusion of superhuman powers, (2) the overcoming of external conditions, including one's past, (3) a view of the world beyond all dualities, including good and evil, and (4) the overcoming of egalitarian humanism.

Batman and the Joker display some of these traits, although nothing close to the essentially magical powers ascribed to yogic adepts. Batman, of course, never goes beyond good and evil, beyond egalitarian humanism. And the Joker, who has achieved moral liberation, does not display any superpowers, although he is remarkably accomplished.

"Nothing in his pockets but knives and lint."

When the Joker is arrested in *The Dark Knight*, Commissioner Gordon is flummoxed: they don't know who he is. They can find no DNA, fingerprint, or dental records. They don't know his name or date of birth. His clothes are custom made, with no labels. As Gordon says, "There's nothing in his pockets but knives and lint."

If the would-be superman sometimes strives to overcome and forget his past, modern society means to keep us all tied to our pasts by compiling records. Of course mere bookkeeping cannot stop the inner spiritual transformation by which man becomes superman, rising above the conditioning of his past. But we are dealing with materialists here. Your karmic records are meaningless to them. But your tax returns and internet traffic are not.

In *The Dark Knight Rises*, Selina Kyle (Cat Woman) is searching for a computer program called Clean Slate that will delete her from all existing computer records, allowing her to completely escape from her past. She craves the Joker's freedom. Batman offers to give her the program in exchange for her help. In the end, both she and Bruce Wayne seem to have used it to escape their pasts and start a new life together in Italy.

Of course, deleting all records of one's past is not the same thing as overcoming the past psychologically and existentially. That is possible only through a fundamental transformation of one's being. But once that transformation is in place, the technology sure can be useful.

"ALL YOU CARE ABOUT IS MONEY."

Contempt for money is another theme common to *The Dark Knight* and *The Dark Knight Rises*. In *The Dark Knight*, the Joker demonstrates his contempt for money by burning his share of a vast fortune.

In *The Dark Knight Rises*, some of Bane's best lines deal with money. His two most spectacular public attacks are on the stock exchange and a football game (as Gregory Hood put it so memorably: the bread and circuses of the decadent American empire).[3]

In the stock exchange, one of the traders speaks to Bane as if he were a common criminal, and a moronic one at that: "We have no money here to steal." To which Bane replies, "Then why are *you* here?"

When Bane breaks a deal with a businessman who has outlived his usefulness, the businessman protests that he has paid Bane a small fortune. "And that gives you power over me?" Bane asks.

Most commentators are somewhat confused about Bane's attitude toward money, because he leads a Communist-style insurrection against the rich. But there are two critical perspectives one can take on money. Figuratively speaking, one can view it from above or from below.

Those who criticize money from below are those who lack it and want it. Their primary motive is envy, which is not necessarily wrong. A hungry man has good reason to

---

[3] Gregory Hood, "The Order in Action: *The Dark Knight Rises*," *Counter-Currents*, July 22, 2012.

envy your bread. And he has good reason to hate you if you prefer to waste it rather than share it. The people who criticize money from below actually have a lot in common with the people they envy: all they care about is money, either getting it or keeping it.

Bane, however, criticizes money from above. His perspective is aristocratic, not egalitarian. He is an initiate, a spiritual warrior against decadence. He realizes there is something higher than money, and he feels contempt for those who are ruled by it, for those who think that money is the highest power in this world. He is, to use the Joker's phrase, "a better class of criminal."

Like the Joker, Bane is free of material concerns even as he masterfully manipulates the base, material world to fight for higher, spiritual aims. Like the Joker, Bane is not above using people who are only interested in money to further his spiritual aims. Thus Bane both makes deals with the rich and incites the envious mob to rise against them, all to hasten the destruction of Gotham.

THE GOOD LITTLE PEOPLE OF GOTHAM

In *The Dark Knight*, the Joker argues that the people of Gotham are only as good as the world allows them to be, and when the chips are down, "they'll eat each other." This sounds like a terrible insult, but from the Joker's perspective it is actually a form of optimism. Being willing to eat one another is a sign of animal vitality unrestrained by egalitarian humanist slave morality. The Joker claims that he is not a monster; he is just "ahead of the curve": meaning that he is already what the rest of Gotham would be if only they were "allowed" by society (or courageous enough to go there without society's permission).

The Joker rigs two boats to explode and gives the detonators to the people in the other boats. He tells them that if they blow up the other boat, he will let them live. If neither boat is destroyed by midnight, he will blow up both of them. One boat is filled with criminals and cops. The other is filled with the good little people of Gotham. In the end, however, neither group manages to blow up the other, and Batman prevents the Joker from destroying both.

Batman draws the false conclusion that the boats were filled with people who believe in goodness, whereas in fact they were merely too craven, decadent, and devitalized to do anything "bad," even to save their own lives. The Joker, it turns out, was a lot farther ahead of the curve than he thought.

In *The Dark Knight Rises*, Bane proves the Joker's point, but he shows that it will take nothing less than a revolutionary mob before the people of Gotham find the courage to eat each other, beginning with the rich. The revolutionary mob gives people permission to act atavistically. But beyond that, they have moral permission as well because, in the end, egalitarian altruism really is a kind of cannibal ethics.

The least convincing part of *The Dark Knight Rises* is the portrayal of the police as improbably idealistic and self-sacrificing. In *The Dark Knight*, the police force consists almost entirely of corrupt, gun-toting bureaucrats counting the days until their pensions kick in. In *The Dark Knight Rises*, Bane lures 3,000 police into the tunnels under Gotham and traps them there. When they finally break out, they charge *en masse* into battle armed only with their sidearms against Bane's heavily-armed fighters. I don't deny that it is possible to awaken such idealism, even in the most cynical public servant. But I needed to see some *reason* for such a dramatic transformation, perhaps something analogous to Bruce Wayne's transformation in his own underground prison.

Cat Woman is motivated primarily by envy of the rich, but the revolution in Gotham has left her thoroughly disgusted. She tells Batman that as soon as she finds a way out, she is leaving. She does, however, linger for personal reasons: she wants to save Batman too. She urges him to follow, telling him that he has given everything for these people. He replies "Not everything, not yet." Then he apparently commits suicide to save the city. But in the end, we learn that Bruce Wayne was not willing to give his life for Gotham. But he was willing to give up Gotham and Batman for a life of his own.

The ending is enigmatic, but as I read it, Bruce Wayne has finally arrived at a higher level of initiation. Again, he has triumphed over his past, this time entirely, and he has used Clean Slate to erase all traces of his life and Cat Woman's. He has also risen above egalitarian humanism. He no longer lives for his inferiors. He lives for himself, and he has found happiness with Cat Woman, which is an interesting change, since it means he has decided to put his happiness above the mere fact that she is a wanted criminal.

Of course, in my eyes, the fact that Bruce Wayne has apparently chosen a private life makes him inferior to Bane. Yes, Wayne has ceased to serve those who are beneath him, but merely serving oneself is inferior to serving a cause that is greater than oneself, which is what Bane did.

TRUTH OR CONSEQUENCES

One of the most important new themes introduced in *The Dark Knight Rises* is the destructiveness of lies. Gordon and Wayne are both debilitated by the burden of the lies they told to protect the reputation of Harvey Dent. Wayne is also crushed by the loss of Rachel Dawes, which is made all the more painful because Alfred chose to conceal the fact that she had chosen to leave Bruce Wayne for Harvey Dent. Finally, near the end of the movie, Robin Blake lies to a group of orphans to give them hope, even though there really wasn't any. The common denominator is that all these lies are told altruistically, to protect people, and particularly "the people," from the truth. Lies are particularly necessary in statecraft, even at its highest and most disinterested. Lies are, of course, a form of bondage to society and the past. Thus they must be rejected by those who would be free, although the initiates seem quite willing to employ deception and violence for a higher cause.

THE LEFT AS THE VANGUARD OF NIHILISM

The Dark Knight Rises is an extremely Right-wing, authoritarian, fascistic movie.

First of all, in this movie, both the good guys (Wayne, Gordon) and the bad guys (the League of Shadows) are united in their belief that Gotham is corrupt and decadent. In the earlier films, the good guys clearly believed that progress was possible. Now they are just looking for excuses to retire, because society no longer has anything to offer them. They have given without reward until their idealism has been extinguished and their souls have been completely emptied. They have become burned-out shells in thankless service to their inferiors.

Second, Nolan's portrayal of the Left is utterly unsympathetic: Leftist values are shown to be nihilistic. Thus promoting Leftism is a perfect tool for those who would destroy a society.

Third, and most trivially, the uncritical portrayal of the police would surely score high on the authoritarian personality inventory, although White Nationalists are not so naïve.

* * *

The Dark Knight Rises is a remarkable movie, a fitting conclusion to a highly entertaining and deeply serious and thought-provoking trilogy. As unlikely as it may seem, these films touch upon—and vividly illustrate—issues that are at the heart of the New Right/Radical Traditionalist critique of modernity. Tens of millions of young whites are eagerly watching and analyzing these films. Thus it is important for us to use these films to communicate our ideas.

Yes, Hollywood always puts our ideas in the mouths of psychotics in order to immunize people against them. But these ideas are one reason why the villains are always more interesting than Batman, who merely comes off as a tool.

I have suggested that these movies incorporate elements from Radical Traditionalism and Nietzschean superhumanism to generate maximum dramatic tension. What conflict could be more fundamental than the one between those who wish to destroy the world and those who wish to save it? That said, I cannot help wondering if Christopher Nolan also feels some sympathy for these ideas, although of course he would deny it. But whatever Nolan's ultimate sympathies, there is no question that somebody in Hollywood knows which ideas offer the most fundamental critique of the modern world. Isn't it time for White Nationalists to learn them as well?

Counter-Currents, July 31, 2012

DOCTOR ZHIVAGO

David Lean's epic anti-Communist romance *Doctor Zhivago* (1965) is a great and serious work of art. *Doctor Zhivago* was initially panned by the critics—probably not because it is a bad film, but because it was very bad for Communism. Nevertheless, it was immensely popular. It is still one of the highest grossing movies of all time, adjusted for inflation. It also won five Oscars—for Best Adapted Screenplay (Robert Bolt), Best Original Score (Maurice Jarre), Best Cinematography (Freddie Young), Best Art Direction, and Best Costume Design. (It was nominated for five other Oscars, but *The Sound of Music* won four of them, including Best Picture and Best Director.) Over the years, critics have also warmed to *Doctor Zhivago*, routinely including it in their "best" lists.

If *Doctor Zhivago* had been the work of almost any other director, it would have been hailed as his greatest film. But *Doctor Zhivago* was directed by David Lean, who had just completed one of the greatest films of all time, *Lawrence of Arabia* (1962). So *Doctor Zhivago* was bound to suffer somewhat from the comparison. But what's really remarkable about *Doctor Zhivago* is how little it disappoints.

The greatness of Lean's film comes into even sharper focus when you read Boris Pasternak's original novel. Pasternak was born in Imperial Russia in 1890 to a cultivated, upper-class Jewish family. His father was a painter, his mother a pianist. He achieved fame as a poet but fell out of favor with the Soviet Communist Party, found publication blocked, and ended up supporting himself as a translator, writing during his off hours "for the drawer."

Pasternak started *Doctor Zhivago* in the 1920s and finished it in 1956. It was smuggled out of the USSR by a dissident Italian Communist and published in 1957 in Italian translation. The first Russian edition of *Doctor Zhivago* was published in 1958 by the US Central Intelligence Agency, which sought to embarrass the Soviets by painting them as repressive cultural philistines who refused to publish one of those great Russian novels that few people manage to finish. Pasternak and *Zhivago* became a liberal *cause célèbre*. In 1958, Pasternak was awarded the Nobel Prize for Literature, which he refused under duress from the Soviet government. He died in 1960.

As a lover of the film, I expected to like the novel. I *wanted* to like the novel. But I found it surprisingly boring: a sprawling, flaccid story cluttered with useless and forgettable characters and digressions. Everything goes on much too long. It also seems unstructured. Good stories are unified from start to finish. They have spines. But Pasternak's *Doctor Zhivago* is a spineless blob, held together with a tissue of increasingly unlikely accidents, as the main characters—in a Moscow of millions, in an empire of tens of millions—keep *bumping into one another*.

As a critique of Communism, Pasternak's novel is unfocused and superficial. We gather that Communism created chaos and unleashed ugliness and nihilism. But we don't really get a sense of why. Pasternak renders surfaces in a wordy, impressionistic blur. But when he tries to go deep, he comes out with lines like this: "Art is always, ceaselessly, occupied with two things. It constantly reflects on death and thereby constantly creates life." It sounds profound, but it is verbose, woolly-minded, and just isn't true.

Finally, the main character of Yuri Zhivago, a doctor

and poet, is not particularly likeable. Thus it comes as a shock when one learns that Zhivago was Pasternak himself in thin disguise. The man must have loathed himself.

But I can't justly review Pasternak's novel, because like many readers, I tapped out before the end. On second thought, that is my review.

A great deal of the credit for turning Pasternak's mediocre novel into a great movie goes to screenwriter Robert Bolt, who also wrote the screenplay for *Lawrence of Arabia*, as well as the stage play and screen adaptation of *A Man for All Seasons*. Bolt removes needless characters and digressions, giving the story more of a spine. He also renders the horrors of Communism more crisply, giving greater insight into why they happened—and what the alternative is.

I will sketch out the film's basic plot, but I will skip over most of the details, leaving much to first-time viewers to discover. Yuri Zhivago is an orphan raised in Moscow by his wealthy godparents, the Gromekos. He is a gifted poet who has chosen medicine as a career. Just before the First World War, Yuri marries Tonya, the Gromekos' daughter, with whom he grew up. When the war begins, Yuri becomes a doctor at the front. After the Revolution, Yuri returns home to find the Gromekos living in one room of their mansion, the rest of which has been given over to seedy proletarians. Moscow is in the grip of the Red terror. Typhus and starvation are rampant.

Worse yet, Yuri is "not liked." His attitudes "have been noticed." His poetry has been deemed too "private" and "bourgeois." He does not conform to the party line, which increasingly consists of managing Communism's failures through lies, excuses, and scapegoating. Yuri's half-brother, Yevgraf, is a Bolshevik secret policeman. He knows Yuri and his family will not survive what is coming (we are now around the winter of 1919) and arranges for them to leave Moscow for the Urals, where they live in a cottage on the Gromekos' former estate.

While in the Urals, Tonya becomes pregnant with their second child, while Yuri begins an affair with Larissa ("Lara") Antipova, a young woman he met in Moscow and again at the front. Yuri is then torn away from both women by a band of Red partisans, who need a doctor and simply kidnap him. Two years later, Yuri manages to return to find the Gromekos have left Russia. He is reunited with Lara briefly but separated again. Lara, it turns out, is carrying his child. Both die some years later without ever being reunited, just two of the many millions of lives blighted and destroyed by a monstrous ideological enthusiasm.

The cast of *Doctor Zhivago* is uniformly strong. Casting an Egyptian Arab, Omar Sharif, as a Russian poet seemed odd to some. He doesn't look like Hollywood's idea of a typical Russian. (Originally, the role was offered to Peter O'Toole.) But the character of Zhivago was based on Pasternak, who didn't look typically Russian either.

The main problem bringing the character of Zhivago to the screen is conveying that he is a poet without actually including any of his poetry. Lean solved this problem brilliantly, perhaps by borrowing a bit from Michael Powell's *The Red Shoes* where composer Julian Craster suddenly goes blank while we hear the music in his head. Lean asked Sharif to look as detached and absent-minded as possible—a pure spectator—while Maurice Jarre's brilliant music (his greatest score) communicates Yuri's flights of poetic imagination.

Julie Christie as Lara is so beautiful I don't think that

the cast had to *pretend* to be in love with her, and her performance is excellent. Alec Guinness as Yevgraf, Tom Courtenay as Pasha, Geraldine Chaplin (Charlie's daughter) as Tonya Gromeko, Ralph Richardson as her father Alexander, and Siobhán McKenna as her mother Anna all turn in strong performances. Klaus Kinski has a memorable bit part as an anarchist turned into a slave laborer. But the most compelling performance is Rod Steiger as V. I. Komarovksy. He has many of the film's best lines. I wouldn't exactly call him a villain, although he's far from pure. Let's just say that he's very much alive.

Even though *Doctor Zhivago* portrays ugliness and horror, it is still a David Lean film, which means that it is a feast for the eyes. Some images are simply unforgettable: a vast throng of workers emerging from a tunnel under a red star; a vase of sunflowers weeping; the Goyaesque horrors of the civil war; the ice palace of Varykino.

But what sets *Doctor Zhivago* apart from most cinema is its fusion of powerful images and emotions with a philosophically insightful critique of Communism.

Before the revolution, *Doctor Zhivago* is constructed out of brilliant contrasts: between the grand boulevards and dirty side streets of Moscow, between the glittering world of high society and the drabness and desperation of the common people, between the healthy, neatly-uniformed men heading toward the front and the starved and ragged deserters fleeing it.

But once the Revolution happens, these contrasts are leveled — downwards, of course — until everyone is cold, starving, dirty, and terrified. The Communist slogans promising freedom, bread, and brotherhood all turn out to be lies. Communism delivered famine, not food — slavery and terror, not freedom. Communism did not ennoble mankind. It empowered cynicism, envy, and pettiness.

But many things didn't change. Russia was still governed by autocrats whom the masses feared. There were still haves and have nots. Both before and after the Revolution, one had to ask people "Can you read?" As the civil war ground on, those caught in the middle could no longer tell Red from White.

But the Soviets recreated the old autocracy on a much lower level, in part due to the sheer chaos and cost of the Revolution, in part because the Bolsheviks being materialists were blind to the essence of the civilization they seized, so they were capable of recapitulating it only as a brute farce. It was the old despotism stripped of all aristocratic magnanimity and refinement and infinitely more violent and cruel.

Four main issues separate the Bolsheviks from the old order.

First, they reject private life. "The private life is dead in Russia. History has killed it," says the Red commander Strelnikov. Private life is disdained as "bourgeois," as if men had never sought their own homes, their own families, and their own happiness before capitalism came along.

The problem with killing private life is that most of life happens in private, which brings us to the second contrast between the Bolsheviks and their enemies: theory versus practice, idealism versus life.

The Bolsheviks are idealists. They are theorists. So is Yuri, for that matter. Although he does choose general practice over medical research, he is by inclination a spectator, always gazing at the world, always trying to clear away the frost and fog to see more clearly.

Perhaps true theories never conflict with practice. But we mere mortals have to make do with half-baked theories, which inevitably clash with the mess of life. Fastidious idealists and dogmatic ideologues think they have the truth, however, which puts them on a collision course with practical life, which has lessons of its own to teach.

The conflict between theory and practice throws light on the climax of the movie, in which Yuri chooses to abandon Lara to Komarovsky. It is a perverse and self-defeating choice. But it is not inexplicable. Yuri is theory. Komarovsky is the mess of life. Yuri is so repulsed by Komarovsky that he is willing to abandon the woman he loves rather than go with him. He may even be condemning himself to death.

What does Yuri do when he decides not to follow Lara? He retreats indoors to *watch* her through a window. Then he smashes out the window *to see her more clearly.*

When private life is suppressed, so are freedom of speech and truth-telling, which is the third gulf between Communism and the old order. Who are you to contradict the party, which is the avatar of universal truth? And since truth is relative to history, and the party is the historical vanguard, truth becomes identical to whatever lie the party declares expedient. When the Party denies starvation and typhus are in Moscow, but Yuri sees them with his own eyes, he believes his eyes. That makes him a thought criminal. But it is truth-tellers, not liars, who pave the upward path for humanity.

(Robert Bolt clearly admired men who were willing to speak their minds and stand by their convictions, even at the risk of their own lives. Hence his depictions not just of Yuri Zhivago but of T. E. Lawrence and Sir Thomas More. Today, people would place all three heroes on the autism spectrum.)

The real center of the story is not Zhivago but Lara, who is loved by the three principal male characters: Zhivago, Pasha Antipov, and V. I. Komarovsky. But the affair between Zhivago and Lara only happens in the last half of the movie. To give the audience an idea of where the whole story was going, Bolt invented a frame for the story, set sometime in the 1940s, after the Second World War.

Yevgraf has come to a construction site. He is looking for his niece, Yuri and Lara's daughter, who had been lost some time in the 1920s. He is convinced that one of the workers, Tanya Komarova, is the girl he seeks. Then he narrates the whole film to her. At the end, Tanya denies she is his niece. "Don't you *want* to believe it?" he asks. This is the voice of the Party speaking, the party that set up wishful thinking as truth and coerced millions to go along with it. Tonya's reply is: "Not if it isn't true." Yevgraf's only comment is: "That's inherited."

This brings us to a fourth divide between Communism and the old order: hereditary gifts versus blank-slate egalitarianism. At the beginning of *Doctor Zhivago*, we learn that Yuri's dead mother had the "gift" of playing the balalaika. The Gromekos wonder if young Yuri has special gifts as well. At the end of the film, as Tanya walks away, Yevgraf learns she has a talent for the balalaika. "Who taught her?" he asks. "No one taught her," comes the reply. "It's a gift, then," says Yevgraf. These are the last words of the movie. In a way, they are the last words on Communism too. Empowering the gifted, not the mediocre, is the upward path for humanity.

Much of the best anti-communist literature is actually Left-wing: Orwell's *Nineteen Eighty-Four* and *Animal Farm*, for example. But a critique of communism that spotlights hereditary inequality belongs objectively to the Right. I have to credit this to David Lean, whose instincts and convictions were Rightist, since there are only the barest traces of this theme in the novel, and Bolt was a card-carrying Communist.

I find the end of *Doctor Zhivago* deeply moving because it offers a ray of hope, which is made visible in the form of a rainbow. Even though Communism can shatter families and whole civilizations, blood has won out in the end.

The Unz Review, September 25, 2021

FIGHT CLUB *

What's philosophical about *Fight Club*? *Fight Club* belongs alongside *Network* and *Pulp Fiction* in an End of History film festival, because it beautifully illustrates ideas about human nature, history, and culture from Hegel and Nietzsche—especially as read through the lenses of Alexandre Kojève and Georges Bataille.

Prehistoric society is relatively egalitarian and focuses on the cycles of nature and the necessities of life. Hegel held that linear history begins with men risking death in duels over honor, which spring from the demand that one's sense of self be recognized by others.

The struggle over honor has winners and losers. Its outcome reveals two kinds of men. The master values honor above life. The slave values life above honor. In terms of Plato's division of the human soul into reason, spiritedness (*thumos*), and desire, the master is ruled by spiritedness, which is intrinsically connected with honor, whereas the slave is ruled by desire.

The struggle over honor gives rise to class structures and class struggles. The ruling class enjoys leisure, which gives rise to the whole realm of high culture, which is driven by the quest for self-knowledge.

The truth about man, though, is somewhat anticlimactic. Mankind has created art, religion, and philosophy—and endured untold suffering in uncounted wars and revolutions—only to discover that . . . we are all free and

---

* These are notes for a lecture on *Fight Club* given on October 25, 2000, in an adult education course called "Philosophy on Film." For a fuller interpretation of *Fight Club*, see Jef Costello's "*Fight Club* as Holy Writ," in Jef Costello, *The Importance of James Bond & Other Essays* (San Francisco: Counter-Currents, 2017).

equal, which is basically how we lived before history.

When we learn the truth about ourselves, history and culture are no longer necessary. When we are all free to pursue our own aims, history and culture will be displaced by mere consumption, the satisfaction of desire, which in a sense is a return to prehistory. Thus the end of history in Hegel's sense brings about the rise of Nietzsche's "Last Man," who believes that there is nothing higher than himself and his petty pleasures.

The protagonist of *Fight Club*, played by Edward Norton, is a man with no name. (He is called Jack in the script, but Jack is a name he adopts from a series of pamphlets about diseases.) He is Everyman. He is the Last Man. He works at a sociopathic corporation. He lives in a condo. He has no apparent religious convictions or cultural interests. He buys clothes and furniture, always with the question, "What does this say about me as a person?" He is single and appears to be celibate. He's free, equal, and has plenty of money to buy stuff. But he feels empty inside. He can't sleep at night, and you know how crazy that can make you.

Everyman seeks out meaning by attending support group meetings under fake names and false pretenses. He doesn't seem to have much truck with the forms of spirituality these peddle, but he does find opportunities for genuine emotional catharses, which help him sleep at night. Unfortunately, another faker has the same idea: Marla Singer (Helena Bonham Carter). Her presence causes our hero to freeze up.

Marla's intrusions drive Everyman to take refuge in an all-male support group. This is significant. History begins not just with isolated men battling for honor, but with bonded male groups, *Männerbünde*, fighting over honor.

Unfortunately, this particular group is called Remaining Men Together. It's for testicular cancer survivors. Emasculated men hugging each other and crying will not restart history. In fact, the group is pretty much a microcosm for everything wrong with the modern world, which would prefer that all men be emasculated, weepy huggers. But it does point to the next step Everyman needs to take.

On one of his business trips, Everyman meets Tyler Durden (Brad Pitt in his most charismatic role). Everyman is a prisoner of the modern world, but he feels above it. He is like a cow shuffling down a chute in a slaughterhouse who feels he is the master of the situation because he keeps up a constant stream of ironic smart-assery. Tyler is genuinely free of the producer-consumer system: He buys his clothes from thrift stores (at best), squats in an abandoned building, and has his own business (he manufactures and sells soap).

Everyman, however, is a Consumer in the hands of an Angry Author. And the Author dictates that Everyman be stripped of all his worldly possessions, because "The things you own, they end up owning you." Then he must be delivered to Tyler Durden, for a new beginning. First, Everyman learns that his luggage has been seized and destroyed because it vibrated. Then, he returns home to find that his condo has been incinerated. He needs a place to stay. Fortunately, he has Tyler's number.

Cut to Lou's Bar, where Everyman and Tyler are drinking and bonding. At the end of the evening, Tyler asks Everyman to hit him. It is a rather shocking suggestion. Neither man has ever been in a fight. Neither man has been tested. Neither man knows how far he would go to win. Would he risk life itself for victory? If so, he is what Hegel called a master. If he is willing to accept dishonor to avoid death, he is a slave. Of course at this point, neither man is willing to risk death. Until now, they haven't even been willing to risk a bloody nose.

After they fight, Tyler and Everyman enjoy a kind of post-coital bliss, then retire to Tyler's place: a crumbling mansion where he squats. It is as if fighting is an initiation into a new world where bourgeois values of comfort and security no longer matter.

Tyler and Everyman have their fights in front of other men, who naturally want to join in. That's how Fight Club is formed. Fight Club is a *Männerbund*. It is structured as a secret, initiatic society. It produces a change of consciousness. "Who you were in Fight Club is not who you were in the rest of your world. You weren't alive anywhere like you were alive at Fight Club. But Fight Club only exists in the hours between when Fight Club starts and when Fight Club ends."

Fight Club also transforms values. "After a night in Fight Club, everything else in your life gets the volume turned down. You can deal with anything. All the people who used to have power over you have less and less." Fight Club breaks the hold that bourgeois society has on us, which springs from a willingness to endure routine forms of dishonor and degradation in exchange for comfort and security.

Not every initiation in Fight Club involves combat, but all of them involve risking death. For instance, one rainy night, Tyler lets go of the wheel of a stolen car, crashing it. When he and the rest of his party crawl out of the wreckage, he declares, "We just had a near-life experience." One cannot really live until one puts aside the fear of death and the desire for comfort, security, and control that are at the foundation of bourgeois society.

As Tyler puts it, "Self-improvement is masturbation. Self-destruction is the answer." The self that must be destroyed is the bourgeois self, the rational producer-consumer. That self must be destroyed so that a higher self may be born, which is, of course, self-improvement in a deeper sense.

Tyler understands that an encounter with death forces one to take life seriously. Modern society is masterful at reducing risks and keeping death at bay. Thus it deprives people of opportunities to really come to grips with their mortality, shed illusions, and live life more seriously.

One night, Tyler demonstrates this by pulling a gun on a convenience store clerk and telling him he is going to die—unless he stops wasting his life as a convenience store clerk. It is an utterly brutal and terrifying encounter, but Tyler thinks he is doing the man a favor: "Tomorrow will be the most beautiful day of Raymond K. Hessell's life"—because of his brush with death at the hands of a gun-toting maniac.

Tyler practices similar tough love with his own friends. One day, he kisses the back of Everyman's hand then dumps lye on it, causing an excruciating chemical burn. Again, his motive is to force a transformative confrontation with death: "First you have to give up. First, you have to know—not fear, know—that someday, you're gonna die. It's only after we've lost everything that we're free to do anything."

When the ordeal is over, Tyler says "Congratulations. You're a step closer to hitting bottom." This is the language of Twelve Step programs. Addiction is sustained by self-deception. Hitting bottom is when the consequences of addiction are so catastrophic that one can no longer evade the reality of one's situation. One confronts it in a moment of clarity, at which point one may embark on the road to recovery.

One of the illusions Tyler is concerned to dispel is the idea of divine providence: "You have to consider the possibility that God doesn't like you. He never wanted you. In all probability, he hates you. This is not the worst thing that can happen . . . We don't need him. Fuck damnation. Fuck redemption. We are God's unwanted children. So be it!"

Tyler's rationale for this line of attack is explained earlier, when he says "Our fathers were our models for God. And, if our fathers bailed, what does that tell us about

God?" If God is just another absent father, then belief in his providence is just another excuse for not taking responsibility for one's life and engaging in self-parenting—or creating a *Männerbund*. (I wonder if Tyler's burning chemical kiss was inspired by the "box" in Frank Herbert's *Dune*. If so, the aim is very different.)

Now I want to discuss two questions. Is Fight Club fascist? And: Is Fight Club gay?

Yes, Fight Club is fascist. After all, Tyler Durden makes his soap out of human fat. That's a joke, but with that detail, the author of the original novel, Chuck Palahniuk, is telling us something. Fight Club is clearly anti-liberal, anti-consumerist, anti-bourgeois, and anti-capitalist. It is also populist, because it empowers ordinary men against the establishment. The only question is: Does Fight Club reject liberalism from the Left or from the Right?

The best way to answer that question is with another question: Does Fight Club admit women? No. Therefore, Fight Club rejects the essential premise of liberalism: human equality. Fight Club is populist, but it is not egalitarian. Fight Club is open to men of all social classes, not because it rejects hierarchy as such, but merely because it rejects the existing hierarchy and wants to create a new one, in which men who are willing to risk combat rule over those who don't. But that's also true of the Nazis and Fascists.

The Unabomber's Manifesto spends a good deal of time critiquing Leftism from a loosely Nietzschean "vitalist" perspective, meaning the idea that a good society gives expression to the life force, thus any institutions that constrict it must be thrown aside. Leftists recoil in fear from such talk, because equality requires leveling and constricting, domesticating and socializing the life force. Leftism is over-socialization. *Fight Club* offers essentially the same critique, but it focuses specifically on *masculine* vitality. Leftism isn't just over-socializing, it is also emasculating.

If Fight Club does not admit women, does that mean it is gay? The Catholic priesthood does not admit women. Does that mean it is gay? Uh-oh. There may be a point here. We can at least say that the movie *plays* with this question.

Fight Club is a bunch of men rolling around half naked and punching each other. Some people find that . . . suggestive. Tyler declares: "We're a generation of men raised by women. I'm wondering if another woman is really the answer we need." Everyman seems to be sexually jealous when Tyler hooks up with Marla. He resents Marla for intruding on his relationship with Tyler. He also clearly feels jealousy of Tyler's affection toward Angel Face, which sends him into a psychotic rage. (Chuck Palahniuk revealed that he is gay in 2004.)

But in a deeper sense, the answer is obviously no. Tyler and Everyman are both heterosexual. Beyond that there is a matter of principle: It does not make men gay to want to work or socialize with one another while excluding women. Women have a great deal of power in pre-historic and post-historic societies because they are relatively egalitarian. Women have a great deal of power over children in all societies. Thus if boys are to mature into men, at a certain point they need to separate themselves from their mothers. They need male-only spheres for that. This is much easier, of course, when they have fathers. But when fathers are absent, they can find father substitutes. One such substitute is the *Männerbund*. Or, in less fancy terms, the gang.

Bonded male groups are not just necessary for the healthy maturation of boys. They are what create and sustain human history and culture. Almost every important institution until quite recently was sex-segregated. Institutions probably work best that way. Feminists, of course, want to break down those barriers, and one of their techniques is to insinuate that any institution that excludes them must be somehow "gay."

Yes, progressive women are not above exploiting "homophobia" to get their way. If they were consistently progressive, they would be saying that men should not think being gay is a stigma at all. Men should not let themselves be manipulated like this. Maybe men should demand that they be allowed into all-female spaces, so that women can absolve themselves of the suspicion of lesbianism. Or better yet, both sexes could call a truce to this childishness. But men are the ones on the retreat, so things will only turn around if they assert themselves.

Fight Club has a cell structure. Fight Clubs can and do pop up everywhere. Fight Club meets once a week and exists only between certain hours. Then Tyler started handing out homework assignments. This is the speech he makes before the first assignment:

> Man, I see in Fight Club the strongest and smartest men who have ever lived. I see all this potential. And I see it squandered. God damn it, an entire generation pumping gas and waiting tables; or they're slaves with white collars. Advertising has us chasing cars and clothes, working jobs we hate so we can buy shit we don't need. We're the middle children of history, man, with no purpose or place. We have no Great War, no Great Depression. Our Great War is a spiritual war. Our Great Depression is our lives. We were raised by television to believe that we'd be millionaires and movie gods and rock stars—but we won't. And we're slowly learning that fact. And we're very, very pissed-off.

Tyler's homework consists mostly pranks and acts of vandalism. But they too are initiations, preparing the way for the next phase.

If the bonded male group is the origin of history, then

we should expect Fight Club to go political. Thus Fight Club morphs into Project Mayhem. At that point, Tyler starts building bunkbeds, because Project Mayhem is a full-time commitment.

Project Mayhem is a cross between a goon squad and a Zen monastery. (But, then again, Zen is the religion of the samurai.) The members of Project Mayhem dress alike, submit to a charismatic leader, chant his cant like robots, and seem ecstatic at the prospect of immolating themselves for the cause. Freedom, equality, individualism, and creature comforts aren't what they want. They want to be "space monkeys" who give their lives for the common good. As Nietzsche said, "Man does not strive for happiness; only the Englishman does that."

The ultimate goal of Project Mayhem is to collapse industrial civilization and start history over again. Tyler envisions going back practically to the stone age:

> In the world I see you are stalking elk through the damp canyon forests around the ruins of Rockefeller Center. You'll wear leather clothes that will last you the rest of your life. You'll climb the wrist-thick kudzu vines that wrap the Sears Tower. And when you look down, you'll see tiny figures pounding corn, laying strips of venison on the empty carpool lane of some abandoned superhighway.

Phase one of collapsing civilization is blowing up the headquarters of the major credit card companies, erasing people's debts. This is easy for Tyler, because if you know how to make soap, you know how to make dynamite.

We never learn what phase two is.

Indeed, near the end, *Fight Club* takes a psychological turn for the worse and becomes as anticlimactic as history itself. It is upsetting, because one really wants to *like* Tyler. But the modern media can't convey profound antimodernist messages without putting them in the mouths of madmen.

What is the lesson of *Fight Club*? The End of History in modern liberal-egalitarian consumer society is good at satisfying our desires for comfort, security, and long life. But we're not satisfied with satisfaction. There's more to the human soul than that. In modernity, masculine *thumos* is, for the most part, unemployed. In fact, it is regarded as a disturber of the peace. But idle hands do the devil's work, and unemployed *thumos*, if mobilized by a charismatic leader and properly directed, can overthrow the modern world and start history over. Maybe next time, we will get it right.

The Unz Review, June 12, 2020

LA DOLCE VITA

Federico Fellini's *La Dolce Vita* (*The Sweet Life*, 1960) is one of the most hailed and fêted films of all time. It was both a commercial and a critical success. It had an immediate and enduring influence on film, fashion, and popular culture in general. It won the Palme d'Or at Cannes in 1960. It was also nominated for four Oscars and won Best Costume Design. Nino Rota's music is also iconic. To this day, *La Dolce Vita* is regularly included in lists of the greatest films of all time.

This is all the more remarkable, given that *La Dolce Vita* lacks a plot. It has interesting episodes and recurring characters. But you are forced to put them together yourself, i.e., you have to do the screenwriter's and director's jobs for them, which is inconsistent with being fully engaged with the film.

La Dolce Vita is filled with beautiful and striking images. Almost every frame can be frozen and endlessly enjoyed. But beautiful images become boring without a story that gives them meaning.

La Dolce Vita also lacks a pulse. The film runs nearly three hours but feels longer because of Fellini's snail-like pacing. Almost every scene outwears its welcome. It is like listening to an interesting story being told by a self-indulgent windbag.

I have sat through *La Dolce Vita* three times, and each time it ended, I felt relieved. I also felt cheated. I felt that my time had been wasted. I vowed that I needed to *do something* with whatever life remained to me. In that sense, at least, the film is therapeutic.

So is the towering reputation of *La Dolce Vita* just another example of pompous critics selling fraudulent "modern art" to the public? That's surely part of it. But it is not the whole story. If it were, I would not have re-watched it. Nor would I be reviewing it. There's actually beauty and depth here. But if you are to take my analysis seriously, I need to be candid about the film's enormous and obvious flaws.

The main character of *La Dolce Vita* is Marcello Rubini, played by Marcello Mastroianni. Marcello is a well-known tabloid journalist who both writes about and lives *la dolce vita*, covering the diversions and dissipations of celebrities, aristocrats, oligarchs, and other beautiful people in Rome.

But Marcello is conflicted. He is drawn away from *la dolce vita* by two forces. First is his fiancée Emma (Yvonne Furneaux), who wants him to marry and settle down. (They currently live together in an almost unfurnished apartment.) Second is his friend Steiner (Alain Cuny), who presides over an intellectual salon in his spectacular apartment. Marcello is working on a novel, although his journalism and partying ensure that progress is slow. Steiner encourages Marcello to devote his talents to more serious, intellectual pursuits. The ambitions of Emma and Steiner are in alliance, for Steiner combines the life of an intellectual with marriage, a family, and bourgeois-bohemian grandeur.

There is another counter-force to *la dolce vita*, which surrounds Marcello on all sides at all times but never seems to reach him: the Catholic church. As the movie wears on, Emma and Steiner drop out of the picture, and Marcello descends deeper into decadence. Only the church remains as a path to salvation. There's a message here, obviously, a deeply Catholic and reactionary one. But Marcello remains unable to hear it. As the movie ends, his prospects seem bleak.

La Dolce Vita opens on a surreal and hilarious note. It is daytime. A helicopter carries a statue of Jesus past ruined Roman aqueducts and new post-war apartment blocs toward Vatican City. A second helicopter follows with

Marcello and his photographer, Paparazzo, covering the event. However, when they see some bikini-clad sunbathers on a rooftop, they stop following Jesus and hover so Marcello can try to get their phone numbers.

Next, it is night. Marcello is in a nightclub, stalking a story, drinks, and women. He meets Maddalena (Anouk Aimée), a beautiful and dissolute heiress with whom he is infatuated. They drive around Rome in Maddalena's magnificent Cadillac convertible. Then they go to the flooded basement apartment of a middle-aged prostitute and make love in her bed while the prostitute drinks coffee in the kitchen.

At dawn, Marcello returns to his apartment to find that Emma has overdosed. He rushes her to the hospital. Emma survives. Marcello pledges his love. But he also slinks away to call Maddalena. Obviously, this will not end well.

Throughout *La Dolce Vita*, we have a pattern of nights, which are times of delusion and irresponsibility, followed by dawns, which reveal both truth and consequences.

Daylight again. Marcello and a horde of other reporters and photographers descend on Ciampino Airport to cover the arrival of Sylvia Rank (Anita Ekberg), a Swedish-American actress, who—aside from a flash of steely imperiousness—is all smiles and charm. Later, at Sylvia's press conference, Marcello calls home to make sure Emma is okay and endures a jealous tirade. Later, Sylvia's boyfriend, Robert (Lex Barker) stumbles in drunk. Next, Sylvia tours St. Peter's, racing up the stairs inside the dome pursued breathlessly by Marcello and photographers. On a balcony overlooking St. Peter's Square, Marcello and Sylvia almost kiss, but she loses her hat. Sylvia is a goddess, and Marcello is clearly captivated, a slave to her every whim.

That evening, Marcello, Sylvia, Robert, and some hangers on end up at a nightclub in the ruins of the Baths of Caracalla. A "divine actor" named Frankie Stout shows up. Frankie looks like a satyr. In fact, he looks like a statue of a satyr, dressed for a night on the town. He's grotesque and ridiculous. When Frankie takes the stage, the party turns into a Bacchanale and a Dithyramb. But Sylvia, not Dionysus, is the focus of the celebration.

Insulted by her bored and drunken boyfriend, Robert, Sylvia flees the baths with Marcello in tow. They wander through the streets of Rome, following Sylvia's every whim. At one point, Marcello is sent to find milk for a kitten Sylvia has decided to adopt. When he returns, he finds the kitten abandoned and Sylvia bathing in the Trevi Fountain. Marcello joins her.

When dawn breaks, Sylvia appears to anoint Marcello with the water of the now still and silent fountain. It is a pagan baptism, further underscoring Marcello's alienation from the church. When Marcello brings Slyvia to her hotel, Robert slaps her and orders her to bed, then beats up Marcello while his "friends" photograph it for the tabloids.

The next episode is set in the afternoon. Marcello is on assignment with a photographer, a model, and a horse. When Marcello sees his friend Steiner enter a modernistic looking church, he follows. Steiner is not there to pray or confess. He's friends with the priest and is picking up an antique grammar. No, it is not Latin, Greek, or Hebrew. It is Sanskrit. Steiner also plays a bit of jazz on the organ before launching into Bach's Toccata and Fugue in D minor. Bach was a Protestant, so it too is out of place. Steiner claims that the church is like a second home to him, but he also claims that this is only because the priests are not afraid of the devil. Steiner is a modern intellectual, and he brings his world with him, even when he enters a church.

The church is in the background of the episode that follows, while Catholicism is very much in the foreground. It is daytime. Marcello, Emma, and Paparazzo are driving to a place in the countryside where two siblings, a boy and a girl, claim to have seen the Madonna. The church is skeptical, but lay Catholics are not. Pilgrims and sick people gather, hoping for a miracle. The media are just there to cover the story, and Fellini puts them very much in the foreground.

After nightfall, the children are released from questioning and return to the field where they reported the apparition. (Does the church have the power to detain and interrogate people about religious visions?) A storm forces the media to shut down their lights. At a certain point, the little girl points to where the Madonna is supposedly appearing and begins running toward her. Mayhem breaks out. The crowd follows the children—who are clearly enjoying the attention—back and forth across the muddy field, while some of the pilgrims shred a small tree said to have given shade to the Madonna, turning every leaf and branch into a relic.

When dawn breaks, we discover that a sick child brought to be healed by the Madonna has been trampled to death by the mob. Marcello is unmoved throughout.

It is during this episode that most viewers start peeking at their watches, wondering where this is all going and how long it will take to get there. The whole sequence could have been cut without loss.

The following episode begins at night. Marcello and Emma have been invited to a salon at Steiner's apartment. Steiner's friends are artists, writers, and academics. An old man discourses on the superiority of the women of the Orient to those of the Occident, because the Orient is closer to nature. A female poet discourses about the importance of never choosing between two options, which is the last thing that Marcello needs to hear, given that he is torn between journalism and literature and between Emma and every other woman in the world.

They then listen to recordings of natural sounds, but only Emma is ingenuous enough to respond to them. She is also enthusiastic about Steiner's two young children, a boy and a girl. Clearly, she would like to have children of her own and envisions Marcello and her living a Steiner-like life. When she speaks of this, Marcello turns away from her. He's clearly ambivalent.

Steiner too is brooding. He is a wealthy dilettante, not a serious intellectual. He too is paralyzed in the face of the choices necessary to follow an intellectual calling. He also fears nuclear war. He does not know what kind of hell his children will inherit. He is hopeless in the face of reality.

This sequence is not followed by a dawn, so we don't know the truth or consequences of what we have seen in Steiner's world—at least not yet.

But the next, brief segment is set during the day. Marcello is on the phone arguing with Emma. He is at a seaside resort. It is summer. He is trying to get away from Rome and write something important. But he is blocked and irritable, not only with Emma but also with Paola, a young blonde waitress from Umbria whom he likens to an angel in an Umbrian church. After a while, Marcello's anger dissipates, and he calls Emma back.

The next episode is set in Rome. It is night. Marcello arrives at one of his hangouts on the Via Veneto, and Paparazzo tells Marcello that his father (Annibale Ninchi) is there eating dinner. Marcello invites his father to a night club and introduces her to Fanny (Magali Noël), a French dancer. After a great deal of alcohol, Fanny takes the father back to her apartment, followed by Marcello and Paparazzo in another car. The apple, it seems, did not fall far from the tree.

Marcello confesses to Paparazzo that when he was growing up, he never really knew his father. He was always gone. Now we have a sense of what he was doing: living *la dolce vita*.

Marcello and Paparazzo take the long way to Fanny's apartment. When they arrive thirty minutes later, Fanny is frantic, because Marcello's father is sick. Marcello is deeply affected. When the episode passes, Marcello's father wishes to return home on the earliest possible train, while Marcello tries to persuade him to stay a while longer. Clearly, Marcello is confronting death. He senses that his father won't be around forever and wants to get to know him better.

But when dawn breaks, the father gets in a cab to leave for the station. This is the truth about the father. He fundamentally does not care about his son. But it is also a vision of Marcello's future, if he does not change the path he is on.

The next sequence begins at the same place on the Via Veneto. Marcello meets Nico, played by Nico herself. She's on her way to a party at her fiancé's castle outside of Rome. She invites Marcello to tag along. It is a wonderfully droll sequence with some stunningly attractive actors.

Marcello meets Maddalena again, who takes him to a room in the castle where he can hear her speaking to him from a distant room. Then she confesses her love to him and asks him to marry her. Marcello is clearly interested. She faces the same choice as him: to whore around or to settle down. She doesn't want to choose, though, and is resigned to being a whore. Marcello tries to talk her out of this, but at a certain point Maddalena goes silent because she begins making out with a handsome partygoer. I guess the wedding is off.

Marcello searches for Maddalena but cannot find her. He tags along when the partygoers decide to relocate to a ruined villa on the estate where they have a séance. Maddalena forgotten, Marcello hits on an aristocrat, who rejects him, then hooks up with a vulgar American artist who later introduces Marcello to her grown son, who is also at the party. It may be a new low for him, but he takes it in stride.

When dawn comes, the partygoers stumble back to the castle, where they meet the prince's mother, a tiny but intense old woman who is headed to mass in the castle chapel. Like ducklings, her son the prince and his three sons fall in line behind her. This is a moment of truth. No matter how dissipated the aristocracy becomes, they will always be able to fall back on their lineages, their manners, and the church. Marcello, however, hangs back with the other guests. These forces have no power over him. Fellini's message here is deeply Catholic and deeply reactionary.

The next episode begins at night. Marcello and Emma are having a shouting match in his car on a road somewhere outside of Rome. A huge industrial light rig stands in the distance, illuminating them. Are they backstage or on stage? Fellini is not even trying to hide the artifice.

Emma wants Marcello to settle down and start a family. She thinks that love is all he needs, and her love should be enough. He disagrees. He's restless. He wants other women, yes, but what he really wants is a life beyond mere domesticity. He wants to make a mark on history. After a lot of "I hate you, don't leave me," Marcello leaves Emma by the roadside. But when dawn breaks he returns to pick her up. The truth revealed here may simply be that both of them have borderline personalities.

Marcello and Emma return home and fall into bed. Later in the day, Marcello is awakened by the telephone. He is called to Steiner's apartment, where a scene of horror awaits. Steiner has killed his two children and himself. This is the daylight truth of Steiner's nighttime brooding: he had no faith in the future, whether religious faith or its secular avatar, progress. He was terrified of nuclear war, terrified that his children would inherit only hell on earth. He gave in to despair, killed his children, and killed himself.

This is devastating for Marcello, for Steiner was one of the main forces pulling against Marcello dissipating his talents into journalism. Now we see that Steiner's life was just another form of nihilism, not a path to salvation.

The final sequence of the film appears to be set some time later. There is more gray in Marcello's hair. He has resolved the tension between journalism and literature by abandoning both. He is a publicist now, an even more superficial job than journalism. There is no sign of Emma. Marcello leads a company of revelers, including his friend Nadia, to the beach house that Nadia shared with her ex-husband Riccardo. Their marriage has just been annulled, and they are going to her ex-husband's house to celebrate "the nullification of her marriage, the nullification of her husband, the nullification of everything." In short, this is a celebration of nihilism. The gate is closed, so they ram it with a car. The house is locked, so Marcello smashes a window to get in.

This is a different crowd than Marcello's old friends. For one thing, there are a lot more homosexuals. They lack the wit of Steiner's crowd. They lack the manners and fashion-sense of the aristocrats. Aside from drinking and music, the entertainment includes vandalizing Riccardo's possessions, a drag show, and a strip tease by the newly nullified Nadia. It isn't just seedy, it's extremely boring.

Eventually Riccardo shows up. He doesn't seem particularly angry or surprised, though, just weary. He's probably seen these kinds of parties before. He orders everyone out. He's pulling an all-nighter too, leaving for Nice at 6:00 am.

But Marcello doesn't want to go. They are all friends. He wants to keep them there. He wants to keep them entertained. The party must never stop. So he closes the curtains on the world and tries to get his own Decameron going. But instead of telling stories, he tries to liven things up by pairing off people to start an orgy. (Can't he get it up himself?) The orgy, however, goes nowhere. So Marcello ends up riding on the back of a drunken woman, throwing feathers from a torn pillow in the air. It is a sad, degrading parody of joy.

When dawn breaks, the revelers depart. But instead of climbing in their cars, they begin wandering through the woods to the beach. "Ah, nature . . . ," one of them says. They've heard of nature. This should be an interesting experience.

When they get to the beach, fishermen are dragging up a dead manta ray from the sea. Is it a symbol? Is it a metaphor? Maybe. But it is also a dead manta ray. It is an encounter with nature and with death: two things that *la dolce vita* must screen out if the party is to continue. But nothing seems to break through. After a few banal remarks, the partygoers begin to drift away.

Marcello has sunk down on the sand. Before he departs, he hears a voice. Just down the beach, across some water, is Paola, the Umbrian angel. She is speaking and gesturing to Marcello, but he can't hear her over the sound of the waves. He doesn't care enough, though, to move closer to her. Eventually, as the last revelers depart, he shrugs, waves goodbye, and follows. Paola watches him leave with a beatific but sad smile. The end.

In Flannery O'Connor's short stories and novels, there are "moments of grace," in which God communicates to mortals, often changing the course of their lives. I read this enigmatic ending as such a moment of grace. Marcello himself likened Paola to an Umbrian angel. That's exactly what she is. She's giving Marcello a choice: listen to her message, which is the message of the Church, or return to the party. He chooses to shrug and walk away.

La Dolce Vita is a self-indulgent film about self-indulgence, an aimless film about aimlessness, a decadent film about decadence. I wish that the message had not corrupted the medium quite so much, because if Fellini had been more disciplined, *La Dolce Vita* really would have been one of the greatest films of all time. As it is, it is still a great film, but a flawed one, with a surprisingly reactionary and pro-Catholic message.

Counter-Currents, November 21, 2024

LAWRENCE OF ARABIA

David Lean directed sixteen movies, fully half of them classics, including three of the greatest films ever made: *The Bridge on the River Kwai* (1957), *Doctor Zhivago* (1965), and, greatest of them all, *Lawrence of Arabia* (1962). *Lawrence of Arabia* is repeatedly ranked as one of the finest films of all time, and when one compares it to such overpraised items as *Citizen Kane* and *Casablanca*, a strong case can be made for putting it at the very top of the list. I am hesitant to speak of "*the* greatest" anything, just because I have not *seen* everything. But when I think of some of my personal favorites—*Vertigo*, *Network*, *Rashomon*—I can't honestly rank any of them higher than *Lawrence of Arabia*.

Everything about this film is epic: from its nearly four-hour running time and its 70-milimeter widescreen image with astonishing detail and depth of focus—to the magnificent settings in Jordan, Morocco, and Spain—to the music by Maurice Jarre—to the cast of thousands crowned by such stars as Peter O'Toole, Alec Guinness, Omar Sharif, Anthony Quinn, Jack Hawkins, José Ferrer, and Claude Rains.

Lean had to go big, simply to do justice to the story. *Lawrence of Arabia* is about one of the most remarkable men of the last century, Thomas Edward Lawrence (1888–1935) and his role in the Arab revolt against the Ottoman Empire during the First World War.

Based on Lawrence's sprawling narrative of the revolt, *Seven Pillars of Wisdom*, the script by Robert Bolt (*A Man for All Seasons*, *Doctor Zhivago*) is a supremely masterful screen adaptation. (Michael Wilson, who worked on the script of *The Bridge on the River Kwai*, also receives screen credit, but the final script is Bolt's.) The timeline is simplified, and certain characters are amalgamated, both to save time and heighten dramatic conflicts, but the truth of the story is conveyed.

Like Lawrence's book, the movie has several layers. First of all, it is a historical narrative. Second, it offers lessons in political philosophy. (The word "wisdom" in the title should have been a warning.) Lawrence was a nationalist, not an imperialist. To fight the Turks, he favored aiding Arab nationalists rather than spending British lives to conquer territory and resources in Mesopotamia. But, against Lawrence's own intention, *Seven Pillars* also makes a case for empire, a case that Lean's film clearly reinforces. Third, there is a strong element of Nietzschean self-mythologization: what Aleister Crowley calls "auto-hagiography" and the Arabs call "blasphemy."

On the symbolic plane, Lawrence overthrows the three Abrahamic faiths by rejecting their doctrines and reversing or rewriting their central stories with himself as the hero. The movie takes this process further, both reflecting upon the process by which Lawrence became a legend and perfecting it: cinema as apotheosis. I want to focus on the latter two layers. Thus I will skip huge stretches of the story and leave those for you to discover on your own.

T. E. Lawrence was one of five illegitimate sons of an Anglo-Irish Baronet, Sir Thomas Chapman, and an English mother, Sarah Junner. Highly intelligent, Lawrence read history at Jesus College, Oxford from 1907 to 1910. From 1910 to 1914, he was an archaeologist in the Holy Land, working with such eminent figures as Leonard Woolley and Flinders Petrie. Woolley and Lawrence also gathered intelligence for the British in the Negev Desert in early 1914.

When the World War broke out, Lawrence enlisted. Fluent in French and Arabic and knowledgeable of Arab history and culture, he received a military intelligence post in Cairo. In June of 1916, when Sharif Hussein, Emir of Mecca, led an Arab revolt against the Ottomans, Lawrence was sent to Arabia to gather intelligence. The rest is history.

The movie begins with Lawrence's death in a motorcycle accident in 1935, at the age of 46. After a memorial service at St. Paul's Cathedral attended by the crème of the British establishment, a priest asks if Lawrence "really belongs here," which introduces the theme of Lawrence as an outsider. The first half of the movie can be seen as an affirmative answer to that question.

Then we flash back nearly twenty years to Lawrence in Cairo. From the start, Peter O'Toole plays Lawrence as slightly autistic and ambiguously gay. He also has a masochistic side. He likes to extinguish matches with his fingers. "The trick . . . is not minding if it hurts." It is a small exercise in self-overcoming, a hint of greater things to come.

Lawrence's commander, General Murray, despises him as an overeducated misfit, but a civil servant Mr. Dryden (a composite character played by Claude Rains) values his intelligence and language skills. Dryden "borrows" Lawrence for an intelligence gathering mission to Arabia. He is to meet Prince Faisal (Alec Guinness), the son of Sharif Hussein, and evaluate his leadership potential.

Lawrence tells Dryden that he thinks this mission will be "fun." Dryden says that the only people who find the desert fun are Bedouin and gods. His unstated premise is that Lawrence is neither. Lawrence flatly declares, "No, it will be fun." If Dryden is right, and Lawrence is not a Bedouin, that implies that Lawrence thinks of himself as a god. To underscore Lawrence's funny idea of fun, he lights a match. But this time Lawrence blows the flame out.

Crossing the desert to find Faisal, Lawrence's guide

Tafas is killed by Sharif Ali (Omar Sharif) for drinking at his well. You see, Tafas is from the wrong tribe. This prompts a bit of political philosophy delivered with autistic frankness that borders on the suicidal, given that it is spoken to a man holding a smoking gun: "As long as the Arabs fight tribe against tribe, they will be a little people, a silly people, greedy, barbarous, and cruel." A nation comes into being when tribes of the same people put aside petty differences and rivalries and embrace a common government, including the rule of law, for a higher good. Throughout his adventures in Arabia, Lawrence's dream of a rising Arab nation is stymied by tribal rivalries and blood feuds.

Out of autistic principledness, Lawrence rejects Ali's help in finding Faisal, preferring to risk it on his own.

When Lieutenant Lawrence reaches Faisal, he is ordered by his British military advisor, Colonel Brighton, to say nothing, observe, and report back to Dryden. But Lawrence is irrepressible. As an autist, Lawrence can't keep his ideas to himself, which intrigues Faisal. Brighton counsels a strategic withdrawal to Yenbo, where the British can resupply him. Faisal wants the British fleet to take the port of Aqaba, but Brighton refuses. It is too well-defended. When Brighton leaves, Faisal bids Lawrence to stay. Faisal naturally fears the English have designs on Arabia, but he is forced to depend upon them: "We need the English, or—what no man can provide, Mr. Lawrence—we need a miracle."

This prompts Lawrence to spend a night brooding in the desert. The next morning, Lawrence suggests to Ali that the Arabs should take Aqaba themselves. Aqaba's guns point toward the sea, because an attack from the land was deemed unlikely. Ali points out that such an attack would require crossing the Nefud Desert, a waste that even the Bedouin avoid. Lawrence proposes crossing the Nefud with fifty men—all members of Ali's tribe—

then raising more troops from the Howeitat tribe on the other side. Ali agrees.

When Lawrence tells Prince Faisal that he is "going to work your miracle," Faisal replies "Blasphemy is a bad beginning." Lean films Lawrence's nocturnal meditations as something more than just a brainstorming session. Now we know that it was a step toward apotheosis.

As Lawrence and his followers make their last push across the Nefud, one of the men, named Gasim, falls off his camel in the dark. When his riderless camel is noticed, Lawrence wants to go back to rescue him. But Ali and the Arabs say they dare not risk it. Gasim's time has come. "It is written," meaning that it is the will of God. Lawrence declares "Nothing is written"—meaning that the will of God is nothing in the face of the will of man—then he goes back on his own to search for Gasim. As he departs, Ali rages at Lawrence's "blasphemous conceit" and says he will not be at Aqaba. Lawrence replies that he will make it to Aqaba: "*That* is written"—by Lawrence himself.

In the space of a single conversation, Lawrence rejects the written laws handed down by Moses and Muhammad. He overthrows God and lays down his own laws. Blasphemy indeed. But Lawrence's blasphemy is not punished. It is rewarded. When he rescues Gasim, the Arabs begin to idolize Lawrence.

As Lawrence sleeps, Ali burns his uniform. The next day, the Arabs dress him in the white and gold robes of a sharif of their tribe, conferring noble status on him. It is proclaimed, "He for whom nothing is written may write himself a clan." Because Lawrence is a bastard in England, he cannot inherit his father's name or title. For Ali, that means he is free to choose his own name. He is free to found his own family, clan, or dynasty. He is free to be somebody's ancestor, not somebody's heir. This is the privilege that descends on all men who bring victory in battle. It is how aristocracies everywhere are born. The Arabs call him "Aurens." Now Ali wishes to style him "El Aurens," which is the equivalent of the German "von." Lawrence is beginning to enter—and alter—Arab society.

The night before Lawrence's men and the Howeitat are to strike Aqaba, a shot rings out. One of the Howeitat lies dead, killed by one of Lawrence's men. The Howeitat demand justice, but if they execute the killer, his own tribesmen are bound to avenge him. Tit-for-tat violence will destroy the alliance. Arab tribalism is about to snatch defeat from the jaws of victory.

But Lawrence has a solution. *He* will execute the prisoner. He will take the blame. He, not the Howeitat, will bear the brunt of the blood feud of the dead man's tribe. Thus the alliance of the two tribes can be maintained for the attack on Aqaba. Lawrence is offering himself as a scapegoat to prevent tribal conflict from spinning out of control.

Of course, in a sense Lawrence can't really serve as a scapegoat, because he knows that he is no danger of actually being punished by Gasim's tribe for executing him. He has already been hailed as a sharif by Gasim's own kin.

The scapegoat here functions as a symbol of the political enemy in Carl Schmitt's sense. If the Arab tribes are to become an Arab nation, they must find a way to take the enmity between them and place it on an outsider. If the Arabs are to become a political "us" they must have an external enemy, a political "them" against whom to define themselves. Lawrence wants it to be the Turks, but he knows that a people in need can create an enemy in its own midst, then externalize it. Lawrence is willing to fill that role in a pinch.

Ironically, though, Lawrence's gesture also undermines nationalism and makes a case for empire. In Xenophon's *The Education of Cyrus*, book 3, we learn of how enemy tribes can be unified not by a common enemy but by a common "friend." Two enemy peoples in the Caucasus, the Armenians and the "Chaldeans," are locked in perpetual warfare. Neither group is strong enough to defeat the other, so their costly conflict can only be terminated by a third party.

Cyrus occupies and fortifies the highlands between the Armenians and Chaldeans. He pacifies them by offering to ally himself to whichever tribe is wronged by the other. Then he delivers the fruits of peace by brokering mutually enriching economic exchanges between the two tribes in place of mutually impoverishing conflict.

None of this would be possible without a third power, an outsider who is above their conflicts and benevolently disposed toward them. This was the legitimating ideology of the Persian empire; hence Cyrus became known as the "prince of peace." Lawrence plays the same role in brokering peace between the tribes. It is, of course, but a small step from hero to emperor. Contrary to the principle of national self-determination, sometimes only an outsider will do.

When Lawrence and the rest of us see the face of the condemned man, it is a punch in the gut. It is Gasim, the man Lawrence risked everything to save. Lawrence asks Gasim if he is guilty. "Yes." Then Lawrence puts six bullets in him. When he flings away his gun in disgust, a mob converges on it, as a holy relic. Lawrence is becoming a legend. (In reality, Lawrence executed a different man. By making Gasim the killer, the screenwriter not only made the story more economical, he also increased its dramatic power.)

After Aqaba is taken, Lawrence basks in victory for a few moments by the seaside, where Ali throws him a garland of flowers, stating "The miracle is accomplished. . . . Tribute for the prince, flowers for the man." Lawrence replies "I'm none of those things, Ali." When asked what he is then, Lawrence says, "Don't know." But he's being coy. If he has worked a miracle, he's a god, or on his way to becoming one.

When the telegraph equipment in Aqaba is smashed by the excitable Arabs, Lawrence proposes taking the news to Cairo by crossing the Sinai desert. "Why not? Moses did it." To which Auda abu Tayi, the leader of the Howeitat (Anthony Quinn in his most compelling role) replies, "Moses was a prophet and beloved of God." But Lawrence is doing more than imitating Moses. He's already tossed away the written laws of Moses and Muhammad. Now he's reversing Moses' journey by going back into Egypt.

When Lawrence arrives in Cairo, he's dressed in Bedouin robes and caked with filth. But Lawrence walks into military HQ like he belongs there. He was an outsider even when he wore the uniform, but now it's obvious. Naturally, he is not welcomed until he is recognized as one of their own. He looks like a beggar. He has gone through hell. But when he reports that he has taken Aqaba, everyone from the top brass to the lowest guardsman knows a good thing when he sees it.

General Murry has been replaced by General Allenby, a far shrewder leader superbly played by Jack Hawkins. Allenby promotes Lawrence to major on the spot. Brighton declares it a "brilliant bit of soldiering" and recommends Lawrence be put up for a commendation. Dryden says, "Before he did it, sir, I would say it couldn't be done." When Allenby summons the lowly Mr. Perkins into his office and asks his opinion of Aqaba, he says "Bloody marvelous, sir." We know Perkins is a lowly fellow because we only see his boots, stamping to attention as he enters and leaves.

Allenby proposes a drink at the officers' bar. The beautifully filmed and choreographed sequence is one of the movie's most memorable. The British HQ was filmed in a magnificent palace in Spain. The music is Kenneth Alford's splendid march, "The Sound of the Guns." (Alford also composed the "Colonel Bogey March," which became an unlikely hit record after Lean and composer Malcolm Arnold used it in *The Bridge on the River Kwai*.) Allenby, Lawrence, and company sweep through the halls and down the grand staircase—past rank after rank of smartly uniformed officers and sentries, standing at attention and saluting—into the sumptuous bar, where all the officers spring to attention until Allenby puts them at ease and begs their permission to drink there, as a guest of Major Lawrence. It is a perfect image of how hierarchy is oiled by magnanimity, manners, and good humor. We pretty much know where David Lean stands on the empire vs. nationalism question. The British Empire has seldom seemed better oiled and more glamorous on screen.

But it is precisely the British ability to look past appearances and to recognize the talents and achievements of an outsider and misfit like Lawrence that made this victory possible. As Allenby and Lawrence continue their conversation in the courtyard, the camera follows Lawrence's eyes to the galleries above, which are lined with onlookers. Again, we see a legend forming. When Allenby takes his leave and Lawrence returns alone to the bar, the officers briefly stand silent then burst out in acclaim. When the priest at Saint Paul's asks, "Does he really belong here?" he means at the very center of one of the world's great empires. Here we see that the answer is yes. It is an enormously moving climax, and we're only at the intermission.

In the first half of the movie, Lawrence makes himself a legend in service of Arab nationalism. In the second half, he meets a rival myth-maker, Jackson Bentley, a fictional American journalist based on Lowell Thomas and played by Arthur Kennedy. Bentley's goal is to use the

Arab anti-colonial revolt and the romantic figure of Lawrence to build American sympathy for the war. Prince Faisal replies: "You are looking for a figure who will draw your country toward war. Aurens is your man." Amusingly, Bentley tells Faisal, "I just want to tell your story." The bastards still say the same thing today.

When Lawrence and the Arabs attack a Turkish train, we see apotheosis in action. A victorious Lawrence stands on top of the train to receive the acclaim of the tribes. A wounded Turk shoots him. Lawrence falls to the sand, where he takes stock of his wound. When a bloodied Lawrence returns to the roof, the tribes are ecstatic. Lawrence prances on the roof of the train like a model on a catwalk, whirling in his robes, drinking up the adulation of his followers.

Looking down through the camera's eyes, we see only Lawrence's shadow across the sands and the cheering crowd. Looking up, we see only his silhouette against the sky. Bentley eagerly snaps pictures, which the Arabs correctly believe will steal their virtue. Bentley *is* stealing—and selling, and exploiting—Lawrence's virtue, his power.

The juxtaposition of the three-dimensional Lawrence and his two-dimensional shadow and silhouette, along with the journalist's camera, is a subtle commentary on myth-making. Lawrence is becoming one of the shadows projected on the walls of the cave of public opinion.

In my essay on John Ford's *The Searchers* (elsewhere in this volume), I comment on Ford's framing effect of moving from silhouette to three-D and back to suggest that the domestic world is less real and more fragile than nature, again an analogue to Plato's Allegory of the Cave. Lean uses the same contrasts to similar effect. Lean carefully studied *The Searchers* before filming *Lawrence* to understand how Ford shot his spectacular Monument Valley settings. He may have taken other inspiration as well.

Sated with loot and desiring to take the winter off, Lawrence's Bedouin allies melt away. But the British campaign rolls on. Lawrence has been asked to besiege Deraa, but he only has fifty men left, the original number he set out with toward Aqaba. Having worked a miracle once before, he presses on. "Who will walk on water with me?" he asks. More blasphemy. But not even Lawrence can motivate fifty men to take a town garrisoned by thousands of Turks.

So Lawrence proposes to go into Deraa alone. Of course with his fair complexion, golden hair, and blue eyes, he's going to have a hard time passing, but for some reason Lawrence *wants* to draw attention to himself—even though he is the most wanted man in the Empire, with a bounty of twenty-thousand pounds on his head. The whole mission makes no sense, and some suspect that it is wholly fictional. Only Ali accompanies him.

Lawrence is arrested, beaten, and most probably raped by a sadistic Turkish general, then thrown into the street. Lawrence's feeling of invincibility is shattered. He wants to return home and bury himself in an ordinary life. "I'm only a man." Ali is incredulous, objecting "A man can do whatever he wants!" Lawrence retorts, "But he can't want what he wants." Meaning that we may be able to reshape the world according to our desires, but we can't reshape our desires. Then he pinches his white flesh and says, "This is the stuff that decides what he wants." Is he referring to his race, which made it impossible for him to pass as an Arab? Is he referring to his sexuality? (Lawrence was most definitely a masochist and most probably homosexual.) Whatever his meaning, Lawrence is doubting his outsider magic.

Lawrence meets with Allenby in Jerusalem and asks to be relieved. "I'm an ordinary man, and I want an ordinary job. . . . I just want my ration of common humanity." Allenby has seen these mood swings before and handles

Lawrence shrewdly. "You're the most extraordinary man I've ever met." Lawrence agrees rather too readily. "Not many people have a destiny, Lawrence. It is a terrible thing for a man to funk it [i.e., lose his nerve] if he has."

This is Lawrence's Garden of Gethsemane moment, when he seeks to renounce or flee his superhuman destiny. But that proves impossible. It is not long before the old Lawrence is back. *He* is going to deliver Damascus to the Arabs. The scene ends dramatically with Lawrence standing in front of a painting of Phaeton falling headlong from the solar chariot declaring emphatically that the Arab tribes "will come *for me*."

Of course, at Deraa he's learned the limits of his charisma. So he demands a great deal of money from Allenby as well, to buy allegiance. When Lawrence sets out for Damascus, he has a paid bodyguard of notorious cutthroats, all of them wanted men.

Lawrence's goal is to beat Allenby to Damascus and install an Arab National Council. He almost loses the race when he comes across an Arab village sickeningly massacred by the retreating Turks. The cutthroats urge "no prisoners." Ali reminds Lawrence of Damascus. When one of Lawrence's men charges the Turks and is gunned down, Lawrence unleashes a massacre. This is his Phaeton-like fall. Faisal prophesied it earlier in the film when he said that for Lawrence, mercy is a passion. For Faisal it is merely good policy. "You may judge which is more reliable." Clearly, Faisal's motive was more reliable in the end.

Despite the massacre, Lawrence beats Allenby to Damascus, occupies key facilities, and declares an Arab National Council in charge. Allenby's response is shrewd. He orders the British army to quarters, including the medical and technical staff. He's going to let the Arabs muck things up, out of tribal pettiness and general backwardness. Eventually, they will get tired of playing at government and leave. Which is pretty much what happens. "Marvelous looking beggars, aren't they?" Allenby remarks as he sees the Bedouin begin to slip back to the desert.

The movie ends with Lawrence, now a full colonel, being sent home so the politicians can take over. Along the road, he passes a troop of Bedouins leaving Damascus and more British coming in. A dispatch rider on a motorcycle passes him and speeds ahead, foreshadowing his death. It looks anticlimactic, but that's history.

It also looks like a defeat, but it wasn't entirely. Prince Faisal held on. He was willing to accept British engineers to run things, but he insisted on flying an Arab flag and declaring himself king. Faisal was eventually run out of Damascus by the French, but he became king of Iraq, which was pretty much a British oilfield with an Arab flag until his grandson was machine-gunned by revolutionaries. His brother became king of Jordan, where his descendants rule to this day. It wasn't what Lawrence wanted, but without his efforts, the Arabs would have had to settle for a lot less. Lawrence's sense of mission wavered from time to time, but he didn't fail the Arabs. Ultimately, they failed themselves.

Visually, *Lawrence of Arabia* is one of the most beautiful films in the history of cinema. It has been studied obsessively by other filmmakers but never equaled. Every new viewing discloses new influences. (For instance, surely Faisal's silent, red-robed guardians gave George Lucas an idea or two.) If a picture is worth a thousand words, *Lawrence of Arabia* is worth a million. Better, then, that you see it for yourself.

What did Lawrence do after Arabia? There were stints at the Foreign Office and the Colonial Office. But having made history, he found office work boring. So he turned his talents to making legend, writing *Seven Pillars of Wisdom* and delivering lectures to enormous audiences.

He also filled his ration of common humanity by joining the Royal Air Force under an assumed name. Apparently he found it relaxing to take orders from fools. When his enlistment was up, Lawrence left the RAF in March of 1935. He had his fatal accident before he could begin the next chapter in his legend.

We can only imagine what Lawrence would have thought of Lean's film. I think he would have found it insightful, but it isn't necessarily pleasant to be spiritually X-rayed. However, if Lean is right about Lawrence's ambitions, I think he would have been pleased to see his apotheosis finally made complete.

The Unz Review, May 31, 2021

THE LEOPARD

Luchino Visconti's masterpiece is his 1963 historical epic *The Leopard* (*Il Gattopardo*, which actually refers to a smaller spotted wild cat, the serval, which is the heraldic animal of the princes of Salina in Sicily). Visconti's film is a remarkably faithful adaptation of the 1958 novel of the same name by Giuseppe Tomasi di Lampedusa. *The Leopard* became the best-selling Italian novel of all time, carrying off many critical laurels as well. In its beauty of language, philosophical depth, and emotional power, *The Leopard* is one of the greatest novels I have ever read, and Visconti's film does it full justice. Both are works of genius.

Set during the Risorgimento, the unification of Italy into a modern nation-state, *The Leopard* is sometimes called "the Italian *Gone with the Wind*," which is an apt comparison, although *The Leopard* is better both as a book and a film. Like *Gone with the Wind*, *The Leopard* is a historical romance set against the backdrop of a war of national unification in which a modern, bourgeois-liberal industrial society (the Northern Kingdom of Piedmont and Sardinia, ruled from Turin by the house of Savoy), triumphs over a feudal, agrarian aristocracy (the Kingdom of the Two Sicilies, encompassing Sicily and Southern Italy and ruled from Naples by the house of Bourbon). Even the time period is basically the same. The novel *The Leopard* is set primarily in 1860–62, and the film takes place entirely in this time frame.

The story begins in May of 1860, when Giuseppe Garibaldi, a charismatic nationalist general, raised an insurgent force of 1000 volunteers and landed in Sicily to overthrow the Bourbons. The Garibaldini fought for no king or parliament. They fought for the nationalist idea. They fought for a unified Italy that did not yet exist.

Garibaldi fought his way to Palermo, declared himself dictator, then raised new troops to take the fight to the mainland, where he overthrew the last Bourbon king, Francis II. Then Garibaldi handed the kingdom over to King Victor Emanuel of Piedmont and Sardinia and retired into private life. Plebiscites were held throughout Italy, except in Venice, which was under Austrian rule. All of Italy, save the Papal States, agreed to unification under the house of Savoy. In 1862, Garibaldi raised an army to march on Rome and forcibly incorporate the Papal States, but he was stopped by troops loyal to the new unified kingdom.

Lampedusa was a Sicilian aristocrat and a partisan of aristocracy. As a study of classical aristocratic virtues, *The Leopard* can be placed alongside Aristotle's *Nicomachean Ethics*. As a meditation on the decline of aristocracy into oligarchy, it can be placed alongside Plato's *Republic*. Visconti, however, was both an aristocrat and a self-professed Communist. Thus his adaptation also highlights other aspects of the novel, dramatizing how the revolutionary energies unleashed by the ideas of the sovereign people and a unified national state were coopted by the old Italian aristocracy and corrupted by the rising middle classes. Although I am a national populist, not a Marxist, there is much truth in Visconti's depiction.

The hero of *The Leopard* is Don Fabrizio Corbera, Prince of Salina, the head of an ancient Sicilian noble family. In the film, he is played by American actor Burt Lancaster, which is perfect casting, for Don Fabrizio is described a hulking blue-eyed blond. Visconti's casting of the whole Corbera clan is remarkable. Princess Maria Stella, played by Rina Morelli, perfectly fits her description in the book, and the couple's children all resemble their parents and their siblings.

Another important character is the prince's nephew and ward, Tancredi, the orphaned and impoverished prince of Falconeri, whom Lampeusa describes as blue-eyed, dark-haired, and rakishly handsome. Tancredi is brought to life on film by Alain Delon. Tancredi is an adventurous lad who has fallen in with liberals, nationalists, and revolutionaries. When Garibaldi lands, Tancredi rushes to join him.

Tancredi is described as charming, ambitious, and somewhat unscrupulous. Thus it is never clear how deep his commitment to the Risorgimento actually is. When he speaks to his uncle, the prince of Salina, he tells him that everything must change so that everything can remain the same. The revolution will ultimately pass away, and Sicily's immemorial customs and ancient aristocracy will quietly reassert themselves. It is never clear if this rather cynical view is accepted by Tancredi himself or simply crafted for his uncle's consumption. But as the story—and especially the film—unfolds, it becomes increasingly clear that if Tancredi ever believed in the ideals of the Risorgimento, he eventually dropped them.

The prince of Salina uses Tancredi's connections to Garibaldi and his wealth and prestige to insulate himself and his family from the chaos of the revolution. With sublime indifference to current events, the family departs Palermo on its annual retreat to the village of Donnafugata, where they have inherited an immense palace.

Visconti's portrayal of their journey and welcome is remarkable. The family arrives, emerging from the enclosed sweatboxes of their carriages, their elegant clothes white with dust from the unpaved mountain roads. Greeted ceremoniously by their retainers and the village notables, they immediately attend a church service. Visconti's camera slowly pans the prince and his family, all of them studies of dignity and decorum although drenched in sweat and caked with filth. Only after thanking God for their safe journey do they retire to their palace and freshen up.

The dignified arrival of the Salinas stands in sharp contrast to Visconti's farcical treatment of the local plebiscite presided over by Don Calogero Sedàra, the mayor of Donnafugata. Sedàra is a strong proponent of the new order. He makes no pretense of partiality. After the prince votes, he proposes a toast with a liqueur in the three colors of the new Italian flag. The prince, who straddles the worlds of the Bourbons and the Savoyards, chooses the Bourbon white, drinks, and winces at the cloying taste.

When Don Calogero reads the results, a brass band continually interrupts him. As it turns out, he has cooked the books. Of the 512 votes cast, 512 are yesses. In truth, the plebiscites were widely fraudulent. The new order had not even legitimated its power, and it was already abusing the public trust.

Who is Don Calogero Sedàra? He is the man of the future. Just as the prince of Salina represents the best of the aristocracy, Sedàra represents the virtues and limitations of the rising middle classes. Sedàra is a man of humble birth but outsized ambition and avarice, which he pursues single-mindedly with boundless intelligence and energy. Now, like the prince, a man of around fifty, Sedàra has amassed a large fortune, become mayor, and is the leader of the revolutionary forces in his district. Sedàra is described as a "beetle of a man," and his portrayal by Paolo Stoppa is of limited success. Stoppa aptly communicates Sedàra's avarice and gaucheries but not his intelligence and hard work.

Sedàra's wife is never seen. She is reputed to be a woman of great beauty but bestial manners, probably due to mental illness. Her father was one of the prince's peasants known as Pepe Cowshit. They have only one child, their daughter Angelica (Claudia Cardinale, almost perfect casting, although she lacks Angelica's green eyes), who has inherited her father's intelligence and ambition as well as her mother's beauty, which—reinforced by her father's wealth and a bit of polishing at a Florentine finishing school—makes her a formidable force.

On the night of his arrival in Donnafugata, the prince holds a dinner for the local notables, including Don Calogero. In the novel, it is explained that the prince does not wear formal evening clothes at this dinner because he knows the villagers don't have them. It is a magnanimous gesture, designed to make class distinctions less onerous on the dignity of the villagers.

But in comes Don Calogero, in white tie and tails, a gesture that in the prince's eyes is more significant than the revolution itself. Indeed, it *is* the revolution itself. Although ill-tailored and ill-shaven, Sedàra's clothes put him above the prince and his family, at least to those who reckon by appearances. Those who know the truth, however, understand that this outcome has occurred only by virtue of the prince's magnanimous condescension and Sedàra's social climbing. (In the film, the prince's magnanimous gesture is not communicated, so the Salinas' surprise at Sedàra being overdressed comes off as mere snobbery, when the truth is precisely the opposite.)

All is forgotten, however, when the radiant Angelica appears. Tancredi is instantly smitten. But this presents a problem. Earlier that very day, the family's Jesuit chaplain, Father Pirrone, told the prince that his eldest daughter, Concetta, wished to marry her cousin Tancredi and believed the feeling to be mutual. The prince, however, dismissed the idea because the timid and submissive Concetta is not a suitable bride for an ambitious man like Tancredi, who needs an equally ambitious wife and a far larger dowry than he could afford to provide Concetta. Angelica, however, is a perfect match, because she is beautiful, intelligent, a wealthy only-child, and a dedicated social climber.

One of the most interesting characters in *The Leopard* is Ciccio Tumeo (played by Serge Reggiani), the local church organist and the prince's hunting companion. Tumeo is an intelligent and thoughtful commoner. He is also a far more zealous guardian of the traditional order than the prince. Tumeo is a Bourbon loyalist because of the patronage and kindness extended to his family by the deposed king's ancestors. He was educated at royal expense, and when his family was in need, they petitioned the court for aid and received it. In his essentially feudal view, this patronage binds and obliges him to the Bourbons. Thus he voted "no" in the plebiscite and was incensed that his vote was changed by Sedàra, whom Ciccio regards as a dishonorable opportunist.

Tumeo tells the prince of Sedàra's bestial wife and her father, Pepe Cowshit. When the prince informs Tumeo that on that very evening he is going to tell Sedàra of Tancredi's proposal of marriage to Angelica, he thinks the match is not appropriate because of Angelica's background. Furthermore, the prince off-handedly informs Tumeo that to prevent him from leaking news of the engagement, he and his hunting dog Teresina will be locked in the prince's gunroom until the deal is struck.

The prince obviously values Tumeo's judgment and companionship. So why doesn't he simply swear Tumeo to silence? Probably because the prince thinks that Tumeo's oath is worthless, because he is not a gentleman. This casual condescension appears earlier in the film as well, when upon his arrival in Donnafugata, the prince greets Teresina before he greets her master. (Actually, such behavior is common among "dog people" of all classes, and nobody takes it personally.)

The final sequence of the film is set two years later at a grand ball in Palermo in which Angelica and Don Calogero are introduced into Sicily's high society. It seems a rather long wait, but the setting is determined by the politics of the times. Garibaldi's attempt to march on Rome has been defeated by troops loyal to the new king in

Turin. The house of Savoy is firmly in control. The revolutionary energies stirred by the Risorgimento's idea of a sovereign Italian people in a united nation-state have been largely coopted and corrupted by the glamor and prestige of the old aristocracy and the avarice of the bourgeoisie.

The aristocracy, however, is doomed to slow displacement. They have expensive tastes and, like Tancredi's father, the prince of Falconeri, are often very bad at managing money. In the past, great aristocratic fortunes could be replenished every few generations by the loot of a victorious war. But in the nineteenth century, the usual route was to marry the daughters of the rising oligarchy, who crave the status and lifestyle of the aristocracy and are better at making and managing money.

We see the process of corruption from the very beginning of *The Leopard*. When Tancredi and two of his fellow Garibaldini visit the prince near Palermo in their dashing red uniforms, a young Northerner, Count Cavriaghi (Terence Hill), addresses the prince as "excellence," an honorific abolished by Garibaldi. An aristocrat himself, with tastes in poetry, music, and painting, Cavriaghi is dazzled by the Salina palace, especially its magnificent frescos. Later, after Tancredi's engagement, Cavriaghi pays court to the prince's daughter Concetta. Later when Tancredi and Cavriaghi appear in Donnafugata, they wear the Prussian blue uniforms of the national army. They have accepted demotions in rank from Garibaldi's forces for a rise in social status.

The aristocracy magically softens Don Calogero's revolutionary fervor as well, to the point that he buys a title for himself. When he informs the prince of this at the end of their engagement negotiations, both the prince and father Pirrone walk away as if he has said nothing. Later, when the prince turns down an invitation to join the senate in Turin, he recommends Sedàra instead, dryly remarking that "his family is an old one, or soon will be."

By the ball, the process of corruption is complete. The leaders of the new army and the jumped-up bourgeoisie like the Sedàras are fêted by the old aristocracy. Colonel Pallavicino, who defeated Garibalidi's last insurgency at Aspromonte, is an especially honored guest. They feast and dance till dawn. Then, in a detail added to the movie, Pallavicino goes off to execute deserters who went to Garibaldi's side at Aspromonte. Tancredi and Sedàra, the former revolutionary now dressed in top hat and tails, approve. It is time for law and order. It is time to get down to business.

At the ball, the prince meditates on mortality. He is in decline. His family is in decline. His class is in decline. After the party, the prince chooses to walk home. Seeing a priest on his way to administer someone's last rites, he kneels and crosses himself, then looks up to Venus, as the morning star, and prays to be delivered from the realm of change. A mathematician and astronomer, the prince is essentially a Platonist. He sees numbers as unchanging and the heavens as a realm of eternal, cyclical change. The prince is both perfectly Catholic and perfectly pagan.

Three chapters of the novel were not adapted to the screen.

Chapter V, "Father Pirrone Pays a Visit," tells of the priest's 1861 excursion to his home village. However, the best lines of the chapter, where Pirrone discourses on the nature of the aristocracy to drowsy peasants, were incorporated into the film, in a scene during the Salinas' journey to Donnafugata.

Chapter VII, "Death of a Prince," narrates the prince's last days in 1883, emphasizing the pagan themes intimated at the end of the ball. The prince has two visions of Venus, at a train station as he returns to Palermo, and on his deathbed, where she appears to guide his soul to the unchanging realm. This chapter is utterly heartbreaking. I wish Visconti had included it in his film.

Chapter VIII, "Relics," is set in 1910 and narrates the total ruin of the great house of Salina, whose prestige and substance have been squandered by the high living and bad business decisions of the prince's male heirs and the superstitious pieties of three of his four daughters, who have become old maids (apparently, they could not find a place in the new order). Angelica, now widowed, seems to have flourished, although there is no mention of any children to carry on the Falconeri name. It is fitting, then, that the last word of the novel is "dust."

The Leopard is obviously a deeply pessimistic meditation on the decline of aristocracy and the rise of the middle classes. Written by the last prince of Lampedusa, whose adopted son inherited his property but not his title, the novel was rejected by both publishers to which it was submitted. Then, before he could submit it to another publisher, the author died of cancer, aged sixty. But *The Leopard*'s pessimism is somewhat belied by its spectacular posthumous success, both as a novel and a film. Because of books like *The Leopard*, we can at least hope that healthy archaic values and institutions can someday return and that, by understanding the seeds of decay, we can perhaps avert it.

Lampedusa was a reactionary and an advocate of aristocracy. I am not. In my view, Garibaldi's only flaw was unifying Italy as a monarchy, not a republic. Although I cannot help but admire the prince of Salina's virtues and magnificent way of life, his political instincts were entirely wrong.

The prince never should have married Tancredi to Angelica or contemplated any alliance with the Sedàras of the world. He should have married Tancredi to Concetta, who because of his cynicism ended up an embittered old maid. He should have taken a seat in the new senate, not ceded it out of cynicism to the likes of Don Calogero Sedàra.

Furthermore, just as the prince was too willing to ally himself with the middle classes, he was entirely too dismissive of improving the lot of the common people, in violation of the feudal ethos that bound the most decent man in the whole book, Ciccio Tumeo, to the deposed Bourbons. Sicily today is objectively better off with paved roads, running water, sewers, and other improvements airily dismissed by the prince.

In short, the best outcome for Italy would have been a marriage of the feudal-warrior ethos of the old aristocracy with a progressive national populism, cutting out the rising oligarchy altogether. This position is actually represented in *The Leopard* by Cavalier Chevalley di Monterzuolo (played by Leslie French), the Piedmontese functionary who asks the prince to join the new senate. In the twentieth century, this synthesis was finally realized by Mussolini, only to be reversed by the Second World War, with some help from the dried-up husk of the house of Savoy.

When the prince bids Chevalley goodbye, he says, "We were the leopards, the lions. Those who will take our place will be jackals, hyenas. And all of us—leopards, lions, jackals, and sheep—we'll go on thinking ourselves the salt of the earth." An accurate prophecy—but a self-fulfilling one. It was the dereliction of men like the prince of Salina who made it so.

The Leopard's depiction of the corruption of Garibaldi's national-populist revolution offers many lessons to national populists today. We should count ourselves fortunate that the old monarchies and aristocracies of Europe are pretty much dead, and those that remain are pretty much politically irrelevant. National populists believe that political sovereignty resides in the nation, not in dynasties. Political legitimacy flows from representing the common good of the people, not from dynastic descent. Social and political hierarchies are justified only by the common good of society, not by divine right or hereditary caste. Monarchy and aristocracy have a seductive glamor, but they are at best imperfect images of just political hierarchies.

However, national populists should emulate the honor-centered warrior ethos of the old aristocracies, as well as their feudal sense of social responsibility, which are the necessary correctives to bourgeois materialism and individualism.

Lampedusa makes clear that the material magnificence of the old aristocracy springs from essentially spiritual and anti-materialist values. Aristocracies arise by subordinating material interests, including the instinct of self-preservation, to the pursuit of honor. Aristocracies transmute material wealth into spiritual values like honor and prestige through munificence and the creation of beautiful and useless things, such as the entire realm of high culture.

But *The Leopard* also shows how high living combined with an ethos of generosity leads to the ruin of great estates and the rise of oligarchy. Oligarchs can better maintain the opulent lifestyles of the aristocracy because they are materialists, individualists, and fundamentally selfish. The bourgeois ethos subordinates honor and culture to self-preservation and commodious living. Obviously, a cash-poor revolutionary movement like national populism needs to adopt the warrior ethos of the aristocracy, but we can't afford aristocratic pretensions in the material realm. We need to be revolutionary ascetics if we are to free ourselves from the trammels of oligarchy.

Everything about this movie is superb: the directing, casting, acting, costumes, camerawork, sets, and Nino Rota's ravishing Romantic score. I have one reservation. Not a criticism so much as a reservation. *The Leopard* is a short novel but a very long movie, clocking in at 185 minutes in its definitive version. The ball sequence alone occupies the last fifty minutes. I resisted watching for years, simply because of the time investment. But there is something magical about this movie. When the ball started, I no longer felt I was watching a movie. I felt I was *in* it. And it made such a strong impression that it was all I remembered about the movie when I re-watched it after more than a decade to write this essay. Buy the Blu-ray and watch it in installments if you must, but you must watch it.

Visconti's film will especially appeal to lovers of historical costume dramas, romances, and comedies of manners. If you like Jane Austen adaptations, you will find *The Leopard* especially appealing, for like Austen, Lampedusa is a student of classical virtue ethics and creates very subtle character portraits. Thus I highly recommend *The Leopard*, the novel and the film. They are two twentieth-century masterpieces that can be appreciated both as escapist entertainment and as profound meditations on politics, morals, and the human condition.

The Unz Review, August 25, 2019

THE MAN WHO SHOT LIBERTY VALANCE

John Ford's last great film *The Man Who Shot Liberty Valance* (1962) enjoys the status of a classic. I find it a deeply flawed, grating, and often ridiculous film that is nonetheless redeemed by raising intellectually deep issues and by an emotionally powerful ending that seems to come out of nowhere.

The stars of *The Man Who Shot Liberty Valance* are John Wayne and Jimmy Stewart, both fine actors given the impossible job of playing men in their 20s, even though they were aged 54 and 53 at the time. It just doesn't work.

There's also too much buffoonery. Ford thought that drunkards and men with funny voices were hilarious. In *The Man Who Shot Liberty Valance*, we get *two* funny drunkards and *three* men with funny voices, including Andy Devine and Strother Martin. There is also a great deal of scene-chewing overacting and overly broad parody that often seem downright cartoonish.

The film is poorly paced as well, burning through screen time and my patience with dramatically needless details of frontier kitchens and political conventions.

Beyond these lapses of taste, *The Man Who Shot Liberty Valance* also contains Left-liberal messages on race. For instance, Devine's Marshal Link Appleyard is married to a Mexican woman. Oddly enough, the same actor's character in Ford's *Stagecoach* (1939) is married to a Mexican as well. In real life, Andy Devine was married to a white woman. Bucking the color bar must have been Ford's preference.

Wayne's character Tom Doniphan has a loyal negro sidekick named Pompey (Woody Strode). Pompey even endures the indignity of being refused service at the saloon, but Doniphan stands up for him, although he does refer to him as "my boy Pompey."

At the very center of the film is a scene in which newly-minted lawyer Ransom Stoddard (Stewart) teaches reading and civics to a class of white adults, plus Pompey and a brood of Mexican children. (All the children in Shinbone are nonwhite, a poignant sign that white civilization has not yet been established there. Now such classrooms are signs of white civilization in decline.) Lawyer Stoddard teaches that the fundamental law of the land is the Declaration of Independence, which holds that "All men are created equal." The Declaration, of course, is not the fundamental law of the land. That would be the Constitution, which says nothing about all men being created equal.

Ford was known as a patriot and an anti-communist, but on race, his politics were aligned with the Hollywood progressive consensus. Ford did not, however, identify with outsiders against America's WASP ethnic core because he was Jewish. Instead, he did so as an Irish Catholic, born John Martin Feeney.

Judging from Ford's cavalry trilogy—*Fort Apache* (1948), *She Wore a Yellow Ribbon* (1949), and *Rio Grande* (1950)—the West could not have been won without the help of golden-hearted, silver-tongued Irish drunkards. These stereotypes seem rather broad and offensive today, but Ford—a heavy drinker himself—obviously regarded them affectionately and thought their inclusion to be progressive.

I list these problems up front, because I don't want you to be surprised or deterred by them. For in spite of its flaws, *The Man Who Shot Liberty Valance* is a worthwhile film. As the title suggests, this is a movie about violence, specifically the relationship of violence to manliness and civilization. The film's message is deeply antiliberal. Indeed, although Ford could not have known it, *The Man Who Shot Liberty Valance* illustrates many of

Carl Schmitt's criticisms of liberalism. Thus I include it among the classics of Right-wing cinema.

The movie opens with a train pulling into the town of Shinbone in an unnamed state in the American Southwest. Shinbone is conspicuously bright, clean, and attractive. Everything looks brand-new. The only thing old and dusty is the stagecoach, a victim of progress suitably abandoned at the undertaker's parlor. Shinbone was built on a soundstage. Ford was known for shooting on location because he loved sweeping vistas and gritty authenticity. But Shinbone's cleanliness and newness—its clear artificiality—were quite deliberate representations of progress and the end of the frontier.

Senator Ransom Stoddard and his wife Hallie (Vera Miles) are met by the former Marshal, Link Appleyard. They have arrived to attend the funeral of their old friend Tom Doniphon (John Wayne), who is being interred in a pauper's grave at public expense. As a sign of the changes in Shinbone, we learn that Doniphon will not be buried with his gun, because he had not carried one in years. When the local newspaper editor demands to know why a sitting Senator is attending the funeral of a pauper, Stoddard agrees to tell the tale.

We flash back some decades. Ransom "Rance" Stoddard, fresh out of law school, has gone West, not so much to seek fame and fortune as to improve the place by bringing law, literacy, and progress from back East. Outside a much rougher version of Shinbone, the stagecoach in which Stoddard is riding is robbed by outlaw Liberty Valance (Lee Marvin) and his gang (including Lee Van Cleef and Strother Martin). When Stoddard objects to the rough treatment of a woman, Valance beats him severely then sends away the coach, leaving him to his fate.

Played to cartoonish excess by Lee Marvin, Liberty Valance is a cold-blooded murderer and thief. He's also a drunkard and a petty bully. The entire town of Shinbone lives in terror of him. He's the kind of man who needs killing, so decent people can plant crops, raise children, and sleep at night.

It seems odd that an American movie would have a villain named Liberty. Isn't America the land of liberty? But Liberty Valance is not really an American. He's a man of the Wild West. America is a Republic with laws. The West is the state of nature. Liberty Valance represents the liberty of savages in the state of nature, where one man's liberty is exercised at the expense of another's. Savage liberty must die so civil liberty can be born. Thus it is appropriate that Liberty Valance is a hired gun of the cattle interests, who oppose statehood and the coming of law and order.

Stoddard is rescued by Tom Doniphon, who owns a small horse ranch outside Shinbone, and brought into town. For no sensible reason except that he likes her, Tom awakens Hallie, who works as a waitress at a local eatery, to help tend to Stoddard's wounds.

Tom quickly pegs Rance as a greenhorn and a tinhorn. He doesn't know how the world works, but he talks like he does. When Tom tells Rance that he'd better get a gun if he wants justice, Rance launches into a speech:

> But do you know what you're saying to me? You're saying just exactly what Liberty Valance said. What kind of community have I come to? You all seem to know Liberty Valance. He's a no-good, gun-packing, murdering thief, but the only advice you give me is to carry a gun. Well, I'm a lawyer! Ransom Stoddard, Attorney at Law. And the law is the only . . .

Jimmy Stewart was brilliant casting because he's obviously in love with his own voice.

Rance doesn't see any difference between force used by criminals and force used by decent men against criminals.

He's an idealist who apparently thinks the laws can magically enforce themselves. In John Wayne's most often-imitated line, Tom calls Rance "Pilgrim," which pretty much sums up his combination of moralism and utopianism. He's a spindly, priggish, progressive zealot. He reminds me of Barack Obama.

Rance settles in Shinbone, working alongside Hallie in the kitchen of the eatery owned by Swedish immigrants Nora and Peter Ericson. Rance's role in the community, however, is distinctly feminine. In a land where men wear guns and settle problems for themselves, he refuses to wear a gun and expects the law to settle disputes . . . somehow. Thus in the Ericsons' restaurant, Rance wears an apron while washing dishes and occasionally waiting tables. (Obama also allowed himself to be photographed in an apron.) When Rance learns that Hallie can't read, he takes on another stereotypically female role: schoolmarm.

When an apron-clad Rance brings Tom his dinner in the restaurant, Liberty trips him, then mocks him. Tom is enraged. It is his steak, after all. Tom demands that Liberty pick it up. Tom is the toughest guy in town, the only one who is not afraid of Liberty. A gunfight almost ensues until Rance, still clad in an apron, picks up the steak for them, ranting about the absurdity of men killing one another over matters of pride. This too is an attitude more commonly associated with women. Ford clearly thinks that manliness is connected with a willingness to fight over matters of honor.

Rance begins to have some doubts, however, when it becomes clear that the local law enforcement, Marshal Appleyard, is a fat, effeminate coward. Devigne's squeaky voice is well-employed, but Ford labors the point endlessly, to the point of cartoonishness.

When Rance allies with the local newspaper editor, funny drunk Dutton Peabody (Edmond O'Brien), to fight the cattle barons and appeal for statehood, Liberty is hired by the ranchers to intimidate the townspeople. At that point, Rance furtively buys a gun and sneaks off to practice shooting. Why the deception? Because he can't really reconcile it with his self-image and the image he has established with the public.

There's also a love triangle in the mix. Tom is in love with Hallie. Everybody sees it. But he hasn't screwed up the courage to propose. It is his one failure of nerve as a man. When Rance enters the picture, Hallie begins by tending his wounds like a mother. Then she works with him in the kitchen like a sister (both in aprons). Then he schoolmarms her along with a brood of Mexican children. Rance is pretty much zilch as a man, certainly nobody Tom would regard as a rival. But when Hallie begs Tom to stop Rance from getting himself killed in a duel over honor, the big lug realizes that he is in danger of losing his girl.

When Rance (still wearing his apron) faces Liberty Valance, Liberty toys with him, shooting a jar first, then wounding his arm, then taunting him to pick up the gun again. Rance does so, takes aim, and shoots Liberty dead. Hallie rushes to tend Rance's wounds. But Rance is no longer a child. He has faced death in a duel over honor. He's a man now. When Tom sees them together, he knows that he has lost Hallie. He gets staggering drunk and burns his own house down in self-pity.

Rance Stoddard enjoyed some esteem for his good heart and his skills as a teacher and a lawyer. But his refusal to carry a gun put him in the category of women and children when it came to defending the community. However, when he shot Liberty Valance, he became a man and a hero. It also launched his political career.

But none of this sits well with Rance's puritanical idealist streak. He feels that he bears the "mark of Cain" and is perhaps unworthy of public office. So Tom takes him aside and tells him a story. Tom was watching the confrontation with Liberty, and when Rance raised his gun to fire, Tom shot Liberty dead with a rifle. Tom is willing to take the guilt—and also the glory—to salve Rance's morbid conscience. "It was cold-blooded murder," says Tom. "But I can live with it." It is telling that Rance can't live with killing in self-defense.

I wonder, though, if Tom's story is even true. Did it really happen, or did he make it up to spare Rance's feelings? True or false, Tom is astonishingly generous. If the story is true, Tom saved Rance's life and lost the woman he loved in the bargain. If the story is false, Tom is admitting to murder simply to make Rance feel better, perhaps because he hopes to promote Hallie's happiness even after losing her.

This is an enormous risk for Tom. If Rance shot Liberty, it was self-defense. But if Tom killed Liberty, he could hang for it. For Tom's sake, Rance is forced to keep the secret. Oddly enough, his conscience allows him to return to politics, where he enjoys an illustrious career: governor, senator, ambassador to England. Granted, he no longer thinks his public esteem is based on killing, but shouldn't he be bothered that it is based on a lie? Perhaps he can live with the lie by telling himself that he is doing good things for the people. But couldn't he say the same thing about killing Liberty Valance?

The deeper truth that Rance evades is that, for civilization to come to the West, *somebody needed to shoot Liberty Valance.* It doesn't really matter who. When Dutton Peabody nominates Rance to represent the territory in Washington, he explains how the West was won. First, it was held by merciless Indian savages. Then it was settled by cattlemen, whose law was the gun. The cattlemen did what was necessary, namely kill and subjugate the Indians. Then came the farmers and businessmen, who need fences and law and order. Liberty Valance is a hired gun of the cattle interests. His type was necessary to deal with the Indians. But now he has outlived his usefulness and stands in the way of progress. Progress requires a new kind of man: Ransom Stoddard, attorney at law. And isn't it poetic that Rance Stoddard is the man who shot Liberty Valance?

The possibility that the story is false is supported by Ford's frank exploration of noble and ignoble lies later in the movie. Although the newspaper editor has pried the story out of Rance by insisting on his "right to the truth," once the tale is told, he burns his notes and tells Rance he will not print the truth. "This is the West, Sir," he says, "When the legend becomes fact, print the legend." What he really means is when facts are *replaced* by legend, print the legend.

But why replace the truth with legend? What's wrong with the truth? The superficial truth deals with who shot Liberty Valance: Tom or Rance? If Tom shot Liberty, he can't be punished now because he's dead. Rance, of course, kept the secret. Perhaps there would be legal consequences for that. But the real need for deception has to do with the deeper truth: *somebody* needed to shoot Liberty Valance so that civilization could come to the West, just as the Liberty Valances of the world were needed to shoot the Indians. This truth needs to be concealed because it does not sit well with liberalism.

Liberalism seeks to do away with force and fraud in human affairs. This is a noble aspiration shared by anti-liberal thinkers as well. Liberal theorists are famous for constructing accounts of how civil order can arise from the state of nature without force or fraud, by means of a social contract between rational agents. It is only because liberals think that political legitimacy depends on the *immaculate conception* of liberal order, without resort to force and fraud, that they are forced to print the legend. Liberalism does not banish force from politics, and especially from the foundation of political order. It merely banishes honesty about force.

Rance Stoddard is a brilliant and scathing portrait of liberalism. When Rance's priggish, effeminate idealism clashes with the grim reality of the state of nature, Tom Doniphon needs to rescue him again and again. If Rance really shot Liberty Valance, it was only by discarding his initial belief that there is no difference between Liberty and Tom—and only by taking Tom's advice to buy a gun. If Tom shot Liberty Valance, the repudiation of liberalism is even deeper, for Rance has the law on his side but isn't up to the task of defeating Liberty, so Tom must commit cold-blooded murder.

Liberalism, in short, depends on illiberal men and extralegal violence for its very survival. But, instead of questioning their own ideological premises, liberals simply lie about this fact. Ford doesn't dispute the benefits of law and order. He just thinks they would be better secured by men who are more honest about the role of violence in founding and maintaining them.

This is an amazing message for a Hollywood film. I have no doubt that this is Ford's intended meaning. Everything about this film, both its virtues and its flaws, is 100% John Ford. He was one of Hollywood's most meticulous *auteurs*, a fact that is somewhat hidden by the formulaic quality of all his films. Ford started making movies in the silent era, when they were everyone's entertainment, which meant that every film had to have something for everyone, including a love story and some crude comic relief, usually involving booze. Of course one could level the same sort of criticisms at Shakespeare.

I chalk the film's flaws up to the self-indulgence of old age. Ford was pushing 70, and his hard-working, hard-drinking life was catching up with him. Perhaps we can credit the film's virtues to another trait of old age: impatience, because time is short, which leads to greater frankness, even though it might ruffle some folks' feathers.

I don't want to spoil the movie's brilliant and heartbreaking final scene, so I will leave you with these words. Since men like Liberty Valance need killing to create political order, nothing is too good for the man who shot Liberty Valance. It is a burning indictment of liberalism that such men lie unsung and unstoried in paupers' graves.

The Unz Review, March 25, 2021

MISHIMA:
A LIFE IN FOUR CHAPTERS

Similar things happen in the United States too: an alienated, bookish radical Right-winger takes up weight-lifting and martial arts, creates a private militia, dreams of overthrowing the government, then dies in a spectacular, suicidal, and apparently pointless confrontation with the state. In the United States, however, such people are easily dismissed as "kooks" and "losers." But when it happened in Japan, the protagonist, Yukio Mishima, was one of the nation's most famous and respected novelists.

Director Paul Schrader's 1985 movie, *Mishima: A Life in Four Chapters*, is an excellent introduction to Mishima's life and work. It is by far the best movie about an artist I have ever seen. It is also surely the most sympathetic film portrayal of a figure who was essentially a fascist, maybe since *Triumph of the Will*.

Paul Schrader, of German Calvinist descent, is famous as the writer or co-writer of the screenplays of Martin Scorsese's *Taxi Driver*, *Raging Bull*, *The Last Temptation of Christ*, and *Bringing Out the Dead*. His other screenplays include Brian De Palma's *Obsession*, Peter Weir's *The Mosquito Coast*, and his own *American Gigolo*. Other movies directed by Schrader include the near-dreadful remake of *Cat People* and the brilliant *Auto Focus*, a biopic about a very different sort of artist, Bob Crane. It is so creepy that I will never watch it again, even though it is a masterpiece.

Mishima, however, is Schrader's best film. He also co-wrote the screenplay with his brother Leonard. (The score, moreover, is the best thing ever written by Philip Glass.)

The narrative frame of the movie is Mishima's last day, which is filmed in realistic color. The story of his life is told in black and white flashbacks, intercut with dramatizations of parts of three of Mishima's novels, *The Temple of the Golden Pavilion*, *Kyoko's House*, and *Runaway Horses*, which are filmed on unrealistic stage sets in lavish Technicolor.

Yukio Mishima was a very, very, very sensitive child. Born Kimitake Hiraoke in 1925 to an upper middle class family with samurai ancestry, he was taken from his mother by his grandmother, who kept him indoors, told him that he was physically fragile, prevented him from playing with other boys, and made him her factotum until she died when he was twelve. Then he returned to his parents.

Highly intelligent and convinced of his physical frailty, Mishima became bookish and introverted: a reader and a writer, a poet and a dreamer. He wrote his first short stories at age 12. Denied an outlet for healthy, boyish aggression, he became a masochist. He was also homosexual.

Imbued with samurai tradition, he longed to fight in the Second World War and die for the Emperor, but he was rejected as physically unfit for duty, a source of lifelong self-reproach. He had a cold when he reported for his physical, and he later claimed that out of cowardice he exaggerated his symptoms so the doctor thought he had tuberculosis.

Mishima's first book was published when he was 19. He wrote at least 100 books—40 novels, 20 collections of short stories, 20 plays (including a screenplay and an opera libretto), and 20-odd book-length essays and collections of essays—before his death at age 45. He also dabbled in acting and directing.

THE TEMPLE OF THE GOLDEN PAVILION

Schrader's dramatization of Mishima's 1956 novel *The Temple of the Golden Pavilion* focuses on the author's Nietzschean exploration of the role of physiognomy and will-to-power in the origin of values. Nietzsche believed that all organisms have will-to-power, even sickly and botched ones. In the realm of values, will-to-power manifests itself particularly in a desire to think well of oneself. A healthy organism affirms itself by positing values that affirm its nature. The healthy affirm health, strength, beauty, and power. They despise the sickly, weak, and ugly.

But sickly organisms have will-to-power too. They affirm themselves by positing values based on their natures, values that cast them in a positive light and cast healthy organisms in a negative light. This is the origin of ascetic and "spiritual" values, as well as the Christian values of the Sermon on the Mount, which Nietzsche calls "slave morality."

The Temple of the Golden Pavilion is loosely based on the burning of the Reliquary (or Golden Pavilion) of Kinkaku-ji in Kyoto by a deranged Buddhist acolyte in 1950. In Mishima's story, the arson is committed by Mizoguchi, an acolyte afflicted with ugliness and a stutter. The acolyte recognizes the beauty of the Golden Pavilion, but also hates it, because its beauty magnifies his deformities.

Mizoguchi's clubfooted friend Kashiwagi tries to teach Mizoguchi to exploit his disabilities to arouse women's pity to get sex. Kashiwagi can use his disability because he lacks pride and will-to-power. Mizoguchi, however, cannot enjoy beauty by means of self-abasement. He cannot own his imperfections. The vision of the Golden Pavilion prevents him. He can like himself only if the Golden Pavilion is destroyed, thus he sets it ablaze.

In Nietzsche's terms, the destruction of the Golden Pavilion is an act of transvaluation. The beauty that oppresses Mizoguchi must be destroyed. For Nietzsche, this act of destruction serves to create a space for new values that will allow him to affirm his disability, just as the destruction of aristocratic values creates a space for slave morality.

Schrader includes this dramatization of *The Temple of the Golden Pavilion* to illustrate Mishima's exploration of his own youthful nihilism. Short even by Japanese standards (5'1"), skinny, and physically frail, Mishima envied and eroticized the bodies of healthier boys, an eroticism that Mishima's *Confessions of a Mask* clearly indicates was tinged with masochistic self-hatred and sadistic fantasies of brutality and murder. (Mishima first became sexually aroused at a photograph of a painting of the martyrdom of Saint Sebastian.)

SELF-TRANSFORMATION

The Temple of the Golden Pavilion, however, is a look backwards, at paths Mishima could understand but not follow. Unlike Kashiwagi, Mishima could not own his physical imperfections. Unlike Mizoguchi, he could not annihilate the ideal of beauty just to feel good about himself. This left Mishima with only one choice: to remake his body according to the ideal of physical beauty. Thus in 1955, Mishima started lifting weights, with impressive results. He also took up kendo and karate.

Mishima documented his physical transformation with a very un-Japanese exhibitionism. He posed frequently for photographers, producing a book, *Ordeal by Roses* (1963), in collaboration with photographer Eikoh Hosoe. Mishima also posed in *Young Samurai: Bodybuilders of Japan* and *OTOKO: Photo Studies of the Young Japanese Male* by Tamotsu Yatō. His acting work was also an extension of this exhibitionism, as was his dandyism. When he wasn't posing nude or in a loincloth, his clothes were almost exclusively Western. He dressed up like James Bond and dressed down like James Dean.

In 1958, his body and self-confidence transformed, Mishima married Yoko Sugiyama. It was an arranged marriage. They had two children. (Among Mishima's requirements for a wife was that she have no interest in his work and that she be shorter than him. As an indication of his social circles, Mishima had earlier considered Michiko Shōda as a possible bride. She went on to marry Crown Prince Akihito and became Empress of Japan.)

In 1959, Mishima built a house in an entirely Western style. Following the Nietzschean principle that every authentic culture has an integrity and unity of style, Mishima rejected multiculturalism, including mixing Japanese and Western lifestyles. Since he could not live in an entirely Japanese house, he chose to live in an entirely Western one, where he could "sit on rococo furniture wearing Levis and an aloha shirt."

KYOKO'S HOUSE

The second Mishima novel Schrader dramatizes is *Kyoko's House* (1959), which cries out for an English translation. According to the literature, *Kyoko's House* is an exploration of Mishima's own psyche, aspects of which are concretized in the four main characters: a boxer, who represents Mishima's new-found athleticism; a painter, who represents his creative side; a businessman, who like Mishima lives an outwardly conventional life but rejects postwar Japanese society; and an actor, who represents his narcissism.

Schrader focuses only on the story of the actor, who takes up bodybuilding when humiliated by a gangster sent to intimidate his mother, who was in debt to loan sharks. The moneylender turns out to be a woman. She offers to cancel the loan if the actor sells himself to her.

The narcissist, whose sense of reality is based on the impression he makes in the eyes of others, realizes that even his newly acquired muscles are not real to him. The realization comes when his lover, on a sadistic whim, cuts his skin with a razor. In physical pain, he finds a sense of reality otherwise unavailable due to his personality disorder. Their sexual relationship takes a sadomasochistic turn that culminates in a suicide pact—foreshadowing Mishima's own end.

Having put so much of himself into *Kyoko's House*, Mishima was deeply wounded by its commercial and critical failure. Schrader had first wanted to dramatize Mishima's *Forbidden Colors*, his novel about Japan's homosexual subculture, but Mishima's widow refused permission. (She denied that Mishima had any homosexual proclivities.) But it is just as well. From what I can gather, *Kyoko's House* is a far better novel than *Forbidden Colors*.

Schrader did not dramatize the story of the boxer in *Kyoko's House*, but it also foreshadows Mishima's life as well. After one of his hands is shattered in a fight, the boxer becomes involved in Right-wing politics. Mishima makes it quite clear that the boxer's political commitment is not based on ideology, but on a physically ruined man's desire for an experience of self-transcendence and sublimity.

The businessman's story is also important for understanding Mishima's life and outlook. He thinks postwar Japan is a spiritual void in which prosperity, materialism, peace, and resolute amnesia about the war years have sapped life of authenticity, which requires that one face death, something that was omnipresent during the war.

Authenticity through awareness of death, pain as an encounter with reality, and Right-wing politics as a form of self-transcendence (or therapy): *Kyoko's House* maps out the trajectory of the rest of Mishima's life.

Mishima's Political Turn

Mishima, like many Western Right-wingers, saw tradition as a third way between capitalism and socialism, which are essentially identical in their materialistic ends and their scientific and technological means. He always had Right-wing tendencies, but his writings in the 1940s and 1950s were absorbed (self-absorbed, truth be told) with personal moral and psychological issues.

Like many Japanese, however, Mishima became increasingly alarmed by the corruptions of postwar consumer society. He saw the samurai tradition as an aristocratic alternative to massification, a spiritual alternative to materialism. He saw the Japanese military and the Emperor as guardians of this tradition. But these guardians had already made too many compromises with modernity. Mishima was particularly critical of the Emperor's renunciation of divinity at the end of the Second World War. In his writings and actions in the last decade of his life, Mishima sought to call the Emperor and the military back to their mission as guardians of Japanese tradition.

In the fall of 1960, Mishima wrote "Patriotism," a short story about the aftermath of the "Ni Ni-Roku Incident" of February 1936, an attempted *coup d'état* by junior officers of the Imperial Army who assassinated several political leaders. The officers wished the government to address widespread poverty caused by the worldwide Great Depression. The coup was cast as an attempt to restore the absolute power of the Emperor, but he regarded it as a rebellion and ordered it crushed.

Mishima's story focuses on Lieutenant Shinji Takeyama and his young wife, Reiko. The Lieutenant did not take part in the coup but was friends with the participants. He is ordered to help suppress it. Torn between loyalty to the Emperor and loyalty to his friends, he chooses to commit suicide by self-disembowelment after a night of love-making. Reiko joins him in death.

Mishima published "Patriotism" in 1961. In 1965, he directed and starred in 28-minute film adaptation which he first released in France. The film of *Patriotism* is erotic, chilling, and cringe-inducingly graphic (people regularly fainted when they saw it in theaters). In retrospect, it seems like merely a rehearsal for Mishima's eventual suicide. The music, fittingly, is the *Liebestod* (Love-Death) from Wagner's *Tristan und Isolde*. Mishima's widow locked up the film after her husband's death. After her death, it was released on DVD by the Criterion Collection. (Mishima also committed suicide on screen in Hideo Gosha's 1969 film *Tenchu!*)

Schrader shows bits of the filming of *Patriotism* and also dramatizes a very similar episode from *Runaway Horses* (1969), the second volume of Mishima's *The Sea of Fertility* quartet (1968–1970). *The Sea of Fertility* is a panorama of Japan's traumatic crash-course in modernization, spanning the years 1912 to 1975, narrating the life of Shigekuni Honda, who becomes a wealthy and widely-traveled jurist.

Runaway Horses, set in 1932–1933, is the story of Isao Iinuma, a Right-wing student who seeks the alliance of the military to plot a rebellion in 1932. The goal is to topple capitalism and restore absolute Imperial rule by simultaneously assassinating the heads of industry and the government and torching the Bank of Japan. The plot is foiled, but when Isao is released from prison, he carries out his part of the mission anyway, assassinating his target. The assassination, of course, is politically futile, but Isao feels honor-bound to carry out his mission. He then commits *hara-kiri*.

Isao's plot is clearly based on the Ni Ni-Roku Incident. The novel also tells the story of the Samurai insurrection in Kunamoto in 1876. But it would be a mistake to conclude that Mishima put his hope in a successful military coup as the most likely path to a renewal of Japanese tradition. Mishima's focus was on the ritual suicides of the defeated rebels.

THE WAY OF THE SAMURAI

Japan enjoyed 300 years of peace under the Tokugawa Shogunate. Conflict had been outlawed; history in the Hegelian sense had been ended. Yet the arts and culture flourished, and the Japanese had not been reduced to a mass of dehumanized and degraded producer-consumers. The cause of this was the persistence of the samurai ethic.

The samurai, of course, like all aristocrats, prefer death to dishonor, and when prevented from demonstrating this on the battlefield, they demonstrated it instead through ritual suicide. They also demonstrated their contempt of material necessity through the cultivation of luxury and refinement. The cultural supremacy of the ideal of the honor suicide served as a bulwark protecting high culture against degeneration into bourgeois consumer culture, which springs from an opposing hierarchy of values that prizes life, comfort, and security over honor.

Mishima's cultural-political project makes the most sense if we view it not as an attempt to return to militarism, but as an attempt to uphold or revive the samurai ethic in postwar Japan so that it could play the same conservative role as it did under the 300-year peace of the Shogunate. (Mishima's outlook would then be very similar to that of Alexandre Kojève, who in his *Introduction to the Reading of Hegel* claimed that Japan under the Shogunate showed how we might retain our humanity at the end of history through an aristocratic culture that rested on the cultural ideal of a "purely gratuitous suicide.")

Mishima produced a spate of political books and essays in the 1960s, most of which have remained untranslated. Two of the most important, however, are available in English. In 1967, Mishima published *The Way of the Samurai*, his commentary on the *Hagakure* (literally, *In the Shadow of the Leaves*), a handbook authored by the eighteenth-century samurai Tsunetomo Yamamoto. In 1968, Mishima published *Sun and Steel*, an autobiographical essay about bodybuilding, martial arts, and the relationship of thought and action which also discusses ritual suicide. (In 1968, Mishima also published a play, *My Friend Hitler*, about the Röhm purge of 1934. He was coy about his true feelings toward Hitler. In truth, he was more a Mussolini man.)

MISHIMA THE ACTIVIST

But Mishima did more than write about action. He acted. In 1967, Mishima enlisted in the Japanese Ground Self-Defense Force (GSDF) and underwent basic training. In 1968, Mishima formed the Tatenokai (Shield Society—Mishima was pleased that the English initials were SS), a private militia composed primarily of Right-wing university students who studied martial arts and swore to protect Japanese tradition against the forces of modernization, Left or Right.

In 1968 and 1969, when Leftist student agitators had the universities in chaos, Mishima participated in debates and teach-ins, criticizing Marxism and arguing that Japanese nationalism, symbolized by loyalty to the Emperor, should come before all other political commitments.

On November 25, 1970, after a year of planning, Mishima and four members of the Shield Society visited the Icigaya Barracks of the Japanese Self-Defense force and took the commander hostage. Mishima demanded that the troops be assembled so he could address them. He had alerted the press in advance. He stepped out onto a balcony in his uniform to harangue the assembled troops, calling them to reject American-imposed materialism and to return to the role of guardians of Japanese tradition.

The speech was largely drowned out by circling helicopters, and the soldiers jeered. Mishima returned to the commander's office, where he and one of his followers, Masakatsu Morita, committed *seppuku*, a ritual suicide involving self-disembowelment with a dagger followed by decapitation with a sword wielded by one's second.

Mishima's stunt is often referred to as a "coup attempt," but this is stupid. Mishima had been talking about, writing about, rehearsing, and preparing for suicide for years. He had no intention of surviving, much less taking power. His death was an attempt to inspire a revival of samurai tradition. In samurai fashion, he wanted a death that mattered, a death of his choosing, a death that he staged with consummate dramatic skill.

Mishima also wished to avoid the decay of old age. Having come to physical health so late in life, he had no intention of experiencing its progressive loss. (His last novel, *The Decay of the Angel*, paints a very bleak portrait of old age.)

Schrader's depiction of Mishima's suicide is far less graphic than *Patriotism* but every bit as powerful. He saves the climaxes of *The Temple of the Golden Pavilion*, *Kyoko's House*, and *Runaway Horses* to the very end, inter-cutting them with Mishima's own suicide, to shattering effect.

This is a great movie, which will leave a lasting impression.

Mishima's Legacy

In the end, though, what did Mishima's death mean? What did it matter? What did it accomplish?

It would be all too easy to dismiss Mishima as a neurotic and a narcissist who engaged in politics as a kind of therapy. Right-wing politics is crawling with such people (none of them with Mishima's talents, unfortunately), and we would be better off without them. If a Mishima wished to write for *Counter-Currents*, we would welcome his work (as we would welcome translations of Mishima's works!). But we would also keep him at arm's length. Such people should be locked in a room with a computer and fed through a slot in the door. They should not be put in positions of trust and responsibility.

But Mishima is safely dead, and the meaning of his death cannot be measured in terms of crass political "deliverables." Indeed, it is a repudiation of the whole calculus of interests that lies at the foundation of modern politics.

Modern politics is based on the idea that a long and comfortable life is the highest value, to be purchased even at the price of our dignity. Aristocratic politics is based on the idea that honor is the highest value, to be purchased even at the price of our lives.

The spiritual aristocrat, therefore, must be ready to die; he must conquer his fear of death; he even must come to love death, for his ability to choose death before dishonor is what raises him above being a mere clever animal. It is what makes him a free man, a natural master rather than a natural slave. It is ultimately the foundation of all forms of higher culture, which involve the rejection or subordination and stylization of merely animal desire.

A natural slave is someone who is willing to give up his honor to save his life. Thus modern politics, which exalts the long and prosperous life as the highest value, is a form of spiritual slavery, even if the external controls are merely soft commercial and political incentives rather than chains and cages.

Thus Mishima's eroticization of death is not a mental illness needing medication. By ceasing to fear death, Mishima became free to lead his life, to take risks other men would not have taken. By ceasing to fear death, Mishima could preserve his honor from the compromises of commerce and politics and the ravages of old age. By ceasing to fear death, Mishima entered into the realm of freedom that is the basis of all high culture. By ceasing to fear death, Mishima struck a mortal blow at the foundations of the modern world.

In my discussion of Christopher Nolan's *The Dark Knight* (elsewhere in this volume), I argued that the Joker is Hollywood's image of a man who is totally free from modern society because he has fundamentally rejected its ruling values—by overcoming the fear of death. An army of such men could bring down the modern world.

Well, Yukio Mishima was a real example of such a man.

And, as usual, the truth is stranger than fiction.

AFTERWORD

In my discussions of Christopher Nolan's *Batman Begins* (in this volume) and Guillermo del Toro's *Hellboy* and *Hellboy II: The Golden Army*,[1] I argued that somebody in Hollywood and the comic book/graphic novel industry must be reading up on Traditionalism, for the supervillains in these movies can be seen as Traditionalists. Since Traditionalism is the most fundamental rejection of the modern world, weaponized Traditionalists make the most dramatically potent foils for liberal, democratic, humanistic superheroes like Hellboy and Batman.

Well, shortly after I wrote that, Savitri Devi's *Impeachment of Man* was ordered by someone at one of the major comics companies.

I can see it all now. Somewhere down the line, Hellboy will be squaring off against the Cat Lady of Calcutta, who will rise from the Antarctic ice with her fleet of Zündel saucers, and Batman will face his new arch-nemesis . . . a five-foot samurai with spindly legs in tights.

Counter-Currents, January 21, 2011

---

[1] In *Trevor Lynch's White Nationalist Guide to the Movies*.

NETWORK

Written by Paddy Chayefsky and directed by Sidney Lumet, *Network* (1976) is a sardonic, dark-comic satire of America at the very moment that its trajectory of decline became apparent (to perceptive eyes, at least).

Network has an outstanding script and incandescent performances, which were duly recognized. Chayefsky won the Oscar for Best Screenplay. Peter Finch won the Oscar for Best Actor for his portrayal of TV anchorman Howard Beale. Faye Dunaway won Best Actress for playing the reptilian, cynical career girl Diana Christensen. William Holden turns in a warm and credible performance as TV news executive Max Schumacher. Beatrice Straight plays Schumacher's wife Louise. She won Best Supporting Actress for basically one scene, where she denounces her cheating husband, a measure of the talent this movie lavished on even minor roles. Robert Duvall is a convincingly loathsome corporate creep named Frank Hackett. Marlene Warfield is electrifying and utterly hilarious as my favorite character, Laureen Hobbs, who introduces herself as a "bad-ass commie nigger."

Remarkably, *Network* has no film score, and it is not really missed. The script and performances stand on their own. We don't need violins to tell us what to feel.

Network is a serious movie of ideas. What's more, these ideas are objectively Right-wing, even though that was surely not the intention of Chayefsky and Lumet.

Network offers a scathing tableau of the cynicism, corruption, and propagandistic agenda of the mainstream media, one of the cultural citadels of the Left. *Network* offers a particularly dark portrait of a scheming, sociopathic career woman (Faye Dunaway's Diana Christiansen) who sleeps with a married superior.

Network also portrays the sixties generation, then rising into positions of influence, as cynical and decadent—disdaining the morals and basic decency of their parents' generation as mere sentiment. Indeed, *Network* portrays the Marxist-terrorist fringe of the Sixties Left as clownish hysterical thugs who instantly sell out when offered a TV contract.

But *Network*'s Right-wing themes that resonate the most today center around the conflict between nationalism and populism on the one hand and globalism and elitism on the other.

The plot of *Network* is fairly simple. Howard Beale (played by Peter Finch) is the evening news anchor at America's fourth television network, UBS, which stands for Union Broadcasting System, but it sounds like "You BS," which means something very different. Beale has been declining personally and professionally for some time, and finally, his old friend Max Schumacher (William Holden), the head of the News Division, was forced to fire him. The two got roaring drunk, and when Howard tells Max he plans to kill himself on the air, Max playfully suggests that it would get a hell of a rating. Then he reels off a whole list of equally lurid shows, which at the time seemed like an obscene parody, but seem like old hat to today's generation, who have easy online access to terrorist and cartel murder videos.

Of course, Max was not serious, and he did not dream that Howard would actually go through with it. But Howard really does go on the air the next day and announce that he will kill himself on live television. The network, of course, cuts the camera. But the stunt garners enormous attention.

Howard begs to go back on the air the next day to say a more dignified goodbye, but when the broadcast goes live, he launches into a tirade about having run out of "bullshit." (This is "You BS," after all.) The broadcast is a hit, but both Max and Howard are canned by the UBS brass, who think gutter language is beneath the dignity of their television network. (Those were the days.)

Enter Faye Dunaway's character Diana Christensen, who is in charge of entertainment programming. She, along with fellow young cynic Frank Hackett (Robert Duvall), persuade UBS to bring back Beale (and Schumacher) for much-needed ratings. (UBS is struggling in fourth rank.) As Diana puts it, "Howard Beale is processed instant God, and right now it looks like he may just go over bigger than Mary Tyler Moore."

What sends Beale into ratings heaven is his famous "Mad as Hell" tirade, which seems even more poignant in the age of Trump and Brexit and at the brink of a global depression.

> I don't have to tell you things are bad. Everybody knows things are bad. It's a depression. Everybody's out of work or scared of losing their job. The dollar buys a nickel's worth, banks are going bust, shopkeepers keep a gun under the counter, punks are running wild in the streets, and there's nobody anywhere who seems to know what to do, and there's no end to it.
>
> We know the air's unfit to breathe, and our food is unfit to eat, and we sit and watch our TVs while some local newscaster tells us today, we had fifteen homicides and sixty-three violent crimes, as if that's the way it's supposed to be. We all know things are bad. Worse than bad. They're crazy. It's like everything's going crazy.
>
> So we don't go out anymore. We sit in the house, and slowly the world we live in gets smaller, and all we ask is please, at least leave us alone in our own living rooms. Let me have my toaster and my TV and my hair-dryer and my steel-belted radials, and I

won't say anything. Just leave us alone.

Well, I'm not going to leave you alone. I want you to get mad—I don't want you to riot. I don't want you to protest. I don't want you to write your congressmen, because I wouldn't know what to tell you to write. I don't know what to do about the depression and the inflation and the defense budget and the Russians and crime in the street.

All I know is first you've got to get mad. You've got to say: "I'm mad as hell, and I'm not going to take this anymore. I'm a human being, goddammit. My life has value." So I want you to get up now. I want you to get out of your chairs and go to the window. Right now. I want you to go to the window, open it, and stick your head out and yell. I want you to yell: "I'm mad as hell, and I'm not going to take this anymore!"—Get up from your chairs. Go to the window. Open it. Stick your head out and yell and keep yelling . . .

There is a deep political truth here. Before we can have any political change at all, we need to get angry. But to get angry, we need to be assertive. And to be assertive, we require self-esteem. It is an amazingly dramatic sequence. If you don't find it stirring, check your pulse, because you might be dead.

In her bid to take over Beale's show, Diana begins an affair with Max Schumacher, who is old enough to be her father and married to boot. Max, however, is disgusted by the desire to exploit Howard Beale, who has obviously gone insane. (Howard shows clear signs of mania.) Eventually, however, Christensen and Hackett team up to fire Schumacher. Then Christensen turns the UBS news program into *The Howard Beale Show*, a grotesque variety program featuring Howard as "The Mad Prophet of the Airwaves."

Diana argues that Howard is popular because he is "articulating the popular rage." She wants a whole new slate of angry, anti-establishment programming. Diana, mind you, doesn't want to *change* society to make people *less angry*. She simply wants to exploit popular discontent and channel it into ratings and money. She wants to make it into a commodity. This is brought home brilliantly in Howard's first speech on *The Howard Beale Show*.

Edward George Ruddy died today! Edward George Ruddy was the Chairman of the Board of the Union Broadcasting Systems—and woe is us if it ever falls in the hands of the wrong people. And that's why woe is us that Edward George Ruddy died. Because this network is now in the hands of CC&A, the Communications Corporation of America.

We've got a new Chairman of the Board, a man named Frank Hackett, now sitting in Mr. Ruddy's office on the twentieth floor. And when the twelfth-largest company in the world controls the most awesome goddamned propaganda force in the whole godless world, who knows what shit will be peddled for truth on this tube?

So, listen to me! Television is not the truth! Television is a goddamned amusement park; that's what television is! Television is a circus, a carnival, a traveling troupe of acrobats and story-tellers, singers and dancers, jugglers, side-show freaks, lion-tamers, and football players. We're in the boredom-killing business! If you want truth, go to God, go to your guru, go to yourself because that's the only place you'll ever find any real truth!

But, man, you're never going to get any truth from us. We'll tell you anything you want to hear. We lie like hell! We'll tell you Kojak always gets the killer, and nobody ever gets cancer in Archie Bunker's house. And no matter how much trouble the hero is in, don't worry: just look at your watch—at the end of the hour, he's going to win. We'll tell you any shit you want to hear!

We deal in illusion, man! None of it's true! But you people sit there—all of you—day after day, night after night, all ages, colors, creeds—we're all you know. You're beginning to believe this illusion we're spinning here. You're beginning to think the tube is reality, and your own lives are unreal. You do whatever the tube tells you. You dress like the tube, you eat like the tube, you raise your children like the tube, you think like the tube.

This is mass madness, you maniacs! In God's name, you people are the real thing! We're the illusions! So turn off this goddamn set! Turn it off right now! Turn it off, and leave it off. Turn it off right now, right in the middle of this very sentence I'm speaking now—

Then Howard collapses in a dead faint. The camera dollies forward and looms up over him. Cue music. Cue applause. The audience goes wild. Thus television turns a critique of television into more television. And, arguably, Chayefsky and Lumet are turning their own critique of the media into more media. A critique of the media becomes just another media experience, which might resonate for a bit but is eventually ousted by yet another media experience. Thus the critical impetus never meshes with anything real; it poses no threat to the existing system.

Howard Beale is like the philosopher in Plato's Allegory of the Cave. He has climbed out of the world of shadows and seen the truth of things. But once he returns to the cave, he is not rejected by the cave-dwellers but instead embraced and turned into one of the dancing shadows that bemuse them.

Howard's speech centers around an important distinction between friendship and flattery. A friend tells you what you *need* to hear, namely the truth, whereas a flatterer tells you what you *want* to hear. Any truth we don't want to hear is basically bad news. But we need to hear bad news. We need to know about problems if we are to overcome them. Bad news about ourselves is usually about personal failings and inadequacies. Friends force us to confront them, which is a necessary condition of growth. Television, however, is a flatterer, not a friend. It dispenses comforting illusions that, at best, promote complacency, but usually promote corruption.

Another important distinction is *edification* versus *pandering*. To edify means to build up: to build up a person's knowledge, character, tastes, and ultimately his individuality. To pander is to stoop down, to cater to a person's existing knowledge, character, and tastes, no matter how inadequate and immature.

Human beings are not blank slates, but we are born ignorant, amoral, crude, fearful, and weak. As Thomas Sowell once put it, every new generation is an invasion of barbarians. We must civilize them, or civilization will perish. The purpose of education and high culture is to edify: to turn barbarians into civilized men.

The culture industry, however, has the diametrically opposite agenda. Its goal is to make money by appealing to people's "given preferences": the given preferences of barbarians. No matter how ignorant, tasteless, immoral, or undifferentiated you may be, you will always find people who will cater to your preferences because they want to separate you from your money.

But the culture industry does not just breed complacency. It also encourages corruption. Having a developed personality—including tastes and morals—means that certain things are beneath you. There are things you will not do, things you will not look at or listen to, things you will not buy. Thus, to sell us more things, the culture industry must break down the inhibitions of morality and taste that forbid certain pleasures. Edification breeds discrimination. The culture industry wants us to be less discriminating, because that means we are willing to consume more. Thus the culture industry has an incentive to dissolve all standards of morals and taste in the acid of cynicism. Civilization can't compete with barbarism in the "free market," which means that capitalism will slowly liquidate civilization, unless education and high culture are preserved from market forces.

Howard's commodified discontent is a hit. It entertains all and threatens none. The big lines kept going up. But then Howard made a speech that actually changed something, something big, something *important*:

> All right, listen to me! Listen carefully! This is your goddamn life I'm talking about today! In this country, when one company takes over another company, they simply buy up a controlling share of the stock. But first, they have to file notice with the government. That's how CC&A—the Communications Corporation of America—bought up the company that owns this network. And now somebody's buying up CC&A! Some company named Western World Funding Corporation is buying up CC&A! They filed their notice this morning!
>
> Well, just who the hell is Western World Funding Corporation? It's a consortium of banks and insurance companies who are not buying CC&A for themselves but as agents for somebody else! Well, who's this somebody else? They won't tell you! They won't tell you, they won't tell the Senate, they won't tell the SEC, the FCC, the Justice Department, they won't tell anybody! They say it's none of our business! The hell it ain't!

Well, I'll tell you who they're buying CC&A for. They're buying it for the Saudi-Arabian Investment Corporation! They're buying it for the Arabs! . . . We know the Arabs control more than sixteen billion dollars in this country! They own a chunk of Fifth Avenue, twenty downtown pieces of Boston, a part of the port of New Orleans, an industrial park in Salt Lake City. They own big hunks of the Atlanta Hilton, the Arizona Land and Cattle Company, the Security National Bank in California, the Bank of the Commonwealth in Detroit! They control ARAMCO, so that puts them into Exxon, Texaco, and Mobil Oil! They're all over—New Jersey, Louisville, St. Louis, Missouri! And that's only what we know about! There's a hell of a lot more we don't know about because all those Arab petro-dollars are washed through Switzerland and Canada and the biggest banks in this country! . . . And there's not a single law on the books to stop them!

There's only one thing that can stop them—you! So I want you to get up now. I want you to get out of your chairs and go to the phone. Right now. I want you to go to your phone or get in your car and drive into the Western Union office in town. I want everybody listening to me to get up right now and send a telegram to the White House. By midnight tonight I want a million telegrams in the White House! I want them wading knee-deep in telegrams at the White House! Get up! Right now! And send President Ford a telegram saying: "I'm mad as hell, and I'm not going to take this anymore! I don't want the banks selling my country to the Arabs! I want this CC&A deal stopped now!"

This is pure red-meat national populism. From a nationalist point of view, it makes no sense to allow crucial industries to fall into the hands of foreign powers, especially global rivals. For instance, the coronavirus crisis has brought home the folly of outsourcing most of our pharmaceutical and medical supply manufacturing to China. Of course, our global business elites see things differently, which is where populism comes in. It is the American masses who must rise up, shove aside the elites, and mobilize the government to intervene in the economy in the national interest.

Howard's speech is a great success. Within hours, the White House was awash in millions of telegrams—six million, to be precise—and the Saudi acquisition of CC&A was halted. It was a glorious outpouring of democracy.

But the head of CC&A, Arthur Jensen (played by Ned Beatty), is not amused. CC&A is deep in debt, and they need the Saudi money badly. So Mr. Jensen calls Howard into this office, with the goal of selling him on globalism rather than nationalism. After ushering him into the CC&A boardroom with the words "Valhalla, Mr. Beale," Jensen closes the curtains and sets the stage for a Mephistophelean harangue:

> You have meddled with the primal forces of nature, Mr. Beale, and I won't have it, is that clear?! You think you have merely stopped a business deal—that is not the case! The Arabs have taken billions of dollars out of this country, and now they must put it back. It is ebb and flow, tidal gravity, it is ecological balance! You are an old man who thinks in terms of nations and peoples. There are no nations! There are no peoples! There are no Russians. There are no Arabs! There are no Third Worlds! There is no West! There is only one holistic system of systems, one vast and immane, interwoven, interacting, multi-variate, multi-national dominion of dollars! Petro-dollars, electro-dollars,

multi-dollars! Reichsmarks, rubles, rin, pounds, and shekels! It is the international system of currency that determines the totality of life on this planet! That is the natural order of things today! That is the atomic, subatomic, and galactic structure of things today! And you have meddled with the primal forces of nature, and you will atone!

Am I getting through to you, Mr. Beale? You get up on your little twenty-one-inch screen, and howl about America and democracy. There is no America. There is no democracy. There is only IBM and ITT and AT&T and Dupont, Dow, Union Carbide, and Exxon. Those are the nations of the world today. What do you think the Russians talk about in their councils of state—Karl Marx? They pull out their linear programming charts, statistical decision theories, and minimax solutions and compute the price-cost probabilities of their transactions and investments just like we do.

We no longer live in a world of nations and ideologies, Mr. Beale. The world is a college of corporations, inexorably determined by the immutable by-laws of business. The world is a business, Mr. Beale. It has been since man crawled out of the slime, and our children, Mr. Beale, will live to see that perfect world in which there is no war and famine, oppression and brutality—one vast and ecumenical holding company, for whom all men will work to serve a common profit, in which all men will hold a share of stock, all necessities provided, all anxieties tranquilized, all boredom amused. And I have chosen you, Mr. Beale, to preach this evangel.

Howard is thunderstruck: "I have seen the face of God!" To which Jensen replies, "You just might be right, Mr. Beale." It is a brilliant scene, but Beatty's delivery verges on parody.

Jensen's speech is a stunning encapsulation of modern political thought and its ultimate telos: what Alexandre Kojève called the "end of history" in a "universal homogeneous state." Modern political philosophy seeks to build a stable social and political order on the broad, low foundation of something shared by all men, namely desire: desire for the necessities of life, desire for comfort and security, desire for a long, healthy life and a peaceful death in the midst of plenty, rather than a short life, ending in want or violence.

To secure this desire-based social order, competing foundations must be eliminated. Since all men share the same basic desires, the modern state is, in principle, global. Therefore, the existence of distinct nations and the patriotic sentiments that dispose us to prefer our homelands to strange lands must be eliminated. Thus Jensen dismisses nationalism as a regressive folly of old men. The world is also divided by ideologies, like Marxism. Jensen dismisses those as well. If mankind is not divided by ideologies or national identities, we will have peace, so we can get down to the business of abolishing want and satisfying desire—business like the CC&A deal with the Saudis.

However, when Howard goes back on the air to preach Mr. Jensen's vision of global capitalist utopia, he paints it in depressingly dystopian tones, for he sees that a world devoted solely to creature comforts and lacking identity, patriotism, and principles is a world without passion, nobility, and soul-expanding sentiments. It is also a world of self-indulgence, not self-edification. So it is a world without the tastes, standards, and strength of character necessary to resist the crowd. Thus it is also a world without individuality. Hence: "It's the individual that's finished. It's the single, solitary human being who's finished. It's every single one of you out there who's finished. Because this is no longer a nation of independent individuals. This is a nation of two hundred odd million transistorized, deodorized, whiter-than-white, steel-belted bodies, totally unnecessary as human beings and as replaceable as piston rods."

The End of History ushers in the age of the Last Man.

This perversely bleak utopia resembles Kojève's description of the universal homogeneous post-historical state as a realm of dehumanization, for desires don't set us apart from the animals, thus a society in which desire is sovereign and reason and sentiments are subordinate puts the distinctly human in service of the subhuman. It is a society of clever animals, not men. Such a depiction of utopia can only lead to its rejection, which was Kojève's intent, as I argue in my lecture "Alexandre Kojève and the End of History."[1]

Howard's depressive utopianism could only provoke revulsion. People started changing the channel, and *The Howard Beale Show* went into steep decline. Mr. Jensen, however, was adamant that Howard remain on the air and on message, regardless of the consequences. Thus Christensen, Hackett, and others at the network hatch a plot to have Beale assassinated, on air.

At this point, we get the payoff for the movie's funniest subplot: Christensen's plan to create a one-hour weekly dramatic series called *The Mao Tse-Tung Hour*, based on the real-life activities of a terrorist group called the Ecumenical Liberation Army (obviously patterned on the Symbionese Liberation Army). Christiansen gives the Communist Party complete control of the ideological content of the show. They can stick any Marxist propaganda they want on television as long as the show makes money, which pretty much sums up television today.

Christiansen's contact with the guerrillas is Laureen Hobbs (who is supposed to remind us of Angela Davis). Hobbs' transformation from pedantically rattling off

---

[1] In Greg Johnson, *From Plato to Postmodernism* (San Francisco: Counter-Currents, 2019).

Marxist duck-speak to hysterically ranting about contracts is absolutely priceless. Actress Marlene Warfield somehow manages to make dialogue like this hilarious:

> Don't fuck with my distribution costs! I'm getting a lousy two-fifteen per segment, and I'm already deficiting twenty-five grand a week with Metro. I'm paying William Morris ten percent off the top! . . . I'm paying Metro twenty percent of all foreign and Canadian distribution, and that's after recoupment! The Communist Party's not going to see a nickel out of this goddam show until we go into syndication!

The name Hobbs is supposed to call to mind Thomas Hobbes, the theorist of dog-eat-dog capitalism, though nobody, in truth, outdoes Marxists in cannibalism. Since Beale's show is in the slot before *The Mao Tse-Tung Hour* and dragging down its ratings, Hobbs agrees to have the Ecumenicals assassinate Howard Beale. It'll be a great two-hour opener for the new season!

The scene in which the network executives decide to murder Howard Beale is quite chilling. Every one of them is a sociopath. Moral considerations never creep in at all.

When the Ecumenicals kill Howard on live television, again the camera dollies forward and looms up over the kill, transmuting it into an image. Then we cut to four television screens, one tuned to each of the four networks. We simultaneously see and hear the coverage of the shooting as well as various commercials. Then the narrator proclaims over the cacophony: "This was the story of Howard Beale, the first known instance of a man who was killed because he had lousy ratings." As far as I know, television networks still do not resort to assassinations, but *Network* was dead right about the plunge of network television into gutter depravity and crude Left-wing agitprop.

Network offers a feast of truth on the media, popular culture, capitalism, feminism, Leftism, nationalism, populism, globalization, and decadence. *Network* is absolutely right that we need to worry about who controls the mass media, especially hostile aliens. But when *Network* raises the alarm about foreign influence on the American media, it names the wrong tribe of Semites.

Indeed, although the American television and movie industries are famously Jewish, *Network* portrays UBS as almost entirely non-Jewish. In the context of a TV network, a name like Max Schumacher sounds Jewish, but William Holden was not Jewish and neither is his portrayal of Schumacher. Of course, if Schumacher is supposed to be Jewish, we also should note that he is the most decent character in the bunch. A minor character—little more than an extra—is named Barbara Schlesinger, a likely Jewish name, but she is played by Conchata Ferrell, who is not Jewish. Jews, however, are not confined to minor roles in the American media.

Everybody else at UBS is conspicuously white. Howard Beale is an English name, and Peter Finch, who played him, was of Anglo-Scottish ancestry. The main villains are named Christensen and Jensen, both Scandinavian names, and Hackett, an English name with Scandinavian roots. (Another corporate sociopath is named Amundsen in the script.) This is such a neat inversion of the truth that it cannot be accidental.

Indeed, the main reason there are so few Jews in front of the cameras in *Network* is that the main people behind the camera, writer Paddy Chayefsky and director Sidney Lumet, were both Jewish. One must give them credit for all the truths that they did put on screen, but it was clearly dishonest of them to omit their own ethnic group's presiding role in the corruption and degeneracy of American television.

There's a lesson in that, too.

The Unz Review, May 13, 2020

ONCE UPON A TIME IN THE WEST

I have had a difficult relationship with Sergio Leone's *Once Upon a Time in the West* (1968). Parts of this film are so emotionally powerful as to be almost unendurable. Indeed, before I began work on this review, I had seen *Once Upon a Time in the West* only one time in full, on a rented VHS tape in the 1990s. I knew it was a great film, so I bought the VHS. But I could not bring myself to watch it again. Then I replaced the VHS with a DVD, but I could not bring myself to watch it in the new format either. Eventually, I sold my unwatched DVD and bought a BluRay. But more than five years passed, and I still could not bring myself to watch it. Finally, before I faced the absurdity of buying the film again in 4K, I forced myself to watch it by agreeing to discuss it on Frodi Midjords' Decameron Film Festival.

After about 30 years, I was surprised at how much I remembered. Whole sequences were simply seared into my memory. Even though I knew what was coming, the emotional impact was not dulled in the least. The only surprise is that the film's dramatic flaws seemed quite glaring. This is a great film, but it could have been so much better.

In some ways *Once Upon a Time in the West* is less successful than Leone's first three Westerns: *A Fistful of Dollars* (1964), *For a Few Dollars More* (1965), and *The Good, the Bad, and the Ugly* (1966), which are nearly perfect movies but not particularly deep ones. *Once Upon a Time in the West*, however, is imperfect because it tries—sometimes fumblingly but usually successfully—to be deep.

Once Upon a Time in the West, like many classic Westerns, is constructed around the contrast between the "wild West" and the creeping civilization that followed the pioneers, pushing back the frontiers until they disappeared. The film is also constructed around a related distinction between the man and the businessman.

Near the end of the film, we have the following dialogue between the two central characters, Frank, a hired killer played by Henry Fonda, and Harmonica, a mysterious gunman who is pursuing Frank, played by Charles Bronson.

> FRANK: Morton once told me I could never be like him. Now I understand why. Wouldn't have bothered him, knowing you were around somewhere, alive.
>
> HARMONICA: So you found out you're not a businessman after all.
>
> FRANK: Just a man.
>
> HARMONICA: An ancient race. Other Mortons will be along, and they'll kill it off.
>
> FRANK: The future don't matter to us. Nothing matters now. Not the land. Not the money. Not the woman. I came here to see you. 'Cause I know that now you'll tell me what you're after.
>
> HARMONICA: Only at the point of dying.
>
> FRANK: I know.

Morton is a railroad tycoon who hired Frank to occasionally intimidate or kill people who got in the way of progress. Morton would not be "bothered" by Harmonica, because Morton is not fundamentally motivated by honor. Morton has been crippled by creeping tuberculosis of the bones, a degradation that Frank thinks a normal man would cast off with a bullet to his brain.

Frank is willing to cast off his life to preserve his honor, but Morton wishes to prolong his life at the expense of honor because he has a dream: building a railroad that reaches the Pacific, which of course would spell the end of the frontier.

Morton loves money. He lives in a luxuriously appointed private train and throws a great deal of cash around. But ultimately his money is in the service of a very Faustian dream: progress, Manifest Destiny, gleaming rails from sea to shining sea. But for all that, he is still spiritually bourgeois, because he places life above honor.

Frank is not just a cold-blooded killer of women and children, he is also a sadist. Beyond that, he kills for money. Yet Frank puts honor above life. He would rather die than exist in Morton's condition. He is also "bothered" by Harmonica enough to seek him out and put his life on the line in a gunfight. Harmonica has bothered Frank in two ways: he has offended his pride, and he has piqued his curiosity. Frank is willing to risk death not just over honor but also truth.

Once Upon a Time in the West begins with a brilliant opening sequence. Three gunmen arrive at a ramshackle station to wait for a train. The gunmen are outlaws, men of the wild West. The train represents civilization. Wherever the tracks extend, the frontier and its wildness end. The geezer who mans the station is decrepit, chatty, and ingratiating. Like Morton, he is the kind of man who would be dead on the frontier, but the railroad enables him to live on. The gunmen, by contrast, are tough, taciturn, and utterly contemptuous of the old man. They don't waste a single word on him.

Everything about the station seems designed to annoy the gunmen: the squeaking of the windmill, the chattering of the telegraph. Leone uses these sounds as well as long silences to build enormous tension and suspense. Finally, there is a cathartic explosion of violence.

The feel of the sequence is epic, Homeric. It is an encounter between vital barbarism and the first probing fingers of decadent civilization.

The gunmen don't wish to travel. They are a welcoming party. Their boss, Frank, has sent them to kill a man who made an appointment to meet him. The man turns out to be Harmonica, who is called that because it seems he'd rather play a harmonica than talk. He is the most laconic frontiersman of the lot. Harmonica can also shoot. When he sees that Frank has sent men to kill him, he guns them down effortlessly.

In the next sequence we meet Frank as he and his henchmen murder an entire family, the McBains: the father and his three children. Their mother is already dead. It is a brutal and shocking sequence, culminating with Ennio Morricone's magnificent "Man with the Harmonica" theme, which associates the harmonica with Frank, not just the Harmonica character. We learn why near the end of the film.

Unbeknownst to Frank, there is a new Mrs. McBain, Jill, played by Claudia Cardinale, who arrives the very day of the massacre to find her husband and stepchildren dead. It is a touching sequence, but Jill's reaction seems a bit cool. Maybe she's just stoic. But a question hangs over the character that will later be resolved.

Morton, played by the great Italian actor Gabriele Ferzetti, is introduced as a grasping hand. His fist closes over the figure of a conquistador, pulling it back to reveal a model train bearing his name. As Morton yanks the conquistador out of the frame, he scolds his own conquistador, Frank, for the senseless murder of the McBains: "You were only supposed to scare them!" Morton values human life, especially his own, but also the lives of others. But for Frank, life is cheap, even his own.

Frank has framed another outlaw, Cheyenne (played by Jason Robards) for the murder of the McBains. Cheyenne shows up at the McBain house to speak to Jill because he wants to clear his name and learn why the family was murdered. Harmonica is pretty sure that Frank is behind the massacre, but he doesn't know why. Soon, Cheyenne, Harmonica, and Jill team up to solve the mystery.

Once Upon a Time in the West falls into roughly three acts. The first and third acts are slow-moving, laconic, epic in feel, and sometimes emotionally shattering. The second act is fast-moving with jarring cuts. It is also chatty, petty, and farcical. Dramatically, it is the weakest part of the film.

The second act commences with a great pile of lumber. Brett McBain has ordered enough lumber to build a small town. But why? Suddenly, Harmonica reveals the answer. A contract is introduced as a *deus ex machina*: McBain's land has plentiful water in the midst of the desert. Morton's railroad needs that water. McBain will have the right to build a town there, as long as a station is built by the time the tracks reach it. The tracks are almost there, so Cheyenne orders his outlaw *Männerbund* to start building a station. Cheyenne and Harmonica suddenly seem interested in striking it rich. It is a jarring change of character.

In the meantime, Frank has kidnapped Jill, and Jill has seduced Frank. It is a cold turn for a grieving widow, but we learn that Jill is a former prostitute. She's a businessman too, like Morton. Frank contemplates forcing Jill to marry him so he can own her land. She would go along with that to save her own skin. But Frank is not the marrying kind, so he decides to force her to auction the land, dispatching his gang to intimidate other bidders so one of Frank's proxies can pick up the land for cheap. Harmonica spoils the plan by bidding $5,000, a handsome sum. Where does Harmonica get the money? By turning in the outlaw Cheyenne for a $5,000 bounty. It is utterly farcical. Is Cheyenne so smitten with Jill that he would risk his life to save her land?

The act ends as Jill goes off to take a bubble bath. She wants to get Frank off her skin. Frank shows up to make Harmonica an offer he can't refuse for the land: $5,000 *plus* a silver dollar, because "Everyone has the right to make a profit." Harmonica drops the silver dollar in an empty glass to pay for his whiskey, leaves the $5,000 on the table, then walks away. This opens act three with a return to the heroic world.

The most charitable interpretation of act two is that it is there to make us heartily sick of Morton's civilization. It is a world of laws, contracts, and business. It is also a woman-centered world. Suddenly two outlaws and an outlaw gang are orbiting an ex-prostitute to help her get rich. Finally, it is the world of Christianity and blasphemies thereof, for when Cheyenne is turned over, he says that Judas settled for 4,970 fewer pieces of silver. But Cheyenne is not sacrificing himself to redeem humanity but merely the widow McBain's farm.

Harmonica bothers Frank because he has dogged him relentlessly without saying who he is or why he is doing it. When Frank asks for his name, Harmonica merely responds with the names of men Frank has killed. Harmonica has also killed five of Frank's men. Now he has refused Frank's offer for the land. Then, to add insult to injury, Harmonica saves Frank from some of Frank's own men who are waiting to kill him as he leaves.

Morton fears Frank and has paid his own gang to kill him. Frank rides off to Morton's train, only to find half-a-dozen dead bodies and Morton dying face down in a mud puddle, the waves of the Pacific roaring in his imagination. Frank planned to shoot Morton, but when he sees that he is slowly dying anyway, he does the sadistic thing and leaves him to suffer and grovel.

Meanwhile, back at the McBain property, Jill watches

the completion of the station as the first train arrives. Harmonica is whittling on a piece of wood, waiting. Cheyenne shows up, having escaped from the law. Jill fully expects both men to try to marry her. But then we learn, no, that's not what either of them had in mind. It wasn't about Jill at all. Both outlaws were simply after revenge. Jill has gotten what she wants but not Cheyenne and Harmonica. We later learn that Cheyenne killed Morton, but Frank is still at large.

Cheyenne tells Jill that she doesn't understand men like Harmonica: "People like that have something inside. Something to do with death." This is true of Cheyenne as well. This thing to do with death is the honor code of the wild West. Honor comes before all else. Frank speaks for them all at the end. For this kind of man, when honor is at stake, "The future don't matter to us. Nothing matters now. Not the land. Not the money. Not the woman." And not life itself. The shootout between Frank and Harmonica is one of the most emotionally shattering climaxes in all of cinema. I'll not spoil it with words. It must simply be seen and heard.

After the gunfight, Harmonica and Cheyenne say goodbye to Jill. But just outside of the McBain property, Cheyenne falters. Harmonica stops and turns with concern. It turns out that Cheyenne was mortally wounded by Morton. Like Jesus, he has a bleeding wound in his side. This comes as some surprise. He must have been putting up a brave front with Jill. But the surprise comes off as a rather contrived plot twist, one of many. Cheyenne doesn't want Harmonica to watch him die. But the men are friends now, friends to the end, and what's a little death between friends? When Cheyenne expires, Harmonica loads his body on his horse. They head West, of course, beyond where the rails have stopped, into the wild. Jill, in the meantime, brings water to the railroad workers who have brought civilization to her doorstep.

The end.

There are many great things about *Once Upon a Time in the West*: a beautiful script, inspired direction, vivid cinematography, meticulously detailed and authentic costumes and sets, and superb performances, especially from Henry Fonda and Jason Robards. Ennio Morricone's magnificent music deserves special mention. Half the emotional impact of the film comes from the music alone.

But be warned: the plot is often a mess, which is hard to forgive in a film that runs nearly three hours. I have already dwelt upon the film's second act. But there's a lot that makes no sense in the rest of the film.

Cheyenne is first introduced at a ramshackle dive in the desert. What is it anyway? A bar? An inn? A stable? Does a cyclops live there? His behavior is so bizarre and menacing that any number of people would be tempted to shoot him dead in self-defense. But all he wants is someone to break the chains on his wrists.

Later, when Cheyenne visits Jill, he is again so menacing that she is tempted to kill him. Yet he is there to declare his innocence and offer his protection. I get it. He's a man of few words. So why doesn't he choose them more carefully? One feels here that Leone is just jerking you around building up false suspense.

Harmonica camps out at the McBain house to protect Jill. But he does not knock at the door and introduce himself. He starts playing the harmonica in the dead of night. Jill thinks he is a bandit and tries to shoot him. It is a natural reaction. Her whole family has just been killed.

The next day, when Jill and Harmonica meet by daylight, he does not greet her politely, exchange names, and explain he is there to protect her. Instead, he throws her around, roughs her up, and tears her clothes as if he is about to rape her. Is this his idea of an acceptable greeting? Does he play the harmonica rather than talk because he's autistic? Then Harmonica abruptly breaks off the assault and asks Jill to get him water from the well, at which point two of Frank's men gallop up to kill her, and Harmonica guns them down. Again, is there a point to this bizarre behavior, or is Leone just jerking us around?

When Frank returns to Morton's train to find the results of a massacre, we are left to wonder who these men were and what happened. Later we learn that Cheyenne led that raid. But why? Was it to take revenge on Morton? I guess that makes sense.

I think it is important to lay all of this film's flaws on the table, because the payoff in the end is worth waiting through them.

Leone's early films are perfect but not particularly moving. The conflicts are merely about money, not principle. In *Once Upon a Time in the West*, Leone stirs us more deeply because this is not just a movie about men; it is a movie about ideas, about the principles from which different lives and different civilizations spring.

The Western lends itself to political philosophy because on the frontier, one leaves behind civil society and enters a state of nature, thus highlighting the distinction between nature and convention.

The frontier is also a realm of clashing tribes—white, Indian, and Mexican—thus highlighting race, identity, and enmity as political forces.

The frontier also stimulates the re-emergence of archaic values like the honor code and archaic institutions like the *Männerbund*, prompting reflections on how these can be integrated into civilized society, if at all.

The frontier is a realm of freedom and adventure, which are especially bracing to men. Can this freedom be preserved under law and civilization?

Finally, the frontier is a dangerous place. It selects for

strength, vitality, and masculinity, posing the question of whether these can find a place in civil society.

Or will it always be the case that hard times produce strong men, strong men produce easy times, easy times produce weak men, and we are doomed to hard times again?

What is the politics of *Once Upon a Time in the West*? The film is clearly anti-capitalist. But is it anti-capitalism of the Left or of the Right? There is not a word about inequality or exploitation in this film, which counts against any sort of Leftist interpretation. The primary victims are not the proletariat, but the McBain family, who are landholders seeking to get rich from a railroad concession.

The central contrast of the film is between *man* and *businessman*, not *capitalist* and *proletarian*. The "ancient race" that the Mortons of the world wish to kill is not the proletariat. It is not colored people. It is men of honor, men who prize honor over life itself. This is the premodern, aristocratic ethos. These are the men of "pride and vainglory," the "contentious and quarrelsome" whom Thomas Hobbes and John Locke wished to replace with the rule of the "industrious and rational." Thus *Once Upon a Time in the West* offers a critique of capitalism from the Right.

I argue that *Once Upon a Time in the West* is *objectively* Rightist, even though this was not the intention of the filmmakers. Leone himself had fashionably Leftish ideas. Bernardo Bertolucci, who co-authored the original story with Leone and Dario Argento, was an avowed Marxist. Yet there is nothing Marxist about *Once Upon a Time in the West*. (Nor is there anything Marxist about his greatest movie, *The Last Emperor*.[1]) The fact that *Once Upon a Time in the West* was hugely popular among the Parisian student Leftists of 1968, who were

---

[1] In *Trevor Lynch's Classics of Right-Wing Cinema*.

crazy about the movie's long "duster" coats, proves nothing either. These kids had great taste in film and fashion. But they were too poorly educated to understand what they were seeing.

Hegel held that the duel to the death over honor was the beginning of man and the beginning of history. Before the duel, men were just clever animals ruled by natural desires, above all self-preservation. By subordinating life itself to the imagination—specifically one's image of oneself—man created the realm of history and culture, which is defined as going against nature. Hegel saw history as a struggle for self-consciousness, which would end when men have realized that we are all free and have built a society that expresses that truth. But Hegel's critics from the Right realized that if making history makes us human, the end of history will be the end of man, the return of merely the cleverest animal.

Once Upon a Time in the West ends by showing us the beginning of history reenacted in the showdown between Frank and Harmonica just as the end of history is pulling into town on Morton's gleaming rails. What do our heroes do? They head West.

We should follow.

It is one thing to write about such ideas, another thing to show them. That's why the end of *Once Upon a Time in the West* feels less like a movie, more like an initiation into some great mystery: why we rise, why we fall, and why there's no stilling or stepping off the great wheel of time.

Counter-Currents, October 31 & November 1, 2023

PULP FICTION

Quentin Tarantino's *Pulp Fiction* is one of my favorite movies. I didn't want to like it. I didn't even want to see it. Everything I'd heard made me think it would be thoroughly nihilistic and quite unpleasant. But then someone at a party described *Pulp Fiction* as a movie about "greatness of soul at the end of history." That caught my attention, because at the time I immersed for the nth time in Plato's *Republic*, the core of which is an account of the human soul, as well as Alexandre Kojève's *Introduction to the Reading of Hegel*, from which Francis Fukuyama derived his "end of history" trope.

The very idea of mentioning Plato and Hegel in the same breath with Quentin Tarantino may seem absurd, but bear with me. *Pulp Fiction* is not a decadent film. It is a film about the most fundamental metaphysical and moral choices we can make—that just happens to be set in the midst of the criminal underclass of a decadent society.

The basic issue to be decided is whether to live according to material or spiritual values—to satisfy one's individual desires or to subordinate these to serve something higher: the common good, one's personal sense of honor, or a religious calling. This deep seriousness makes *Pulp Fiction* more than just clever, dark-comic nihilism. It is a genuinely great movie.

The three main characters of *Pulp Fiction* are two hit men, one black (Jules Winnfield, brilliantly played by Samuel L. Jackson) and one white (Vincent Vega, played by John Travolta), and a corrupt boxer, Butch Coolidge (Bruce Willis).

Each of these men represents a particular spiritual type, defined in terms of which part of his soul rules the others. Jules Winnfield is a spiritual man, meaning that in a conflict between spiritual and material considerations, he follows the spiritual path. Butch Coolidge is an honor-driven man, meaning that in a conflict between honor and the satisfaction of his desires (even to the point of preserving his life), he chooses honor. Vincent Vega is ruled entirely by his desires, meaning that in a conflict between his desires and honor or spiritual motives, he chooses his desires.

These types of individuals correspond to the three fundamental Indo-European social "functions"/castes as explained by Georges Dumézil and reflected in Plato's *Republic*. The spiritual man corresponds to the priestly function/caste. The honor-driven man corresponds to the warrior function/caste. The desire-ruled man corresponds to the economic function/caste.

Pulp Fiction tells the overlapping stories of these three men in a complex, non-linear fashion. The meaning of the movie becomes clearer, however, if we discuss the story in chronological order.

THE OUTLINE OF THE MOVIE

The titles in quotes are Quentin Tarantino's. The others are mine.

> **Part 1**: The Diner: Two criminals known as "Pumpkin" (Tim Roth) and "Honey Bunny" (Amanda Plummer) decide to rob a diner.
>
> **Part 2**: The Killing: Hit men Vincent Vega and Jules Winnfield kill several people and recover a briefcase containing something stolen from their employer, gangster Marsellus Wallace (Ving Rhames).
>
> **Part 3**: "Vincent Vega and Marsellus Wallace's Wife": Vincent Vega takes Marsellus Wallace's wife Mia out for dinner and dancing.

Part 4: "The Gold Watch": Boxer Butch Coolidge double-crosses Marsellus Wallace and prepares to flee town when he discovers that he must return to his apartment to recover his father's gold watch. (The prologue of this scene is a flashback that explains the significance of the watch.)

Part 5: "The Bonnie Situation": Vincent Vega and Jules Winnfield must dispose of the body of one of their associates who is accidentally shot in their car in broad daylight.

Part 6: The Diner Again: After disposing of the body, Vincent and Jules decide to have breakfast at a diner, only to have their meal interrupted by Pumpkin and Honey Bunny's robbery.

THE CHRONOLOGY OF EVENTS

1. The flashback to Butch's childhood
2. The Killing
3. "The Bonnie Situation"
4. The Diner/The Diner Again
5. "Vincent Vega and Marsellus Wallace's Wife"
6. "The Gold Watch"

Pulp Fiction is set in Los Angeles and its environs in the early 1990s. The movie was filmed in 1993 and released in 1994.

JULES WINNFIELD, THE SPIRITUAL MAN

Let's begin the story with the killing. It is early morning. Jules Winnfield has come to pick up Vincent Vega for a job. When we meet Vincent Vega he has just returned to Los Angeles from three years in Amsterdam.

After three years in one of Europe's greatest cities, what has rubbed off on him? Vincent's conversation focuses entirely on fast food, drink, and drugs: what the Dutch eat with their French fries, what the French call a Quarter Pounder with Cheese (Royale with Cheese—on account of the metric system), where you can buy beer, the laws governing marijuana use in Holland, etc. Vincent, as we come to learn, is not stupid. He is intelligent and witty. But he is totally ruled by his desires.

Vincent and his partner Jules Winnfield go to an apartment occupied by four young thieves, three white and one black, who have stolen a briefcase from the black gangster Marsellus Wallace, who is Vega and Winnfield's employer. The two hit men are let into the apartment by the black thief Marvin, who has betrayed his white friends to the black gangster Wallace and his black enforcer Winnfield. After recovering the briefcase, Winnfield kills two of the white thieves, sadistically toying with their leader, Brett, including shooting him in the leg and quoting the Bible at him before finishing him off. This ends Part 2, "The Killing."

The storyline resumes in Part 5, "The Bonnie Situation," when the third white, who has been hiding in the bathroom, bursts out firing a .357 Magnum. All six shots miss. Jules and Vincent then shoot the gunman, collect the briefcase, and depart with Marvin in tow.

Jules interprets the fact that the bullets missed as "divine intervention." "God came down from heaven and stopped the bullets." Vincent interprets it as merely "luck," a "freak occurrence," "this shit happens." These fundamentally different interpretations reveal fundamentally different characters. Vincent is ruled by his desires. Thus it makes sense that he would interpret the event in fundamentally materialistic terms as a meaningless freak accident. Jules, by contrast, gives the event a spiritual interpretation, revealing an openness to a higher reality and thus to motives higher than the satisfaction of mere material interests.

In the getaway car, Vincent turns to Marvin for his opinion of the event. Vincent is holding his gun, pointed at Marvin. Marvin, who seems none too bright, says he has no opinion. Then Vincent blows Marvin's head off, drenching the interior of the car in blood. Vincent claims it is an accident, although he was none too pleased that Marvin had not mentioned that the third white thief was hiding in the bathroom with a "hand cannon." Still, Vincent is a rather calculating and risk-averse individual. Before the hit, he meticulously questions Jules about the number of people they are facing and keeps insisting that they should have brought shotguns. Thus intentionally killing Marvin in a car in broad daylight seems uncharacteristically reckless.

To avoid being pulled over driving a car bathed in blood, Jules drives to the nearby house of his friend Jimmy (played by Quentin Tarantino himself). Jimmy is not amused. He tells his friends that he is not in the "dead nigger storage" business. His wife Bonnie, a nurse working graveyard at a hospital, will be home in an hour, and the killers, the corpse, and the car will have to be gone. Jules calls Marsellus, who dispatches Winston Wolf (Harvey Keitel), who apparently has some experience in these matters. The whole scene is played in a darkly comic way, wallowing in the grossness of the blood and the corpse, as well as the moral sordidness of its casual disposal. Marvin is "nobody who will be missed," and, truly, there are plenty more where he came from.

After Wolf disposes of the body and departs, "The Bonnie Situation" has been resolved, and the last part of the movie commences: Part 6, The Diner Again.

Jules and Vincent decide to have breakfast at a local diner (it truly has been a long morning). Vincent orders pancakes and bacon, Jules coffee and a muffin. When Vincent offers Jules some bacon, Jules refuses on the ground that pigs are unclean animals, to which Vincent retorts in a childish voice, "Bacon tastes *good*. Pork chops taste *good*." Again Vincent shows that he is fundamentally ruled by his desires, whereas Jules has higher standards, in this case aesthetic. (Jewish dietary laws are explicitly rejected as his motive, but spiritual men routinely codify their moral and aesthetic preferences as religious commandments.)

Then the conversation returns to the bullets that missed. Vincent again dismisses it as a freak accident. Jules again insists that it was divine intervention, a message from God. He has decided to quit "the life"—meaning the life of a killer—and "wander the earth like Kane in *Kung Fu*," getting in adventures and meeting people until God tells him he is where he ought to be. Vincent, who is immune to the spiritual and focused entirely on the material, knows exactly what people with no jobs and no money who wander the earth are. They are bums. Jules is proposing to be nothing more than a bum. Vincent, whose entire life seems to be ruled by his digestive tract, then interrupts the conversation "to take a shit."

When Vincent is in the toilet, Pumpkin and Honey Bunny launch their robbery, and the movie comes full circle. It goes quite well, until Pumpkin tries to take Marsellus' case from Jules. Jules gets the drop on him, then in an absolutely riveting speech, explains that he will not kill them because he is "in a transitional period" (transitioning out of "the life"). His brush with death has brought on "a moment of clarity." He now sees through the excuses and self-deceptions he has used to rationalize his life as a criminal. He sees that he has been nothing more than a tool of "the tyranny of evil men." He keeps the briefcase. Pumpkin and Honey Bunny depart, followed by Jules and Vincent.

At this point, the movie ends, but we are not even halfway into the story. If Tarantino had originally meant to present the movie in chronological order, Samuel L. Jackson's absolutely riveting delivery makes it easy to understand why he chose to make this the final scene. Everything after it would seem like an anticlimax.

Next in the story is Part 3, "Vincent Vega and Marsellus Wallace's Wife." Vincent and Jules, having departed the diner, arrive at a bar owned by their employer, Marsellus Wallace. The scene begins with Wallace speaking to Butch Coolidge, the boxer, but I will save my discussion of this scene until later, when I discuss "The Gold Watch." Although we do not see it happen, Jules presumably tenders his resignation and departs on his spiritual quest. We learn nothing more about his fate.

Since Jules Winnfield is now departing from the story, this is the appropriate place to explore another way in which spiritual themes play a role in *Pulp Fiction*. What is in Marsellus Wallace's briefcase? When Vincent opens the briefcase in The Killing, a golden light shines out of it. Vincent takes a drag on his cigarette and stares, transfixed. In The Diner Again, when Pumpkin demands that Jules open the briefcase, again we see a golden glow. With a look of awe on his face, Pumpkin asks: "Is that what I think it is?" Jules nods yes, then Pumpkin says, "It's beautiful."

An interpretation that I find appealing has been floating around the internet since 1994: The briefcase contains Marsellus Wallace's soul.[1] He has sold it, or it has been stolen, but in any case he wants it back. This interpretation fits in with a number of details in the movie in addition to the strange glow and the looks of awe: The combination of the briefcase is 666, the Number of the Beast. Jules tells Pumpkin that the briefcase contains his boss's "dirty laundry," and indeed, Marsellus Wallace has a lot of dirty laundry, a lot of sins upon his soul.

---

[1] http://www.snopes.com/movies/films/pulp.asp

The first thing we see of Marsellus Wallace is the back of his shaved head. At the base of his skull is a large Band-Aid. One wonders if something has been removed. It has been suggested that his soul was removed through the back of his head, although the idea apparently has no basis in myth or tradition. If Jules and Vincent were trying to recover Marsellus Wallace's soul, it would also explain why God might indeed want to intervene on their behalf. And as for the death of the four thieves: well, they are the devil's little helpers anyway.

VINCENT VEGA: THE DESIRE-DRIVEN MAN

Although Jules Winnfield quits "the life," Vincent Vega stays in Marsellus's employ, and his next job is to take Mrs. Wallace out for a night on the town while Mr. Wallace is away.

Am I the only one to whom this does not sound like a good idea? During the opening sequence of The Killing, we learn that Marsellus' white wife Mia (Uma Thurman) is a failed actress. (She was in a pilot.) We also hear that Marsellus had another of his associates, Atwan Rockamora, thrown off a fourth-storey balcony for giving Mia a foot massage. (Those of us who on this basis suspected Tarantino of being a foot fetishist were vindicated by the *Kill Bill* movies.)

For Vincent, the first order of business in taking out his boss's wife is to buy some heroin. He goes to the house of his dealer Lance (Eric Stolz). As Vincent waits for Lance, he listens to a disquisition on body piercing from Lance's wife Jody (Rosanna Arquette). Having purchased and injected some spendy gourmet heroin, Vincent departs for the Wallace residence to pick up Mia.

We soon learn that Mia is cut from the same cloth as Vincent: she is witty, playful, and entirely dominated by her desires. Cocaine is her drug of choice, along with alcohol and cigarettes. Everything about this couple is extremely cool, from Vincent's car to their clothes, their music, their witty repartee, and their wonderful dance scene. But their most disarming traits are their sensitivity and old-fashioned manners. It is impossible to dislike Vincent and Mia. It is hard not to envy them. Their lives would be a fun vacation from our lives. This whole segment of *Pulp Fiction* does full justice to both the allure and the emptiness of their postmodern hedonism.

Mia has Vincent take her to Jack Rabbit Slim's, a '50s nostalgia restaurant in which the booths are classic cars and the waiters and waitresses dress up like '50s movie and pop stars. (The prices, however, are very much in the '90s.) Vincent sums the place up brilliantly, in one of the movie's best lines: "It's like a wax museum with a pulse." After Buddy Holly takes their order, Mia slips into the bathroom to snort some coke. After dinner, they doff their shoes then compete in, and win, the Jack Rabbit Slim's twist contest. There is a great deal of clever dialogue, but the overall impression is that Vincent and Mia have only one use for their intelligence: to accumulate novel experiences and undergo pleasant sensations.

Cut to the end of the evening. Vincent and Mia stagger back to the Wallace residence. Having eaten, drunk, danced, laughed, and shot up, Vincent's desires are now moving in a sexual direction. But first he has "to take a piss." He ducks into the bathroom to get a grip on himself. Here we see the roles of reason and morality in a desire-dominated life.

For Plato, reason is a multifaceted faculty embracing everything from induction from sense experience to calculating options and outcomes to mystical insight into transcendent truths. All human beings use reason, but only the spiritual individual accesses its highest powers. Jules Winnfield's conviction that God was sending him a message is an example of the highest, mystical function of reason, although it seems none too reasonable to the rest of us.

For desire-ruled individuals like Vincent, however, reason is merely a tool to satisfy their desires. It is empirical and calculative. Modern philosophy, no matter how rational it professes to be, tends to define reason merely as a tool for the satisfaction of desire, which makes even professed rationalists hedonists in the end.

Vincent wants to fuck Mia. (There is no point in putting a finer word on it.) This, he claims, is "a test of character," and he shows that modernity defines character, like reason, in a way that leaves desire firmly in control. Vincent would enjoy fucking Mia. But he would not enjoy the probable consequences if Marsellus finds out. (Mia denies the foot massage story, but who knows . . . ?)

Vincent does not choose against sex with Mia based on his sense of the honorable or the sacred. Rather, he masters one desire by rationally counter-posing other, greater desires: the desires to remain alive and on good terms with his boss. Thus he resolves that he is going to have a drink, say goodnight, be a perfect gentleman, then go home and jerk off.

Vincent, in short, achieves self-mastery though rational self-indulgence. Reason for Vincent means hedonistic calculus. Character means the ability to sacrifice present pleasures for future pleasures. These are the highest virtues to which a hedonist can aspire.

While Vincent is communing in the toilet with the cleverer demons of his nature, Mia is getting bored in the other room. Vincent has gallantly offered Mia his coat, which she is still wearing. In a pocket, she finds his bag of heroin. Thinking it is cocaine, she snorts some of it, sending her into an immediate overdose. When Vincent finds her—glassy-eyed, foaming at the mouth, bleeding from the nose, a grotesque parody of Man Ray's "Tears"—he panics. He is a no-doubt wanted criminal. So is his boss. So he cannot take Mia to an emergency room.

Too many questions. So he drives her to the house of his dealer Lance, where, after a good deal of dark-comic hysteria, he revives Mia by stabbing her in the heart with a huge syringe full of adrenaline, shocking her back to consciousness. ("Pretty trippy" chortles Jody. Then her friend Trudi celebrates life with another bong hit.)

As the bedraggled pair stumble back to the Wallace house, they no longer look so cool and attractive. They look like death warmed over. One knows that all their coolness, cleverness, and wit—not to mention what passes for reason and character in their lives—will not be enough to save them from the consequences of their affluent hedonism: addiction, degradation, and death by misadventure. (As an "anti-drug" film, *Pulp Fiction* is second only to *Requiem for a Dream*.)

Postmodernism, Hedonism, & Death

The story of "Vincent Vega and Marsellus Wallace's Wife" beautifully illustrates two philosophical theses: (1) there is an inner identity between postmodern culture and hedonism, and (2) hedonism, taken to an extreme, can lead to its self-overcoming by arranging an encounter with death—an encounter which, if survived, can expand one's awareness of one's self and the world to embrace non-hedonistic motives and actions.

"Postmodernism" is one of those academically fashionable weasel words like "paradigm" that have now seeped into middlebrow and even lowbrow discourse. Those of us who have fundamental and principled critiques of modernity quickly learned that postmodernism is not postmodern enough. Indeed, in most ways, it is just an intensification of the worst features of modernity.

For my purposes, postmodernity is an attitude toward culture characterized by (1) eclecticism or *bricolage*, meaning the mixing of different cultures and traditions, i.e., multiculturalism, and (2) irony, detachment, and playfulness toward culture, which is what allows us to mix and manipulate cultures in the first place. The opposite of multiculturalism is cultural integrity and exclusivity. The opposite of irony is earnestness. The opposite of detachment is identification. The opposite of playfulness is seriousness.

The core of a genuine culture is a worldview, an interpretation of existence and our place in it, as well as of our nature and the best form of life for us. These are *serious* matters. Because of the fundamental seriousness of a living culture, each one is characterized by a unity of style, the other side of which is an exclusion of foreign cultural forms.

After all, if one takes one's own worldview seriously, one cannot take incompatible worldviews with equal seriousness. (Yes, cultures do borrow from one another, but a serious culture only borrows what it can assimilate to its own worldview and use for its greater glory.)

The core of a living culture is not primarily a set of ideas, but of *ideals*. Ideals are ideas that make *normative* claims upon us. They don't just tell us what *is*, but what *ought* to be. Like Rilke's "Archaic Torso of Apollo," ideals demand that we change our lives. The core of a living culture is a pantheon of ideals that is experienced as *numinous* and *enthralling*.

An individual formed by a living culture has a fundamental sense of identification with and participation in his culture. He cannot separate himself from it, and since it is the source of his ideas of his nature, the good life, the cosmos, and his place in it, his attitude toward culture is fundamentally earnest and serious, even pious. In a very deep sense, he does not own his culture, he is owned by it.

In terms of their relationship to culture, human beings fall into two basic categories: healthy and unhealthy. Healthy human beings experience the ideals that define a culture as a challenge, as a tonic. The gap between the ideal and the real is bridged by a longing of the soul for perfection. This longing is a tension, like the tension of the bowstring or the lyre, that makes human greatness possible. Culture forms human beings not merely by evoking idealistic longings, but also by suppressing, shaping, stylizing, and sublimating our natural desires. Culture has an element of mortification. But healthy organisms embrace this ascetic dimension as a pathway to ennoblement through self-transcendence.

Unhealthy organisms experience culture in a radically different way. Ideals are not experienced as a challenge to quicken and mobilize the life force. Instead, they are experienced as a threat, an insult, an external imposition, a gnawing thorn in the flesh. The unhealthy organism wishes to free itself from the tension created by ideals—which it experiences as nothing more than unreasonable expectations (unreasonable by the standards of an immanentized reason, a mere hedonistic calculus). The unhealthy organism does not wish to suppress and sublimate his natural desires. He wishes to validate them as good enough and then express them. He wants to give them free rein, not pull back on the bit.

Unfortunately, the decadent have will-to-power too. Thus they have been able to free themselves and their desires from the tyranny of normative culture and institute a decadent counter-culture in its place. This is the true meaning of "postmodernism." Postmodernism replaces participation with detachment, earnestness with irony, seriousness with playfulness, enthrallment with emancipation. Such attitudes demythologize and profane the pantheon of numinous ideals that is the beating heart of a living culture.

Culture henceforth becomes merely a wax museum: a realm of dead, decontextualized artifacts and ideas. When a culture is eviscerated of its defining worldview, all integrity, all unity of style is lost. Cultural integrity gives way to multiculturalism, which is merely a pretentious way of describing a shopping mall where artifacts are bought and sold, mixed and matched to satisfy emancipated consumer desires: a wax museum jumping to the pulse of commerce. This is the world of *Pulp Fiction*.

Yet, as *Pulp Fiction* also shows, even when desire becomes emancipated and sovereign, it has a tendency to dialectically overcome itself. As William Blake said, "The fool who persists in his folly will become wise." As much as hedonists wish to become mere happy animals, they remain botched human beings. The human soul still contains longings for something more than mere satiation of natural desires. These longings, moreover, are closely intertwined with these desires. For instance, merely natural desires are few and easily satisfied. But the human imagination can multiply desires to infinity. Most of these artificial desires, moreover, are for objects that satisfy a need for honor, recognition, status, not mere natural creature comforts. Hedonism is not an animal existence, but merely a perverted and profaned human existence.

If *animal* life is all about contentment, plenitude, fullness—the fulfillment of our natural desires—then a distinctly *human* mode of existence emerges when hominids mortify the flesh in the name of something higher. Hegel believed that the perforation of the flesh was the first expression of human spirit in animal existence.

This throws light on the discourse on body piercing delivered by Jody, the wife of Lance the drug dealer. Jody, it is safe to say, is about as complete a hedonist as has ever existed. Yet Jody has had her body pierced sixteen times, including her left nipple, her clitoris, and her tongue. And in each instance, she used a needle rather than a relatively quick and painless piercing gun. As she says, "That gun goes against the whole idea behind piercing."

Well then, one has to ask: "What is the whole idea behind piercing?" Yes, piercing is fashionable. Yes, it is involved with sexual fetishism. (But fetishism is not mere desire either.) Yes, it is now big business. But the phenomenon cannot merely be reduced to hedonistic self-indulgence. It hurts. And it is irreversible.

Thus, in a world of casual and meaningless self-indulgence, piercing and its first cousin tattooing are deeply significant; they are tests; they are limit experiences; they are encounters with something—something in ourselves and in the world—that transcends the economy of desire. They are re-enactments of the primal *anthropogenetic* act within the context of a decadent and dehumanizing society.

But to "mortify" the flesh means literally to kill it. Each little hole is a little death, which derives its meaning from a big death, a whole death, death itself. And it is an encounter with death itself that is truly anthropogenetic—at least potentially so.

Jules and Vincent had a brush with death, but the bullets missed. For Jules, this brought on a moment of clarity. His self-deceptions were breached, he saw his life for what it really was, and he changed it. But the experience was wasted on Vincent.

Vincent and Mia Wallace also had a brush with death. (Mia's death would surely have entailed Vincent's death.) But again, it was wasted on Vincent. (We never learn how it affected Mia.)

For Hegel, however, the truly anthropogenetic encounter with death is not a mere "near miss," but rather *an intentionally undertaken battle to the death over honor*, which is the subject of Part 4, "The Gold Watch," to which we now turn.

THE GOLD WATCH

We first encounter boxer Butch Coolidge at the beginning of Part 3, "Vincent Vega and Marsellus Wallace's Wife." The setting is a tittie bar owned by Marsellus Wallace. The time is mid-morning, so the bar is empty. Butch is a small timer near the end of his career. If he was going to make it, he would have made it already. So he is looking to scrape up some retirement money by throwing a fight. Marsellus Wallace offers him a large sum of cash to lose in the fifth round. Wallace plans to bet on Butch's opponent and clean up.

Butch accepts the deal, then Wallace dispenses a bit of advice: "Now, the night of the fight, you may feel a slight sting. That's pride fuckin' wit ya. Fuck pride! Pride only hurts, it never helps. Fight through that shit. 'Cause a year from now, when you're kickin' it in the Caribbean, you're gonna say, 'Marsellus Wallace was right.'" Butch replies, "I've got no problem with that, Mr. Wallace."

Just before Butch leaves, Vincent Vega and Jules Winnfield enter, fresh from their encounter with Pumpkin and Honey Bunny. As Butch approaches the bar, Vincent, who (as we all know) has had a really bad morning, taunts him as "palooka" and "punchy." Butch is clearly incensed but lets it drop. Apparently, his pride is well in check.

We meet Butch again in Part 4, "The Gold Watch," which begins with a flashback. It is 1972. Butch is about eight years old. He is watching TV when his mother introduces him to Captain Koons (Christopher Walken), who was in the same North Vietnamese prisoner of war camp as Butch's father, who died there.

Captain Koons has come to keep a promise to Butch's father. He is delivering a wristwatch that was bought by Butch's great-grandfather Ryan Coolidge when he went off to fight in World War I. Twenty years later, he gave it to his son Dane Coolidge, who went off to fight in World

War II as a Marine. Dane was killed at the battle of Wake Island. Knowing that he had little chance of survival, he entrusted a man named Winocki, a gunner on an Air Force transport plane, with the task of delivering his watch to his infant son whom he had never seen. The gunner kept his promise, and that same watch was on the wrist of Butch's father when he was shot down over Hanoi. To keep the watch from being confiscated, Butch's father hid it in his rectum. When he died, he entrusted it to Captain Koons, who hid it in his rectum until he was released. "And now, little man," says Captain Koons, "I give the watch to you."

As young Butch reaches out for the watch, the older Butch wakes up with a start. It is the night of the fight. His trainer opens the door: "It's time, Butch." We hear the roar of the crowd.

Cut to the aftermath of the fight. A female cabbie, Esmeralda Villa Lobos, is listening to the radio as she waits outside the arena. We hear the announcers say that the other boxer, Floyd Ray Willis (a black man, according to the script) was killed and that Butch Coolidge fled the ring. Then Butch exits the arena from a window and jumps into the cab. He has broken his deal with Marsellus Wallace and is clearly on the run. But the question is: "*Why* did he fight to win, to the point of killing the other boxer?"

The natural interpretation is that his pride got the best of him. What stirred up his pride? The most plausible answer is his dream/recollection of the story of the gold watch. After all, everything in the story is connected to honor: the three generations of his family (patriotic folk from Tennessee) who fought in America's wars, two of them giving their lives. The fact that we know that these wars were not in America's interests, and that American men were sent to their deaths by aliens and traitors, does not alter the fact that the military cultivates an ethos of honor to overcome the fear of death. Furthermore, Winocki and Captain Koons both honored their promises to deliver the gold watch to the next Coolidge heir.

Thus the watch represents honor, the honor of fighting men, a fact that is not stained but enhanced by the detail that both Butch's father and Captain Koons kept it hidden in their rectums for years. As Butch later says, his father "went through a lot" to give him that watch. What they went through commands respect.

So my initial interpretation was that Butch's honor was stirred up by the recollection of the watch, thus he went into the ring and fought, not for money, but for honor. And since he had made a deal with Marsellus Wallace to throw the fight, he was risking his life to fight for honor. And he fought all-out, killing the other boxer. So Butch seems to have proved himself to be a man ruled by honor, not by desire.

HEGEL ON THE BEGINNING OF HISTORY

The duel to the death over honor is a remarkable phenomenon. Animals duel over dominance, which ensures their access to mates. But these duels result in death only by accident, because the whole process is governed by their survival instincts, and their "egos" do not prevent them from surrendering when the fight is hopeless. The duel to the death over honor is a distinctly human thing.

Indeed, in his *Phenomenology of Spirit*, Hegel claims that the duel to the death over honor is the beginning of history—and the beginning of a distinctly human form of existence and self-consciousness.

Prehistoric man is dominated by nature: the natural world around him and the natural world within him, namely his desires. History, for Hegel, is something different. It is the process of (1) our discovery of those parts of our nature that *transcend* mere animal desire, and (2) our creation of a society in accord with our true nature.

When we fully know ourselves as more than merely natural beings and finally live accordingly, then history will be over. (History can end, because as a process of discovery and construction, it is the kind of thing that can end.) Hegel claimed that history ended with the discovery that all men are free and the creation of a society that reflects that truth.

When two men duel to the death over honor, the external struggle between them conceals an internal struggle within each of them as they confront the possibility of being ruled by two different parts of their souls: *desire*, which includes the desire for self-preservation, and *honor*, which demands recognition of our worth by others.

When our sense of honor is offended, we become angry and seek to compel the offending party to respect us. If the other party is equally offended and intransigent, the struggle can escalate to the point where life is at stake.

At this point, two kinds of human beings distinguish themselves. Those who are ruled by their honor will sacrifice their lives to preserve it. Their motto is: "Death before dishonor." Those who are ruled by their desires are more concerned to preserve their lives than their honor. Thus they will sacrifice their honor to preserve their lives. Their motto is: "Dishonor before death."

Suppose two honorable men fight to the death. One will live, one will die, but both will preserve their honor. But what if the vanquished party begs to be spared at the last moment at the price of his honor? What if his desire to survive is stronger than his sense of honor? In that case, he will become the slave of the victor.

The man who prefers death to dishonor is a natural master. The man who prefers dishonor to death—life at any price—is a natural slave. The natural master defines himself in terms of a distinctly human self-consciousness, an awareness of his transcendence over animal desire, the survival "instinct," the whole realm of biological necessity. The natural slave, by contrast, is ruled by his animal nature and experiences his sense of honor as a danger to survival. The master uses the slave's fear of death to compel him to work.

History thus begins with the emergence of a warrior aristocracy, a two-tiered society structured in terms of the oppositions between work and leisure, necessity and luxury, nature and culture. Slaves work so that the masters can enjoy leisure. Slaves secure the necessities of life so the masters can enjoy luxuries. Slaves conquer nature so masters can create culture. In a sense, the whole realm of culture is a "luxury," since none of it is necessitated by our animal desires. But in a higher sense, it is a necessity: a necessity of our distinctly human nature to understand itself and put its stamp upon the world.

THE END OF HISTORY

Hegel had the fanciful notion that there is a necessary "dialectic" between master and slave that will eventually lead to universal freedom, that at the end of history, the distinction between master and slave can be abolished, that all men are potential masters.

Now, to his credit, Hegel was a race realist. He was also quite realistic about the tendency of bourgeois capitalism to turn all men into spiritual slaves. Thus his view of the ideal state, which regulates economic life and reinforces the institutions that elevate human character against the corrupting influences of modernity, differs little from fascism. So in the end, Hegel's high-flown talk about universal freedom seems unworthy of him, rather like Jefferson's rhetorical gaffe that "all men are created equal."

The true heirs to Hegel's universalism are Marx and his followers, who really believed that the dialectic would lead to universal freedom. Alexandre Kojève, Hegel's greatest twentieth-century Marxist interpreter, came to believe that both Communism and bourgeois capitalism/liberal democracy were paths to Hegel's vision of universal freedom. After the collapse of communism, Kojève's interpreter Francis Fukuyama declared that bourgeois capitalism and liberal democracy would create what Kojève called the "universal homogeneous state," the global political and economic order in which all men would be free.

But both capitalism and communism are essentially materialistic systems. Yes, they made appeals to idealism, but primarily to motivate their subjects to fight for them. But if one system triumphed over the other, that necessity would no longer exist, and desire would be fully sovereign. Materialism would triumph. (And so it would have, were it not for the rise of another global enemy that is spiritual and warlike rather than materialistic: Islam.)

Thus Kojève came to believe that the universal homogeneous state would not be a society in which all men are masters, i.e., a society in which honor rules over desire. Rather, it would be a world in which all men are slaves, a society in which desire rules over honor.

This is the world of Nietzsche's "Last Man," the world of C. S. Lewis's "Men without Chests" (honor is traditionally associated with the chest, just as reason is associated with the head and desire with the belly and points below). This is the postmodern world, where emancipated desire and corrosive individualism and irony have reduced all normative cultures to commodities that can be bought and sold, used and discarded.

This is the end of the path blazed by the first wave of modern philosophers: Thomas Hobbes, John Locke, David Hume, etc., all of whom envisioned a liberal order founded on the sovereignty of desire, in which reason is reduced to a technical-instrumental faculty and honor is checked or sublimated into economic competitiveness and the quest for material status symbols.

From this point of view, there is no significant difference between classical liberalism and Left liberalism. Both are based on the sovereignty of desire. Although Left liberalism is more idealistic because it is dedicated to the impossible dream of overcoming natural inequality, whereas classical liberalism, always more vulgar, unimaginative, and morally complacent, is content with mere "bourgeois" legal equality.

The great theorists of liberalism offered mankind the same deal that Marsellus Wallace offered Butch: "Fuck pride. Think of the money." And our ancestors took the deal. As Marsellus hands Butch the cash, he pauses to ask, "Are you my nigger?" "It certainly appears so," Butch answers, then takes the money. In modernity, every man is the nigger, the spiritual slave, of any man with more money than him—to the precise extent that any contrary motives, such as pride or religious/intellectual enthusiasm, have been suppressed. (Marsellus, a black man, calls all of his hirelings niggers, but surely it gives him special pleasure to deem the white ones so.)

History Begins Again

But history can never really end as long as it is possible for men to choose to place honor above money. And that is always possible, given that we really do seem to have the ability to choose which part of our soul is sovereign.

It is, moreover, possible as long as the examples of our ancestors, better men than ourselves, can still stir us. When Esmeralda asks Butch what his name means, he replies "I'm an American, honey, our names don't mean shit." It is one of the funniest lines of the movie, but also one of the saddest. Americans are such a sorry lot of spiritual slaves because we don't know who we are. We don't know who our ancestors are. We don't know what our names mean. So we don't have to live up to them. Or if we do know, we allow the Marsellus Wallaces of the world to bribe us into forgetting about it.

Of course "Butch" means something. It is a fighting man's name. Butch is a fighting man, from a long line of fighting men. Although he fights for money, not honor. But then, when he has reached the rock bottom of spiritual sordidness—when he sells himself as the nigger of a black gangster—he redeems himself. This is what makes Butch Coolidge seem so heroic.

But then we discover that we were completely wrong. Butch stops to make a phone call, and we learn that he has taken Marsellus's money then leaked the word that the fix was in, which tilted the odds dramatically in favor of his opponent. Then Butch bet all of Marsellus's money on himself and beat the other boxer—and he *had* to beat him, so he fought all-out and killed him—in order to win a huge payout. So Butch turns out to be a bigger crook than Marsellus Wallace. And we all know what happens to people who steal from Marsellus Wallace.

Butch meets his French girlfriend Fabienne at a cheap motel. They are cute together, and she obviously wants to have his children, explaining at length about how she wants to have a large, perfectly round potbelly. They plan to leave town the next morning, but Butch discovers that Fabienne forgot to pack his father's gold watch.

Again, Butch is faced with a conflict between honor and desire, a conflict in which his life is at stake. Honor tells him to retrieve the watch, although he knows that he will have to risk his life to do so, because Wallace will surely stake out his apartment. Desire, most eminently the desire to stay alive, tells him to take the money and run. So now we see, for real, what kind of man Butch is. He chooses honor, risking his life to retrieve the watch.

Butch cautiously returns to his apartment and retrieves

the watch. Astonished at the ease, he ducks into his kitchen for a snack (he has had no breakfast). As he waits for the toaster, he is startled to see a submachine gun with a huge silencer lying on the counter. As he hefts the gun, he hears the toilet flush. The bathroom door opens, and there stands Vincent Vega, reading material in hand. The two men freeze, staring at each other. Then the toaster pops, breaking the spell, and Butch pulls the trigger, reducing Vega to a bullet-riddled corpse sprawled in the bathtub.

It could have been Jules Winnfield, but he followed his spiritual enthusiasm and left "the life." Vincent, ruled by his desires, stayed in. Vincent, ruled by his desires, mocked Butch as "palooka" and "punchy," daring him to retaliate. Which, eventually, he did. And given Vincent's character, it is singularly appropriate that Butch got the drop on him while he was "taking a shit."

Butch flees in Fabienne's Honda. As he waits at a light, Marsellus Wallace crosses the street in front of him with coffee and donuts for the stake out. When the two men recognize each other, Butch floors it, running Marsellus down. But his car is hit by oncoming traffic. When Marsellus comes to and sees Butch, injured in the wrecked Honda, he pulls out a .45 and starts firing wildly as he staggers across the street. Butch ducks into a pawnshop, and when Marsellus follows, Butch knocks him down and starts punching him furiously: "Feel that sting? That's pride, fuckin' wit ya."

Unfortunately, they have blundered into no ordinary pawnshop. Maynard, the shop-keeper gets the drop on Butch with a shotgun then knocks him out cold. When he comes to, he and Marsellus are tied to chairs in a basement dungeon with red S&M ball gags in their mouths. Maynard explains that nobody kills anyone in his place of business except himself or Zed, who is arriving presently. Zed and Maynard are two homosexual hillbilly sadists who apparently plan to rape, torture, and murder Marsellus and Butch.

When Zed and Maynard take Marsellus in the other room to reenact a scene from *Deliverance*, Butch manages to free himself. He could just sneak out, saving himself and leaving Marsellus to a well-deserved fate. But Butch can't do it. He chooses a riskier but more honorable path. He decides to rescue Marsellus. He looks around for a suitable weapon. First he hefts a claw hammer. Then a small chainsaw. Then a baseball bat. Finally, his eyes light on a samurai sword—the perfect symbol of honor.

He returns to the dungeon. Zed is raping Marsellus (who does look just like a hawg—a roasted one, complete with an apple in his mouth) while Maynard watches. Butch dispatches Maynard and taunts Zed. Marsellus, in the meantime, gets up, grabs Maynard's shotgun, and blasts Zed in the groin. At this point, Marsellus could have killed Butch as well. (Butch was very, very stupid to let Marsellus get the drop on him.)

But Marsellus responds to Butch's gallant gesture in kind. He agrees to drop his grievance against Butch if he does not tell anyone about what has happened and if he leaves L.A. never to return. I know it is unlikely. But if he got his soul back, maybe it is starting to kick in. (But not soon enough to save Zed from a "medieval" fate.)

Butch accepts the deal and roars off on Zed's chopper to meet Fabienne. They still have time to catch their train to Tennessee. And on that happy note, the story (as opposed to the movie) of *Pulp Fiction* ends.

* * *

Even its detractors admit that *Pulp Fiction* is a stylishly directed, superbly acted, darkly comic movie. I hope I have convinced you that it is a deeply serious movie as well. Yes, Quentin Tarantino is a thoroughly repulsive and nihilistic human being, and everything he directed before and since *Pulp Fiction* reflects that.[2] But repugnant people create great art all the time, in spite of themselves.

Yes, *Pulp Fiction* contains interracial couples, villainous bumbling whites, and noble, eloquent blacks. One just has to look beyond the casting to the story itself. But *Pulp Fiction* is only superficially anti-white. On a deeper level, it can aid us in rejecting modernity and recovering the spiritual foundations of something better.

Pulp Fiction is valuable for our cause as a critique of modernity in its final decadent phase, what Traditionalists call the Kali Yuga, Hegelians call the "end of history," and idiots celebrate as postmodernity. Philosophically speaking, modernity is the emancipation of desire from reason, honor, culture, and tradition.

Pulp Fiction takes such philosophical abstractions and pairs them with unforgettably dramatic concrete images and events. Modernity is Marsellus Wallace telling us to fuck pride, take his money, and become his nigger. Modernity is coke, smack, and Jack Rabbit Slim's. Modernity is Vincent Vega sprawled dead in a bathtub, Mia Wallace with a huge syringe stuck in her heart, and Jules Winnfield scooping up bits of brain and skull in the back seat of a blood-soaked car.

But *Pulp Fiction* does much more than just critique modernity. It also shows us an alternative. Not an alternative vision of society, but rather *the spiritual basis* of an alternative to modernity. Spiritually, modernity is the rule of desire. Part of the grip of modernity is that even people who intellectually reject it are still modern men

---

[2] See my reviews of *Kill Bill: Vol. 1*, *Inglourious Basterds*, and *Django Unchained* in *Trevor Lynch's White Nationalist Guide to the Movies*.

who have no idea of how they could become anything else.

Most modern people lack the concepts necessary to think of themselves as anything more than desire-driven producer-consumers. Reason to them is just calculating options. Honor is just the narcissistic display of commodities that we are told symbolize status.

Pulp Fiction brilliantly concretizes and dramatizes the moments of decision when one chooses to be something more than a mere modern man: Jules Winnfield's choice to follow his desires or his mystical conviction that God is sending him a message; Butch Coolidge's choice to be a sneaky, bourgeois coward or a man of honor.

The spiritual man is Jules Winnfield, honestly confronting the fact that he has been lying to himself all his life, that he has been the tool of the "tyranny of evil men" (from Hobbes and Locke down to Marsellus Wallace), and instead "trying to be the shepherd." The warrior is Captain Koons keeping his word and delivering the gold watch; the warrior is Butch Coolidge descending back into hell with a samurai sword to do justice. These are the kinds of men who can start history again and deliver our people from evil.

Plato claims that society is the soul writ large. If democracy is the rule of desire writ large, then the regime that corresponds to Butch Coolidge's soul is a warrior aristocracy. The regime that corresponds to Jules Winnfield's soul is a form of theocracy in which social order is based on a transcendent metaphysical order, what Evola called the idea of the Imperium. If Tarantino had tried to show us the political big picture, he would have gotten it all terribly wrong. But what he does show, he gets dead right. Mapping out the political alternative is our job.

Counter-Currents, June 29 & July 6, 2011

RASHOMON & REALISM

Akira Kurosawa's *Rashomon* (1950) is commonly found on lists of the world's greatest movies, and deservedly so. *Rashomon* features avant-garde narrative techniques (flashbacks, multiple points of view), dynamic black-and-white cinematography by Kazuo Miyagawa, compelling Ravel-like music by Fumio Hayasaka, subtle and intensely dramatic performances, and a complex but tightly edited script, all combined into a fast-paced 88-minute masterpiece with an emotionally devastating climax. *Rashomon* is also distinguished by featuring one of the most loathsome and twisted female villains in all of cinema ("Let's you and he fight, and I'll go with the survivor").

When *Rashomon* won the Golden Lion at the 1951 Venice International Film Festival, it did more than lay the foundations for the enduring world-wide fame of Kurosawa and his star, Toshiro Mifune; it opened the eyes of the world toward Japanese cinema as a whole.

Rashomon is the story of a rape and murder committed in twelfth-century Japan. Or, rather, it is four radically divergent stories of the same rape and murder. *Rashomon* is constantly trotted out by coffee-house intellectuals as an illustration of the subjectivity of our perceptions and the relativity of truth. But this is a superficial misreading of the film.

The stories in *Rashomon* do not diverge because of the ineluctable subjectivity of all claims about the world. The witnesses are simply *lying*. Furthermore, if we pay attention to their testimony, the characters of the witnesses, and the enduring facts of human psychology, *we can reconstruct what really happened*. Finally, *Rashomon* does not just presuppose that reality is objective and knowable, but that there is a *moral order* that is objective and knowable as well, an objective *ought* as well as an objective *is*. In short, *Rashomon* is not a relativist film but a deeply realist one.

The film opens in a downpour. Two men, a woodcutter and a priest, have taken refuge from the rain in the ruins of the Rashomon gate of Kyoto. It is a time of war, famine, natural disasters, and social breakdown. The woodcutter speaks the first words of the film: "I can't understand it. I can't understand it at all." The two men look at each other and then turn to morosely watch the rain.

Soon they are joined by a third man, who turns out to be a cynic and a thief. Hearing the woodcutter repeating "I just can't understand it," the cynic asks what he is talking about. The woodcutter and the priest both state that they have heard troubling testimonies that day. The cynic asks to hear all about it. When the priest begins to sermonize, though, the cynic cuts him off. He only wants to hear the facts for his amusement. The priest can keep his moralizing to himself.

THE WOODCUTTER'S FIRST STORY

According to the woodcutter, three days before, he went to the forest to gather wood. Walking along a forest path, he first encounters a woman's hat with a veil hanging on a bush, then a samurai's hat trampled in the leaves, then a length of rope, then an amulet case, then the dead body of a man. Horrified, he rushes off to tell the police. Next we see the woodcutter testifying in court. When asked by the judge if he saw a sword, he answers no.

THE PRIEST'S TESTIMONY

Next, we see the testimony of the priest, who passed the murdered man on the road on the afternoon of his death. The murdered man was a samurai, carrying a sword and a bow and arrows. His young wife was on horseback. The priest, who does love to sermonize, then begins to speak of the fragility and fleetingness of human life.

The Policeman's Testimony

Next we see a policeman sitting next to the bound bandit, Tajomaru (Toshiro Mifune). The policeman claims that he captured the bandit after he had been thrown from a horse, which turns out to be the horse of the samurai's wife. The policeman also found the samurai's bow and arrows.

Tajomaru's Testimony

Tajomaru scoffs at the policeman's claim that the great bandit Tajomaru had been thrown from a horse. Instead, he claims, he had been sick with dysentery from drinking polluted water. He then admits that he killed the samurai and tells how it happened.

It was a hot day, and Tajomaru was resting alongside the road. The samurai and his wife passed by, and a breeze momentarily lifted her veil. Struck by her beauty, the bandit decided that he would have her, even if he had to kill her husband. (This sort of contingency brings to mind Camus' *The Stranger*, in which the protagonist Patrice Meursault ends up killing an Arab because it is an especially hot day on the beach.[1])

Tajomaru quickly hatches a plan. He approaches the samurai and tells him that he found a treasure of swords and mirrors buried in the woods. He offers to sell them to him at a good price. The samurai follows the bandit down a forest path and into a grove, where the bandit springs on him and ties him up. The bandit returns to the wife and tells him her husband has taken sick. Her childlike concern made him feel jealous of her husband. He wanted to show her his disgrace and led her into the grove.

When she sees that her husband has been captured,

---

[1] Greg Johnson, "A Leveling Wing: Reading Camus' *The Stranger*," in *From Plato to Postmodernism*.

her expression goes cold. Then she pulls out a dagger and attacks the bandit fiercely. He evades her blows, and as she tires, he seizes her. She breaks down in tears as he rapes her, dropping the knife as she gives in.

After the rape, the bandit prepares to leave and allow them to continue on their journey, but the wife stops him with a shocking proposal. She has been shamed. Two men cannot know of her shame. One of them must die. The two must fight, and she will go with the survivor. The bandit is horrified by this proposal. He cuts the husband's bonds. The husband seizes his sword and attacks. There is an epic swordfight, and the samurai is killed. It is an honorable death, but it was not what the bandit intended.

When the fight was over, the bandit discovered that the woman had run off. So he took the husband's sword and bow and arrows. Then he found the wife's horse and left. He sold the samurai's sword. But he forgot to collect the dagger, which he calls his "biggest mistake."

Throughout his testimony, and in the flashbacks as well, Tajomaru's testimony is filled with bravado, boasting, boyish hi-jinks, and loud, hollow laughter. At times, he seem maniacal. Even though he has been captured and will surely die, he pretends that he is in control, speaking haughtily to the policeman and judge. Genuine laughter is an expression of a sense of superiority. Nervous or forced laughter is an expression of a feeling of inferiority trying to mask itself as superiority. The same is true of boasting. The bandit has been shamed, and he is trying save face. We must bear this motive in mind.

Japan, like other Far Eastern societies, is a shame culture, not a guilt culture. In shame cultures, one's infractions of morals and manners cause intense shame if seen by others. In guilt cultures, one's infractions of morals and manners cause pangs of conscience, even if nobody else knows about them. In shame cultures, one does not suffer pangs of conscience if one's infractions go unnoticed or can be covered up with a face-saving lie. All the lies in *Rashomon* are motivated by the desire to hide shame and save face. If one bears this motive in mind, one can reconstruct what actually happened from the four widely diverging stories.

After Tajomaru's story, the movie returns us to the Rashomon gate. Much to the cynic's surprise, the wife was found alive, hiding in a temple, and was brought to the court to testify. The woodcutter then declares that both Tajomaru and the wife were lying. How does he know this? It turns out that he saw the whole thing and lied about it to the court.

THE WIFE'S TESTIMONY

In the court, the wife is far from being the virago described by Tajomaru. Instead, she is tearful and submissive. According to the wife, after the bandit raped her, he told her his name and mocked her husband. The husband struggled in his bonds, and the wife ran to his side to help. The bandit laughed and ran away. The wife was frozen by her husband's glance, which was aloof and filled with loathing. She screamed for him to kill her, but not to hold her in contempt. She fetched her dagger, freed her husband, and asked him to kill her. Then she grew hysterical and fainted. When she awoke, she found her husband dead, the dagger in his chest. It is never made clear whether he died at her hand or his. She said that she did not remember leaving the woods. She found herself by a pond and tried to drown herself, but failed. Then she took refuge in a temple. She ends her testimony by asking, "What could a poor, helpless woman like me do?" The whole thrust of her story is to establish her good intentions and to absolve her of all responsibility for what happened. She does not even have the agency to secure the honorable death that she claims she desired.

The movie then returns us to the three men conversing

at the Rashomon gate. The cynic doubts the woman's testimony, accusing women of fooling themselves and using tears to manipulate men. Then we learn that the dead samurai also testified in court, through a spirit medium. The woodcutter, however, declares that the dead man's story is a lie as well. Again, he can say this because, as revealed later, he actually witnessed the whole crime.

THE HUSBAND'S TESTIMONY

The medium's testimony is one of the most imaginative sequences in the film. The medium is played by a woman, who engages is some sort of shamanic ritual, then speaks in a raspy, unearthly male voice.

According to the husband, after the rape, the bandit tried to console his wife and persuade her to run away with him. The wife agrees to go with the bandit, but then she implores him to kill her husband, again to hide her shame. The bandit is horrified by this and feels sympathy for the husband. He turns to the husband and says that he will kill her if he wishes it. The husband says that for these words, he almost forgave the bandit. The woman then fled, and the bandit chased her. Later, the bandit returns alone. The woman has escaped. The bandit frees the samurai and leaves. The samurai, sickened by his dishonor, takes up the wife's dagger and stabs himself. As he dies, he feels someone approach and remove the dagger from his chest.

At this point, we return to the gate, and the woodcutter blurts out that the story is untrue, for the samurai was killed by a sword, not a dagger. At this point, the canny cynic realizes that the woodcutter had seen more than he let on and persuades him to tell the whole story.

THE WOODCUTTER'S SECOND STORY

As in his original story, the woodcutter first found the woman's hat on a branch. But then he heard a woman weeping. He crept closer and found the samurai tied up and the bandit begging the woman to stop crying. The bandit has just raped her, but now he begs for her forgiveness. He offers to marry her. He even offers to work to support her. He then threatens to kill her if she refuses.

The wife gets to her feet and uses her dagger to free her husband. She does not wish to choose between the two of them. She wants the men to fight to the death, and she will go with the winner. The husband, however, holds her in complete contempt. He will not risk his life for a shameless whore and tells her to kill herself.

The bandit too is repulsed by her. He begins to leave but she begs him to stay. When her husband continues to insult her, however, the bandit stops and sticks up for her. Pressing her new opportunity, the wife manically shames both men, saying that if they were real men, they would fight each other. She says that women can only be won by strength, by the sword.

At this point, both men are still united by loathing for the woman, but they are also shamed by her into a half-hearted battle, a battle that they think will restore their honor but which simply deepens their own feelings of self-loathing. Instead of the epic show of swordsmanship in Tajomaru's story, we witness an utterly degrading farce in which two men, sword hands trembling, advance hesitantly then quickly retreat, rolling in the leaves and dirt. Eventually, almost by accident, the husband—begging for his life—is killed by the bandit who throws his sword at him, almost to renounce responsibility for the killing in the very act. He is utterly sickened by his victory. (This long-drawn, sordid murder brings to mind the killing scene in Hitchcock's *Torn Curtain* some years later.) The woman then flees, dishonoring the bandit still further. The bandit picks up the samurai's weapons, finds his horse, and flees, full of furtiveness and self-loathing.

When the woodcutter finishes his story, the cynic

questions the truth of the tale, and the woodcutter bristles and says that he is telling the truth. A bit later, the cynic asks him why he omitted any mention of the dagger, and the woodcutter admits that he stole it and sold it.

WHAT REALLY HAPPENED?

We can determine what really happened in *Rashomon* if we understand that all the lies and omissions in the various tales—save one, which is crucial to the movie's end—spring from the same motive: the desire to conceal shame and save face. I think it is most plausible to work backwards from the woodcutter's second tale. The woodcutter's account is most likely to be accurate because he was merely a witness, not a participant in the events. But even he conceals something out of shame, namely his theft of the dagger. But that was after the rape and murder took place.

If we take the woodcutter's account as basically accurate, then remove everything from it that the bandit, the wife, and the samurai would find shameful, we will arrive at the tales they tell.

The woodcutter did not see how the samurai and his wife ended up in the grove, or how the rape took place, so we simply must take the bandit's account of those events at face value.

The humiliating events that the bandit omits from the woodcutter's tale are begging the woman to marry him, the woman's verbal abuse and shaming, and the disgraceful duel at the end. Instead, as the bandit told it, he was prepared to leave and let the samurai and his wife to continue their journey, but she begged him to kill her husband. He was horrified by this proposal and released the husband. The husband then attacked. A gallant duel followed, ending with the samurai's honorable death.

The woman's tale omits everything after the rape that casts her in a shameful light. Gone is her proposal to have the two men fight to the death, which is present in all the other accounts. Gone is the bandit's horror at this proposal, which is also present in the other three accounts. As the wife tells it, the bandit simply leaves, the husband treats her contemptuously, she begs him to kill her, then faints. When she comes to, she finds her husband dead with her dagger in his chest—perhaps at his own hand, perhaps at hers. Her story does not account for what happened to the dagger, which was not found at the scene of the crime.

The tale told by the samurai's ghost also omits everything personally shameful to him: his wife goading the men to fight and his death at the end of their degrading duel. Instead, he claims that he committed suicide, but, unlike the wife, he had the presence of mind to explain why he was not found with a knife in his chest.

What remains to be explained is the discrepancy between the woodcutter's first and second accounts. Why did he completely omit the events after the rape leading up to the murder? To answer this question, we need to examine the final scene of the movie.

THE FOUNDLING

After the woodcutter finishes his second story, the priest bemoans the fact that human lies and selfishness create hell on earth, and they are living through it.

The ruined Rashomon gate is not just a place where people take refuge from the rain. It is also a spot where unclaimed corpses and unwanted babies are abandoned. After the priest finishes his lament, they hear the cries of a baby.

The woodcutter and the priest are horrified to find the cynic stealing the baby's clothes and an amulet left for its protection. The cynic defends himself by claiming that if he did not do it, someone else would. The woodcutter accuses him of being evil and selfish. The cynic deflects that by claiming that the parents of the foundling are evil and selfish for abandoning it.

The woodcutter disagrees. The amulet was left for the baby's protection. It must have been hard for the parents to abandon their child. The cynic mocks the woodcutter's compassion for the parents and leaves. The woodcutter then tells the priest that he will adopt the baby. He has six children already. One more won't matter. The priest then tells the woodcutter that he has restored his faith in humanity. The rain stops, sun breaks through the clouds, and the woodcutter departs with the foundling. The End.

How has the great Rashomon gate of Kyoto become a ruin where rotting corpses and unwanted babies are abandoned? How did life on earth become hell?

Rashomon's answer is: because of Japanese honor culture, because of the selfish desire to save face, to construct and propagate an image of oneself, which requires lies, manipulation, and the domination of others. How does one get beyond selfishness, lies, and violence to heal the world? The woodcutter shows us the way: through compassion. I read *Rashomon* as a critique of Japanese honor culture, including the code of the samurai, from the point of view of a Buddhist ethics of compassion.

The woodcutter's compassion even explains why he omitted so much when testifying in court. Granted, he had selfish reasons not to mention the theft of the dagger. But then again, he had six children to feed. However, he did not omit the story of the murder to hide his own shame, but because he felt compassion for the shame of the bandit, the samurai, and his wife. It was painful for him to watch. It is painful for *us* to watch. We want to look away, and we can understand why the woodcutter did not want to compound their shame by revealing it to the world.

If *Rashomon* is a deeply realist work, presupposing that both facts and morality are objective and knowable, why has it become the favorite film of relativists? Why has such a superficial reading become the dominant one? What sort of bovine mind could view four completely contradictory accounts of what the rest of us naïvely call "the same events" and conclude that there's nothing more to the film than that? How can one watch *Rashomon* all the way to the end and never advance beyond the opening words, "I can't understand it. I can't understand it at all"? What sort of mind would wish to repeat and recommend such an experience? And what do such viewers make of the ending of the film, which I interpret as a repudiation of everything that the relativists praise?

I believe that the relativist reading of *Rashomon* is popular because we today are living in the same kind of world depicted by the film: a Dark Age of selfishness and lies. Relativism is just a philosophical rationalization of the egocentrism and dishonesty that turned the world of *Rashomon* into a hell. Which means that today we face the same problem explored in the film itself: how can we awaken the forces of compassion and solidarity, forces that can free us from the deep solitude of spirit to which this Dark Age confines us, allowing us to redeem this hellish fallen world and make it a place we can all call home?

Counter-Currents, October 16, 2017

The Searchers

The Searchers (1956) has been acclaimed not just as one of John Ford's greatest films, and not just as one of the greatest Westerns, but as one of the greatest films of all time. This praise is all the more surprising given that *The Searchers* is a profoundly illiberal and even "racist" movie, which means that most fans esteem it grudgingly rather than unreservedly.

I think *The Searchers* is absurdly overrated, for it is far from flawless. But it is still a great work of art that plumbs deep themes and stirs deep feelings. It should be seen by everyone, even people who generally don't watch movies.

Although *The Searchers* is set in Texas in 1868, Ford's treatment goes beyond the historical to the mythic and epic. The movie begins in a dark room. A door opens on a magnificent Monument Valley landscape. The silhouette of a woman appears in the doorway. As she steps forward, into the light, she moves from being two-dimensional to three. It is like watching a specter, a shade, taking on an embodied form. It has the feel of a creation myth.

But what is being created? The answer seems to be civilization, and it is a very different myth than the one told by liberal social contract theorists. The opening also suggests that the interior realm of family and domesticity is less real than the exterior world. It certainly proves to be less harsh and far more vulnerable.

A rider approaches across the desert. This is a lawless land, where every stranger is regarded with apprehension. The wife is joined on the porch by her husband, then her daughters, then her son, all scanning anxiously. The figures are shot from a low angle. They move with dignity. They barely speak. The whole feel is monumental, epic.

As the rider comes closer, they recognize him as a

long-lost member of the family: Ethan Edwards, played with searing charisma by John Wayne. After eight years of fighting, first with the Confederacy then as a mercenary for the Emperor Maximilian in Mexico, the wanderer Ethan has come to the ranch of his brother Aaron, Aaron's wife Martha, and their three children, Lucy, Ben, and Debbie.

Ethan clearly aims to stop fighting and make a home there. He gives his sabre to Ben and a Mexican medal to Debbie. He presents Aaron with a substantial amount of money to "pay his way." But Ethan's attempt to return to society and enjoy the fruits of peace does not last a single day, for there's trouble afoot.

The next morning, Ethan goes off with a group of Texas Rangers to recover the stolen cattle of a neighboring rancher, Lars Jorgenson. When they find the cattle slaughtered with Comanche lances, Ethan concludes that the cattle theft was a diversion to pull the men from the ranches, leaving them vulnerable to attack. The party splits up, riding to defend both the Jorgenson and Edwards ranches.

When Ethan arrives back at his brother's ranch, he finds it in flames. Aaron, Ben, and Martha are dead. Lucy and Debbie have been abducted by a band of Comanches led by a warrior known as Scar. After a brief funeral, Ethan and a group of Rangers go in search of the girls.

After a battle with the Indians, the party splits in two. Most of them return home, while Ethan continues the search accompanied by Lucy's fiancé Brad Jorgenson (Harry Carey, Jr.) and Martin Pawley (Jeffrey Hunter), an orphan who was adopted by the Edwards and considers the kidnapped girls his sisters. When Ethan finds Lucy dead, a distraught Brad charges into the Indian camp and is killed. The searchers are thus reduced to Ethan and Martin, so we need to pause a bit and examine both characters.

Who is Ethan Edwards? He is a warrior and a wanderer in wild spaces: the space between warring civilizations and the space between civilization and savagery. He lives in the state of nature, not civil society. In the state of nature, there is no overarching power to enforce the peace, so a man needs to know how to protect himself. Thus Ethan knows how to thread his way between hostile peoples, negotiate treaties with enemies, strike bargains with crooks, and deploy both trickery and violence in a fight. He knows Spanish, Comanche, and probably some other Indian tongues.

Ethan fought on the side of the Confederacy out of loyalty. (He won't swear another oath to the Texas Rangers.) Once the Confederacy was defeated, he fought for the Emperor Maximilian for money. But war is a young man's game. Ethan is getting too old for it. Thus, he wants to take his earnings and make a home for himself with his brother's family in Texas.

Ethan is a dark character. He has done dark deeds. He fits "any number of warrants," which doesn't necessarily mean he is guilty of anything. But the local Rangers would rather be his friend than his enemy. On two occasions, the Ranger Captain Clayton chooses to ignore Ethan's possible crimes because they need his help. They sense that Ethan is like them: a guardian of peace and family life, even though he has known precious little of them himself.

For instance, when a fight breaks out at a wedding at the Jorgenson home, Ethan shoos Mrs. Jorgenson inside because he doesn't think a woman should see such things. When Ethan finds the bodies of Martha and Lucy, both of whom were presumably raped, he spares others the sight. He has peered into the abyss so that others don't have to.

Ethan doesn't wish to remain in the state of nature. But he understands that he may never see civil society. He may have to give his life so that others will see it. He may have to do things that render him unfit for civil society, so that others can enjoy it in innocence and peace.

At one point, Mrs. Jorgenson says, "A Texican's nothin' but a human man out on a limb . . . This year and next and maybe for a hundred more. But I don't think it'll be forever. Someday this country will be a fine good place to be . . . Maybe it needs our bones in the ground before that time can come . . ."

Texas is a pagan land that demands human sacrifices before it becomes a decent place to live. This is why Ethan interrupts the Christian burial of his family to begin the search for the killers. Texas is not yet ready for such niceties. It needs more blood and bones, and Ethan is ready to lay down his own.

Ethan is a man in a hurry. The proximate reason for haste is that with each passing minute, the girls are closer to rape, torture, and death. The deeper cause is that he's over the hill, so his time is short. Thus he's rude and abrasive. He treats weakness with contempt. He is focused on action and has no time for social niceties. He is cold and ruthless, using Martin as bait to trap and kill the treacherous merchant Futterman. He is also increasingly savage. He shoots out the eyes of a dead Indian, because mutilated men "can't enter the spirit land" but must "wander forever between the winds." He scalps another Indian corpse for the same reason. He even slaughters buffalo simply to starve the Indians.

Ethan's search for Debbie quickly takes on the quality of an obsession. He barely knew the girl. She was eight years old when he returned from eight years of wandering. But she is all that remains of his family, and he searches for her for five years, long after most men would have given up. He is Odysseus, who returns home for a day, then becomes Captain Ahab.

There's a lot to dislike about Ethan Edwards, but he's the only man who could have rescued Debbie. As in *The Man Who Shot Liberty Valance*, Ford wants to confront liberals with the fact their civilization could not have been built without illiberal men and illiberal deeds.

The central hangup of most critical writing about *The Searchers* is that Ethan is a "racist," even a "virulent" one. "Racism" is a recently invented sin, a bogus moral concept that means hating people "for no reason whatsoever" except the fact that they are "different." A racist, in the words of Jim Goad, means "a vicious loser who hates people with different continental ancestry . . . merely to compensate for being an inadequate psychopath and to avoid taking responsibility for his own problems."[1] Racists, we are always told, are "ignorant," for apparently to know Indians or blacks or Mexicans is to love them.

Ethan clearly isn't a racist in this sense. First of all, he is not ignorant of the Comanches. He knows their language and their myths. He respects them as enemies. He clearly hates them. But he doesn't hate them because they are merely "different" or because he is a "loser." He hates them because of their treachery, violence, and cruelty. They butchered his family after raping the women, something they did to countless other white families.

Critics are also exercised over the fact that Ethan would rather kill Debbie than allow her to stay with the Indians. Surely this is an expression of irrational "racism" and "hate." But is it? Plan A was always to rescue Debbie. At one point during their search, Ethan and Marty encounter some white women and girls rescued from Comanche captivity. They have clearly been driven mad by the experience. "Hard to believe they are white" says their rescuer. Ethan says, "They're not white anymore." Arguably, this is a fate worse than death. At this point, Ethan formulates Plan B: to kill Debbie if he can't rescue her.

Ethan also knows that once Debbie reaches puberty she will be raped. Maybe she will be killed then. Maybe

---

[1] Jim Goad, "I'm Not a Racist, But . . . ," *Counter-Currents*, April 15, 2021.

she will be made into a squaw. Ethan would rather die than suffer that fate. He wants to spare Debbie from it. This isn't racism and hate. It is an act of love in a terrible situation.

Martin Scorsese was deeply influenced by *The Searchers*. In *Taxi Driver*, Scorsese modeled the characterization of the pimp Sport (played by Harvey Keitel) on Scar. Scorsese saw the relationship of Sport and the teenage prostitute Iris (Jodie Foster) as an exploration of how someone like Scar would establish his hold on a captive like Debbie. (Screenwriter Paul Schrader originally made the pimp black, which was true to life. The producers thought it would be too "racist" to have a black pimp, so Scorsese had a Jewish actor play him as an Indian.)

The Searchers is based on Alan Le May's 1954 novel of the same name, which is based on the true stories of James W. Parker and Brit Johnson, both of whom searched for years to rescue female kin kidnapped by Indians. In the novel, the conflict is neatly racial: whites versus Indians. But in Ford's movie, these neat lines are blurred in two important cases.

First, Ford makes Martin Pawley one-eighth Cherokee. He first appears riding a horse bareback, then neatly dismounts while it is still trotting. He's also late to dinner. Later we see that he is highly emotional and impulsive, although he is still a teenager. When he is a little older, he does not fight "fair" in a fist-fight. All this suggests that he has a bit of Indian wildness in him.

Ethan rescued Marty as a child after his parents had been killed by Comanches. He was adopted by Aaron and Martha and regards the Edwards as family. When Ethan sees him, he blurts out that he could be mistaken for a half-breed. In truth, he cannot. Played by Jeffrey Hunter, Marty has strikingly handsome Caucasian features, with a dark tan—but no darker than Aaron—and flashing, pale blue eyes. Ethan also rejects Martin calling him "Uncle

Ethan," because they are not blood kin.

Second, the Comanche chief Scar is played by a German actor, Henry Brandon. Like Marty, he has handsome white features, a dark tan, and pale blue eyes.

I don't think Ford was trying to lessen the racial conflict in the movie so much as to create additional dramatic conflicts. Blood loyalties drive the whole story: Ethan wants to avenge his dead kin and rescue or kill Debbie. Scar wants to avenge his two dead sons killed by whites. But there are other loyalties. Marty is not blood kin to the Edwards, but he was raised by them and feels loyalty to them, a tie that Ford brings into sharper relief with a taint of Indian blood. Scar, by contrast, has white blood and Indian loyalties.

Ethan himself recognizes that blood kinship is not everything. The rescued whites who have gone mad in captivity may be racially white, but they no longer belong to white society. Which opens the disturbing possibility that some whites can embrace "going native." When Ethan and Marty finally find Debbie, she claims that the Comanches are now her people, but she also tries to save Marty and Ethan from them. When Ethan sees she has gone native, he tries to shoot her. It looks like he will shoot Marty as well to get her. But he is wounded by a Comanche arrow.

When Ethan and Marty reach safety, Marty tends to Ethan's wound, and Ethan informs him that he is disowning Debbie and leaving his property to Marty. Clearly, he is giving up the search. Earlier, Ethan offered Marty some of his property to settle down and marry Laurie Jorgenson. Clearly, he doesn't think a taint of Cherokee blood makes him a bad match for Laurie. Blood matters a great deal in this world, but so does loyalty, and sometimes it cuts across the lines of blood and race. When Laurie suggests that it might be better for Debbie to die than stay with the Comanches, it is obviously not because she has a horror of miscegenation. Instead, she has a horror of rape.

The characters of Marty and Laurie bring us to the main faults of *The Searchers*. They are incredibly annoying: less characters than caricatures. Perhaps these characters could have been saved by good acting, but both Jeffrey Hunter and Vera Miles as Laurie are committed overactors. Marty is annoyingly whiny and buffoonish, and Laurie tends to be shrill. There is a great deal of childish flirting and bickering. It is often painful. But the worst thing about it is that Ford left nothing to accident. He clearly wanted it exactly this way, which is a terrible lapse of taste.

George Lucas claimed that Ethan's return to the flaming ruins of the ranch influenced the scene in *Star Wars* where Luke Skywalker returns to the moisture farm after the Stormtroopers have destroyed it. Anakin Skywalker's massacre of the Tusken raiders in *Attack of the Clones* clearly takes some inspiration from *The Searchers* as well. I wish to suggest the terrible possibility that Lucas also copied Luke's annoying whining from Marty and the juvenile bickering between Luke, Leia, and Han from similar scenes in *The Searchers*.

The character of Marty does develop, making *The Searchers* something of a coming-of-age tale. Marty starts out as a callow teenager who is simply sucked into the vortex of Ethan's maniacal charisma and drive. By the end of the film, he is man enough to defy Ethan then fight off Laurie's would-be groom, a grinning, drawling buffoon about whom the less said the better.

The end of *The Searchers* baffles the critics who see Ethan as simply a racist hater. A short time after Ethan almost kills Debbie, Scar's Comanches show up in Texas. The Rangers, along with the US Cavalry, go in search of them. Marty insists on going into the camp alone, to rescue Debbie. He kills Scar, then the Rangers and Cavalry attack. Debbie runs off. Ethan scalps Scar's corpse, then goes looking for Debbie. She flees from him in terror, but he rides her down, dismounts, scoops her up, and says "Let's go home, Debbie."

What happened? Obviously, Ethan has had a change of heart. But it makes perfect sense. He wanted to kill Debbie when she wanted to stay with Scar. But Scar is now dead, his people will be killed or captured, and Debbie has run *away* from the Comanches. So she has had a change of heart too. Now Ethan *can* rescue her, so he does. But that was Plan A all along.

The final scene of *The Searchers* is utterly heartbreaking. Returning to the epic laconicism of the opening, it is entirely without words. Ethan, Marty, and Debbie return to the Jorgenson ranch, where the family is gathered on the porch. Then we see through the door of the darkened Jorgenson home. Mr. and Mrs. Jorgenson welcome Debbie and take her inside while Ethan watches. Then Marty and Laurie pass Ethan and enter together. Two new families are forming. As they enter the dark interior, their figures become two-dimensional silhouettes. They are entering the realm of shades, the happily ever after.

Ethan stands for a moment, then turns and walks away. He will not enter the domestic world that he has given everything to secure. He is a mutilated man who will wander between the winds and know no peace. Then the door closes, and we see only darkness.

The Unz Review, April 16, 2021

WATCHMEN

Watchmen is one of the most thoroughly Right-wing, even fascistic works of recent popular culture, despite the right-thinking Leftism of the creators of the original graphic novel, Alan Moore, who wrote the story, and Dave Gibbons, who illustrated it—and of Zack Snyder, who directed the movie adaptation, which to my mind is the greatest superhero movie of all time, a movie that not only does justice to the original novel but actually improves upon it in fundamental ways.

Watchmen was not a Leftist parody of the Right that went off mark. Moore is too good a writer to fail in a big way. When Moore engages in parody, such as his sendup of far-Right Cold War journalism in *The New Frontiersman*, he hits the mark nicely.

Snyder also introduces elements of satire into the movie's treatment of Richard Nixon. In the graphic novel, Nixon is portrayed as a lonely, dignified, and thoughtful figure who rejects rash decisions. (This is quite telling in itself.) The movie takes us into *Dr. Strangelove* territory, but it gives Nixon some great lines—contemplating the nuclear destruction of the Eastern Seaboard: "The last gasp of the Harvard establishment. Let's see them debate their way out of nuclear fission"—that we find ourselves laughing with him, not at him. But Snyder's treatment of the main characters follows Moore in being serious, not satirical.

Thus the Right-wing flavor of *Watchmen* is a product of design, not accident. At heart, it is a gallery, not of Right-wing caricatures, but of complex and compelling characters with a range of far-Right outlooks. These characters are placed in an extraordinary plot driven by fundamental moral and political, and even metaphysical and religious conflicts. With its archetypal characters and high-stakes plot, *Watchmen* is a nineteenth-century Romantic novel disguised as a comic book.

THE SETTING & BACK STORY

The main events of *Watchmen* take place in October and November 1985. They are set primarily in New York City, in Antarctica, and on Mars, within an alternative history in which Richard Nixon has been President since 1968 and superheroes, called "Watchmen," actually exist.

There are two generations of Watchmen.

THE FIRST GENERATION

The Watchmen began in 1938 as eight individual costumed crime-fighters, six men and two women. In 1939, they teamed up and were referred to collectively as "Minutemen," after the rapid-response partisan militia of the American Revolutionary War. These superheroes were physically fit and public-spirited but otherwise ordinary individuals who donned masks and costumes to fight crime.

Five of them play little or no part in the graphic novel and movie: Silhouette (a lesbian who was murdered with her lover), Captain Metropolis (Nelson Gardner), Hooded Justice (missing in 1955, presumed dead), Dollar Bill (killed by bank robbers when his cape got caught in a revolving door), and Mothman (confined to a mental hospital). (Zack Snyder, who is a brilliant silent movie director, shows these stories under the opening credits of the film.)

Three first-generation Watchmen play important roles in the graphic novel/movie: Nite Owl (Hollis Mason), Silk Spectre (Sally Jupiter), and The Comedian (Edward Blake), all of them in their late 60s at the time.

The Minutemen rapidly fell apart. The Comedian was expelled in 1940 for trying to rape Silk Spectre. He went on to fight in the Second World War and after the war became a government "black ops" specialist who, among other things, assassinated John F. Kennedy from the grassy knoll near Dealey Plaza. Silhouette was murdered in 1946; Dollar Bill was gunned down around the same time; then, in 1947, Silk Spectre quit to have a family. In 1949, the Minutemen officially disbanded as a group, although some members continued to fight crime on their own.

The Second Generation

Despite their failure, the Minutemen did inspire a second generation of Watchmen, which formed in the late 1960s under the name Crimebusters. In the novel, they are called together by Captain Metropolis (Nelson Gardner), thus establishing a link with the first generation. (Gardner was to die in a car accident in 1974.) In the movie, they are convened by Ozymandias (Adrian Veidt). The Comedian also returned to costumed crime-fighting. Silk Spectre's daughter Laurie took over her mother's identity. Dan Driberg replaced Hollis Mason as Nite Owl. And three new personas emerged: Ozymandias, Rorschach (Walter Kovacs), and Dr. Manhattan (Dr. Jon Osterman).

The second generation of Watchmen includes some genuine superheroes. Although the Comedian, Rorschach, and Silk Spectre are all-too-human vigilantes dependent on will and athleticism, Ozymandias and Nite Owl have to some extent transcended human limitations, Veidt through physical and mental exercises which made him the smartest man alive and fast enough to catch a bullet, and Dreiberg primarily through technology which he could afford to develop because of the money left to him by his father, a wealthy banker. (Nite Owl, therefore, resembles Batman in more than just the costume.)

Dr. Manhattan, however, is a true superman. He is virtually indestructible and can see the future, mold matter with the power of thought, and transport himself and anything else instantaneously over great distances.

The second generation of Watchmen operated for about a decade, and they were more than just crimefighters. The Comedian walked out of the initial meeting because he saw little point in fighting crime in a world menaced by nuclear war. But he involved himself anyway, because his objections were taken seriously by both Dr. Manhattan and Ozymandias. Instead of being mere vigilantes trying to save New York, they began to think geopolitically about saving the whole world. The high point of their operations came when Dr. Manhattan intervened to win the Vietnam War for the United States. (The Comedian came along for laughs.)

But only a few years later, in 1977, public opinion had sufficiently turned against the Watchmen that the US Congress passed the Keene Act banning costumed vigilantes, and Nixon signed it.

In the eight years from the Keene Act to the opening of the story in 1985, Adrian Veidt (whose true identity was already known before the Keene Act) focused on building up a multi-billion-dollar business empire. Dr. Manhattan and the Comedian returned to doing secret work for the government, the former in research and development, the latter in black ops, knocking over Marxist republics in Latin America. (Nixon also has the Comedian keep tabs on the former Watchmen.) Laurie Jupiter went on the government payroll as Manhattan's lover. Dan Dreiberg went into retirement, never revealing his true identity. Rorschach, however, remained active, but entirely outside the law.

THE PLOT

My primary focus is on the cast of *Watchmen* as a gallery of Right-wing archetypes. But before I deal with the characters in greater depth, I must sketch out the plot.

Both the novel and the movie open with the murder of

Edward Blake by an unknown assailant. Rorschach investigates and discovers that Blake was the Comedian. Rorschach then breaks the news to the other members of his fraternity—first Dreiberg, then Veidt, then Jupiter and Manhattan—warning them, also, that they might be targets. (In the movie, Dreiberg warns Veidt.)

When Rorschach observes the former supervillain Moloch paying his respects at the grave of the Comedian, he tails him to his apartment and forces him to talk. Moloch reveals that he has terminal cancer. He also reveals that Blake broke into Moloch's apartment, drunk and weeping, and told Moloch that he had discovered a terrible conspiracy involving Dr. Manhattan, his ex-girlfriend Janey Slater, and Moloch himself. But Blake never mentioned the details or who was behind the conspiracy. A week later, he was dead, apparently silenced by the conspirators before he could talk.

Meanwhile, Dr. Manhattan's relationship with Laurie is fraying as he becomes increasingly detached from the human condition. Laurie walks out and goes to Dan Dreiberg, Nite Owl II, for company. Reminiscing about their crime-fighting days, they walk through a dangerous area looking for trouble and end up in a fight with members of a gang, the Knot Tops, whom they trounce.

That same evening, Dr. Manhattan goes on *Nightline* and is accused on live television of giving cancer to Janey Slater, his friend Wally Weaver, and other associates. Enraged, Manhattan teleports himself to Mars. The Soviets take advantage of the absence of America's ultimate deterrent to launch an invasion of Afghanistan, setting the United States and the USSR on the path to nuclear war.

Rorschach's theory that someone is targeting the Watchmen receives further confirmation when a gunman tries to kill Adrian Veidt. The gunman, however, swallowed a cyanide capsule before he could be compelled to reveal who was pulling his strings. Then Moloch was murdered. Rorschach was framed for the crime and arrested, but he is rescued in the middle of a prison riot by Nite Owl II and Silk Spectre II, who have grown closer, begun a sexual relationship, and returned to crime-fighting.

After the prison break, Manhattan teleports Laurie to Mars, where she tries to persuade him to return to Earth to prevent an imminent nuclear war. Meanwhile, Nite Owl and Rorschach investigate Roy Chess, the gunman who attempted to kill Veidt. They eventually discover that Chess, Moloch, and Janey Slater all worked for Pyramid Transnational, and that Pyramid was secretly owned by Adrian Veidt himself. They also discover a psychological profile on Manhattan that makes clear that Veidt was behind an elaborate plot to drive Dr. Manhattan to sever his ties with humanity, the success of which had brought the world to the brink of nuclear annihilation. They immediately depart for Veidt's Antarctic research center (a kind of Fortress of Solitude) to get some answers.

Veidt reveals that he has engineered Manhattan's exile not to start a nuclear war but because Manhattan is the only person who could foil Veidt's plans to *stop* it. At this point, the plots of the graphic novel and the movie diverge significantly. In the graphic novel, Veidt destroys New York City by faking an attack by a huge squid-like monster of apparent extraterrestrial origin. In the movie, he destroys a number of cities with explosions that bear the energy signature of Dr. Manhattan. In both cases, the result is that the United States and the Soviet Union call off their war and unite to face a greater threat: extraterrestrial invasion in one case, Dr. Manhattan in the other. In both the novel and the movie, Manhattan and Laurie return to Earth too late for him to do anything to stop it.

As a Lovecraftian, I am, of course, a sucker for tentacles. But I have to admit that the climax of the movie is far more elegant.

First, it provides a more plausible motive for driving Dr. Manhattan off the planet. Veidt had already successfully prevented Manhattan from seeing through his plot by creating tachyons, which obscured his vision of the future. Thus Veidt had no need to send Manhattan to Mars—as if such a piddling distance would matter to Manhattan anyway.

Second, the movie's climax heightens Manhattan's heroism. In the novel, Manhattan, Dreiberg, and Laurie agree not to reveal what Veidt has done, because to bring Veidt to justice would undo the unity he created and set the world back on the path to war. In the movie, however, Manhattan does more than just keep Veidt's secret. He also *takes the blame* for Veidt's crimes. Thus he plays a unique and supreme role in saving humanity by accepting, like Christ, the role of the scapegoat for the sins of others.

The dénouement of both the book and the movie are essentially the same: Rorschach refuses to keep Veidt's secret, so Manhattan is forced to kill him. Manhattan then leaves Earth forever, perhaps to create life on another planet. The threat of nuclear war having passed, New York rebuilds (with Veidt Industries profiting handsomely). Dreiberg and Laurie decide to marry. And Rorschach's diary, which tells the whole story up to his departure to Antarctica, when he dropped it in the mail, is fished out of the crank file at his favorite Right-wing periodical, *New Frontiersman*, bringing the story back to its beginning.

Principal Characters: First Generation

Nite Owl I (Hollis Mason)

Hollis Mason's primary role is as chronicler of the first generation of Watchmen and as a murder victim.

According to Mason's memoirs, which are excerpted in the graphic novel, the Minutemen were called "fascists" and "perverts," and there was an "element of truth in both those accusations," although "neither of them are big enough to take in the whole picture." In particular, Hooded Justice was heard "openly expressing approval for the activities of Hitler's Third Reich," while Captain Metropolis "has gone on record making statements about black and Hispanic Americans that have been viewed as both racially prejudiced and inflammatory." As Mason sums it up, "Yes, we were crazy, we were kinky, we were Nazis, all those things people say."

But, he adds significantly, "We were also doing something because we believed in it. We were attempting, through our personal efforts, to make our country a safer and better place to live in."

This is an important point to bear in mind, for in mainstream comics, Right-wing political views are not the mark of superheroes, but of supervillains. Even the most macho vigilante scofflaw, like Batman, still has to pay lip-service to humanistic, egalitarian morals. But in the *Watchmen* universe, Right-wing superheroes are still superheroes. Indeed, as we shall see, they are the only kind.

Mason is killed by a gang known as the Knot Tops in retaliation for a beating meted out to their members by Nite Owl II (Dreiberg) and Silk Spectre II (Laurie Jupiter). (The gang members either don't know or don't care that there are two Nite Owls.) Dreiberg feels great guilt for Mason's death, because he and Jupiter sought out the confrontation as they edged themselves toward resuming crime-fighting.

SILK SPECTRE I (SALLY JUPITER)

Sally Jupiter (born Juspeczyk) was a model turned crime-fighter. As one might suspect, she was no demure little flower. She drank and cussed with the guys, and also slept with some of them. Sally's principal role in the plot is not, however, as a crime-fighter, but as a mother. The Comedian was drummed out of the Minutemen for trying to rape her. But later they had consensual sex (while she was married to her agent), producing Laurie (Silk Spectre II).

THE COMEDIAN (EDWARD BLAKE)

Edward Blake is one of the most enigmatic characters in *Watchmen*. He is called the Comedian because he wears a mask of cynicism and irreverence. He is capable of cold-blooded brutality and sadism. At first glance, he seems to be a sociopath. Ozymandias characterized him as "practically a Nazi." But the Comedian is no Joker. Blake has a conscience. When he discovers that Ozymandias is committing crimes far more terrible than anything he has done, he is horrified and distraught and tries to confess to Moloch, one of his old foes.

Blake, moreover, is not just a cynic. He is best understood as a disillusioned idealist. Blake loves America. But he is a political realist enough to know that America has enemies, foreign and domestic, who must be killed. He knows that maintaining law and order sometimes requires going outside the law. Thus he is capable of assassinating President Kennedy and killing countless Communists in Vietnam and Latin America, and probably a lot of innocents who just got in the way.

But at some point, Blake lost his faith in America. Since he began as a conservative American, Blake surely saw liberalism as a decadent deviation from American ideals. But Blake had changed his views by the time of the police strike and riots of 1977, which were followed by the Keene Act, all of which sprung from a Left-liberal rejection of vigilantism.

The Comedian realized that liberal decadence was not a deviation from American principles, but their fulfillment. Exasperated by the ingratitude of the rioters, Nite Owl II asked the Comedian, "Whatever happened to the American dream?" To which the Comedian responded: "It came true." America had been a giant joke after all, and the joke was on him.

PRINCIPAL CHARACTERS: SECOND GENERATION

RORSCHACH (WALTER KOVACS)

Rorschach is the narrator of *Watchmen*. We see the story through his eyes. Veidt creates the conspiracy, and Rorschach's investigation creates the plot. Rorschach also has the best lines in *Watchmen* and is by far the most popular character.

But he is also deeply problematic, for as his origin story makes clear, he is a hero out of the most unheroic of motives: *ressentiment*. The son of a prostitute, young Walter Kovacs suffered from abuse, neglect, and scorn. He was placed in a juvenile home at the age of 11, after savagely attacking two older bullies. Walter's anger and embitterment give rise to a powerful desire to punish, both others and himself. Thus he adopts an absolutist, objective, black-and-white moral code which he applies without mercy or compromise.

Rorschach became a masked vigilante in 1964. He teamed up with Nite Owl II to fight crime. In the late '60s, he joined the "Crimebusters" group. Rorschach was known for roughing up criminals, but he delivered them to the police alive. But America's increasingly soft and liberal criminal justice system could no longer be trusted to mete out justice, so in 1975 Rorschach began killing criminals, starting with Gerald Grice, who had kidnapped a little girl, Blair Roche, butchered her, and fed her to his dogs.

Rorschach's excesses were surely a factor that led to the Keene Act, banning masked vigilantes altogether. The other Watchmen retired or went to work for the government, but true to his uncompromising code, Rorschach remained in the fight. Thus Rorschach was on the scene after the Comedian's murder, and his investigation brought the other Watchmen back into action.

But this same uncompromising character leads to Rorschach's death in the end. After Ozymandias has used mass murder and trickery to pull the world back from the brink of nuclear war, Rorschach vows to tell the world. He is so wedded to punitive moral absolutism that he prefers that justice triumph even though the world might very well perish.

When Dr. Manhattan offers Rorschach the choice of silence or death, he chooses death. Rorschach's attachment to principle seems admirable. But the root of his attachment is ultimately a punitive bitterness and spite that turns suicidal when Manhattan blocks him from unleashing it on the world.

NITE OWL II (DAN DREIBERG)

At first glance, there is nothing particularly Right-wing about the character of Dan Dreiberg, who became Nite Owl II. But the mere fact that he is a costumed vigilante in the first place should rate rather high on the F-scale. Thus I would argue that all costumed superheroes should be treated as *de facto* Right-wingers in the absence of any express allegiance to liberal humanism, which is entirely absent in Dreiberg's case.

Dreiberg and Laurie Jupiter are drawn together because they were the only two Watchmen who actually retired into private life after the Keene Act. Rorschach went rogue, the Comedian and Dr. Manhattan went to work for the government, and Ozymandias became a publicly-traded commodity.

Although both of them deny it, they very much miss "the life." Laurie resents being reduced to Manhattan's consort, for which she receives a government paycheck, although it turns out that her principal role in the plot is not as an independent agent but as the object of Manhattan's affections.

If Laurie's retirement reduces her to a sexual companion, Dreiberg's has reduced him to sexual solitude and impotence. Laurie and Dreiberg are first drawn together by loneliness and nostalgia, but they can conquer their discontent only by inching back into crime-fighting. After their dust-up with the Knot-Tops, Laurie moves their relationship in a sexual direction, but Dreiberg is impotent. He only recovers his sexual potency after a full-fledged return to superherodom, right between saving people from a burning tenement and breaking Rorschach out of jail.

The character of Dan Dreiberg is a combination of Bruce Wayne (Batman) and Clark Kent (Superman). Nite Owl II's costume looks like Batman's, more so in the movie. Also, like Batman, Dreiberg is independently wealthy and uses his wealth to create technology that helps him transcend his human weaknesses.

Like Clark Kent, Dreiberg has a bespectacled, nebbishy persona, complete with spit curls. But in the graphic novel, Dreiberg is far more Jewish than Superman. Indeed, with his hook nose, 'berg name, and banker father, he is almost explicitly Jewish, but not quite.

There is, however, nothing distinctly Jewish about Dreiberg's psychology as written by Moore. Dreiberg is earnest, not ironic. His psychological emasculation is not rooted in an overbearing mother or some other mind-twisting childhood trauma, but in the adoption of an emasculating lifestyle. Thus in the movie, Zack Snyder completely Aryanizes the character by casting Patrick Wilson in the role.

As a side note, the graphic novel is filled with Jewish touches. We read an excerpt from Dr. Milton Glass's book on Dr. Manhattan. Mrs. Hirsch is interviewed by the police after her husband kills himself and their two children. Rorschach's mother's maiden name was Glick. Dreiberg is questioned by a detective Fine. Veidt sends a memo to

Miss Neuberg. There are also numerous references to the Third Reich, National Socialism, and the Second World War.

Part of this can be explained by the fact that the novel is set mostly in New York City. Another factor, surely, is Moore's desire to fit into the comic book industry, which has an overwhelmingly Jewish culture due to its principal founders. It may also have been calculated by Moore to somewhat counterbalance the political incorrectness of the novel with a little Semitical correctness, in effect giving it a "neoconservative" character.

Snyder, however, scrubs the Jewishness of the novel from the film, except for Veidt's description of the Comedian as "practically a Nazi." Interestingly enough, in 300, Snyder also mutes the strong Jewish and neoconservative nature of Frank Miller's original graphic novel.[1]

DR. MANHATTAN (JON OSTERMAN)

In 1959, nuclear physicist Jon Osterman was seemingly annihilated in an experiment with an "Intrinsic Field Subtractor." But he managed to reassemble himself into a being who can see past, present, and future simultaneously and bend matter to his will. The birth of Dr. Manhattan was greeted by the news that, "The superman exists, and he is American." But Wally Weaver, who was present at Osterman's death and resurrection, went further, declaring that, "God exists, and he is American."

And indeed, Dr. Manhattan is portrayed as a god, and not just a god, but a savior. Like Osiris and Dionysus, he was killed through dismemberment, then reassembled and resurrected, showing mankind the way to conquer death. Like Jesus, who also died and was resurrected, Dr. Manhattan appears floating in the air in a halo of light.

He is also portrayed as an avatar of the Hindu god

---

[1] See my review of 300 in *Trevor Lynch's White Nationalist Guide to the Movies.*

Vishnu, specifically Krishna: muscular, with glowing blue skin, and a circular "bindi" mark on his forehead, which to a Hindu indicates expanded consciousness. He even appears in a lotus position.

But of course Dr. Manhattan does not just *look* the part of a savior. He actually plays it, saving mankind from nuclear annihilation by assuming, like Christ, the role of scapegoat for the sins of others, in this case Adrian Veidt. The use of such symbols and myths is part of the emotional power of *Watchmen*.

SILK SPECTRE II (LAURIE JUPITER)

Just as Sally Jupiter's primary role in *Watchmen* is not as a crime-fighter but as the object of the Comedian's lust and mother of his child, Laurie Jupiter, Laurie's primary role is not as a crime-fighter, but as the object of Dr. Manhattan's affections. Needless to say, this is a very traditional and anti-feminist conception of the true power and proper role of women.

When Manhattan learns that Laurie was produced through the sordid union of Sally and the Comedian, he is snapped out of his estrangement with humanity and resolves to save mankind. This is the crucial moment in the plot, marking the emergence of one of its deepest themes: Love for an individual human being can redeem the whole universe.

If you love someone, you are implicitly saying "yes" to his existence. You are glad of his existence and wish it to continue. Logically, you cannot love someone and wish that the causes of his existence were otherwise, for then one's beloved would not exist. And since everything in the universe is causally connected with everything else, if you really love someone, you cannot wish that the universe were otherwise. And this is true even though the universe is filled with many things that, in themselves, are terrible.

At the end of the story, this theme is reprised with

great emotional power when Laurie is reconciled with her mother. Laurie can forgive her mother because she loves herself, which entails accepting all the conditions that made her life possible, including the union of her mother and the Comedian. Laurie says, "I love you, mom. You always did right by me." Sally is also reconciled with the Comedian because he gave her Laurie, whom she loves.

Ozymandias (Adrian Veidt)

Ozymandias is the only openly liberal character in *Watchmen*. He is 46 when the story of *Watchmen* begins. The hyper-Nordic child of wealthy German immigrants, Adrian Veidt is a self-made superman. He has used meditation and other physical and mental training techniques to become the smartest and fastest man alive. When he was young, he gave his vast inheritance to charity and pursued the life of a costumed crime-fighter, taking the name Ozymandias, a name for the Egyptian Pharaoh and megalomaniac Rameses II. But when the Keene Act forced Ozymandias into retirement, he went into business and became a billionaire in his own right.

Ozymandias is a vegetarian and a pacifist. He is unmarried, and Rorschach thinks he is a "possible homosexual." In the graphic novel, he is portrayed as beefy and also—despite his gymnastics exhibition—as macho, posturing in victory like a quarterback after a touchdown. In the movie, he is portrayed by the wiry and epicene Matthew Goode, who heightens the character's liberal do-gooder "vibe."

Ozymandias is also a materialist who believes that war is caused by the poor seeking wealth and the rich trying to hold onto it. He believes, therefore, that free, unlimited energy will bring about universal abundance and end the Cold War. He is a utilitarian governed by the principle of the greatest good for the greatest number. He reckons in terms of human quantity rather than quality. (He believes that anybody can become a superman through the Veidt Technique.)

In short, Ozymandias is a quintessential egalitarian humanist, which is the moral code of virtually every superhero outside the *Watchmen* universe. But Ozymandias is the only egalitarian humanist in the cast of *Watchmen*. Ozymandias would seem to be a counter-example to my thesis that *Watchmen* is a Right-wing comic, were it not for the fact that he is also the *villain* of the story, the cold-blooded, calculating murderer of millions.

Ozymandias is no less the villain because his scheme worked to prevent nuclear war. Indeed, his scheme to goad Dr. Manhattan into exile brought the world to the brink in the first place. Moreover, he is no less a villain because he in effect uses nuclear blackmail to force the other Watchmen to remain silent, and Dr. Manhattan to kill Rorschach, all in order to keep his secret.

There is a sense in which even Ozymandias is a Right-wing archetype, namely a Right-winger's archetype of a villain: the egalitarian, humanist, pacifist mass murderer.

Although egalitarian humanists like Lenin, Stalin, and Mao are the biggest butchers in world history, within the world of comics, the heroes are always egalitarian humanists, and the villains are always people who reject that morality, e.g., traditionalists, Nazis, fascists, racists, eugenicists, and the like.[2] *Watchmen* neatly and completely inverts this code. That is why it is the supreme masterpiece of pop fascism.

Counter-Currents, February 18, 2014

---

[2] See my essays on *The Dark Knight Trilogy* in this volume and *Hellboy,* and *Hellboy II* in *Trevor Lynch's White Nationalist Guide to the Movies.*

INDEX

Numbers in **bold** refer to a whole chapter or section devoted to a particular topic.

300 (film), 215
'60s, 15

A
Abrahamic faiths, 82
adepts (yogic), 44–45
Afghanistan, 207
Ahab, Captain, 197
Aimée, Anouk, 73
Akihito (Japanese Prince, later Emperor), 121
Alford, Kenneth, 89; "Colonel Bogey March," 89; "The Sound of the Guns," 89
Allenby, General Sir Edmund, 88–89, 91–92
altruism, 18, 48–49
American Gigolo, 117
American History X, 37
American Revolutionary War, 204
Amsterdam, 158
Animal Farm, 59
anti-modernism, 69–70
apotheosis, 82, 85, 90, 94
Arabs, 82, 84–86, 88, 90, 92–93, 138–39
archetypes, 2, 33, 204, 206, 218

Argento, Dario, 154
aristocracy, 78, **95–98**, **101–105**; samurai, 123; vs. egalitarianism, 27, 47; warrior, 175–82
aristocratic civilization, 21; culture, 125; ethic, 27; ethos, 19, 154; fortunes, 101; magnanimity, 57; morals, 32–33; politics, 128; pretension, 105; values, 119; virtues, 96
aristocrats, 72, 77, 79, 125; spiritual, 128
Aristotle, 96
Arnold, Malcolm, 22, 89
Arquette, Rosanna, 163
asceticism & ascetics, as element of culture, 168; revolutionary, 105; spiritual, 119; warrior, 24
Attack of the Clones, 201
Austen, Jane, 106
authority, 18
autism, 60, 83, 84, 153
Auto Focus, 117

B
Bach, Johann Sebastian,

74
Badalamenti, Angelo, 2
Bale, Christian, 23, 39
Bataille, Georges, 61
Batman, 24–25, 51, 129, 205, 210, 214; see also: The Dark Knight Trilogy
Batman Begins, **23-26**, 29, 38, 39–40, 43
Bay, Frances, 3
Beatty, Ned, 139
beauty, 72, 95, 98, 119–20, 185
Beginning of History, 40, 61–62, **69–70**, 155, **173-75**, **177–80**, 182; see also: End of History
Being, in Heidegger, 35–36; in Vedanta, 44–45
Bertolucci, Bernardo, 154; *The Last Emperor*, 154; *Once Upon a Time in the West*, **145-55**
Bible, 159
blank slate theory, 59, 136
Blake, William, 169
blasphemy, 82, 85, 91
blood (race), 60, 200; blood feud, 84, 86
Blue Velvet, **1-16**
Bolsheviks, 54, 57
Bolt, Robert, 52, 54, 58, 81
Bond, James, 120
bondage, 7, 12, 50
Boreanaz, David, 23
Boulle, Pierre, 17, 18, 21, 22
bourgeoisie, 101–102, 103–104; see also: middle-class
Brandon, Henry, 200
bricolage, 166
The Bridge on the River Kwai (film), **17-22**, 81, 89
The Bridge on the River Kwai (novel), 17–18, 20
Bringing Out the Dead, 117
British Empire, 89
Bronson, Charles, 146
Buddhist ethics of compassion, 192
Bunker, Archie, 134–35
bushido, 19
businessman, 46, 121, 122; vs. man, 146, 154

C

Caine, Michael, 23, 39
Camus, Albert, 185
cannibalism, 143
capitalism, 122, 124, 137, 143, 154, 176; anti-capitalism, 66, 154
Cardinale, Claudia, 98, 148
Carey, Harry, Jr., 195
Carter, Helena Bonham, 62
Casablanca, 81
Cat People (remake), 117
Catholic Church, 67, 72, 78, 80, 102, 108
Central Intelligence Agency, 53
chaos, 2, 21, 25, **34-37**, 53, 57, 97, 126

Chaplin, Charlie, 56
Chaplin, Geraldine, 56
Chapman, Sir Thomas, 82
character (moral), 21, 106, 136, 141, 149, **165–66**, 175, 179, 196, 201, 213; national, 18
charisma, 24, 39, 63, 69, 92, 95, 195, 201
Chayefsky, Paddy, 130, 135, 144
China, 23, 139
Christ, 209, 215; see also: Jesus
Christie, Julie, 55–56
Citizen Kane, 81
civil society, 110, 153–54, 196
civil war (Russian), 56, 57
civilization, 2, 15, 24, 40, 60, 114, 146–47, 151, 153, 194, 198; aristocratic, 21; decadent, 148; industrial, 69, 95; vs. barbarism, 136–37, 148, 196; white, 108
class (social), 27, 33, 47, 52, 61, 99, 102, 118
Clooney, George, 23
Comanches, 195, 196, 198–202
comedies of manners, 106
comic book industry, 215
Communism, 21, 46, 52–54, **56–60**, 176
Communist Party of the Soviet Union, 52
Communist Party USA, 142
compassion, 192–93; see also: mercy
Confederate States of America, 195, 196
conservatism, 2, 15, 21, 211; neoconservatism, 215; see also: Rightism
consumer society, 70
contingency, **35–36**, 38, 185
convention, 16, 153
coronavirus, 139
Costello, Jef, 61n1
costume dramas, 106
Cotillard, Marion, 39
Counter-Currents, 127
Courtenay, Tom, 56
Crane, Bob, 117
Crowley, Aleister, 82
Cruise, Julee, 14
culture industry, 136–37
culture(s), 62, 67, 82, 105, 124, 155, **166–67**, 175, 181; aristocratic, 125; authentic, 121; consumer, 125; counter-, 168; genuine, 167; guilt, 186; high, 25, 61, 125, 128, **136–37**; Jewish, 215; normative, 176, 168; popular, 23, 71, 143, 203; postmodern, 166–67; shame, 186; culture industry, 136–37
Cuny, Alain, 72
cynicism, 21, 57, **103–04**,

130, 137, 211
Cyrus II of Persia (Cyrus the Great), 86–87

D

dandyism, 120
Dark Age, 24, 26, 40, 193
The Dark Knight Rises, **38–50**
The Dark Knight Trilogy, 23–51; 129; see also: Batman
The Dark Knight, **26–38**, 39, 41–42, 44–46, 128
darkness, 2–4, 12–13, 16, 43, 202
Davis, Angela, 142
De Palma, Brian, 117; *Obsession*, 117
Dean, James, 120
death, **19–21**, 25, **28–35**, 37, 41–42, 53, 58, 61, **63–65**, 75, 77, 80, 83, 93, 102, 112, 118, **122–28**, 141, 147, 151, 155, 161, 163, 166, 170, **173–75**, 184, 186–87, **189–91**, 197–98, 210, 213, 215; fear of, 28, 30, 64, 128–29, 173, 175; see also: mortality
decadence, 24–25, 46–48, 72, 80, 131, 144, 148, 156, 168, 170, 181, 211
Decameron Film Festival, 145
Declaration of Independence, 108
del Toro, Guillermo, 26, 129; *Hellboy*, 26, 129; *Hellboy II*, 26, 129
Deliverance (film), 180
Delon, Alain, 97
demythologizing, 168
Dern, Laura, 4
detachment, 167–68
Devine, Andy, 107
Devlin, F. Roger, 15
Dickerson, George, 3
Divine providence, 65–66
Django Unchained, 181n2
Doctor Zhivago (film), **52–60**, 81
Doctor Zhivago (novel), 52–54, 60
Dr. Strangelove, 203
drag shows, 9, 78
dreams, 9–10,
drugs, 15, 159
Dumézil, Georges, 157
Dunaway, Faye, 130, 132
Dune (David Lynch film), 16
Dune (novel), 66
duty, 18, 118
Duvall, Robert, 130

E

earnestness, 167–68
Eckhart, Aaron, 33
edification vs. pandering, 136–37, 141
egalitarian-humanism, 27, 41–42, 45, 47, 49, 210, 218; see also: humanistic ethic
egalitarianism, 44, 59

egocentrism, 193
Ekberg, Anita, 73
The Elephant Man, 16
elitism & elitists, 131, 139
Emperor (Japanese), 118, 123, 126
End of History, 61, 62, 70, 125, **141–42**, 155, 156, 174, 177, 181; see also: Beginning of History; Last Man
enemy, 18, 38, **86–87**, 176, 196
envy, **46–48**, 57, 164
equality, 25, 66, 69, 154, 177
Eraserhead, 1–12, 16
Ereignis, 36
establishment, 66; British, 83; East Coast, 203; anti-establishment, 134
ethos, aristocratic, 19, 21, 33, 105, 154; bourgeois, 19, 105; feudal, 104; feudal-warrior, 104, 105; of honor, 173
eugenicists, 218
evil, 3–4, **12–13**, 16, **44–45**, 161, 182, 191–92
Evola, Julius, 26, 182

F
Faisal bin Abdulaziz Al Saud, 83–85, 90, 92–93
faith, 78, 192, 211
fascism & fascists, 50, 66, 117, 175, 203, 209; pop fascism, 218
fathers, 65–67
fear, 41, 43, 66; see also: death, fear of
Fellini, Federico, 71, 75, 78, 80
Ferrell, Conchata, 144
Ferrer, José, 81
fetish, fetishism or fetishist, 6, 8, 10, 160, 170
fetishism, 6, 10, 163, 170
feudalism, 95, 100, **104–105**
Fight Club (film), **61–70**
Fight Club (novel), 60
Finch, Peter, 130, 131, 144
First World War, 54, 81, 171; see also: Great War
A Fistful of Dollars, 145
Fonda, Henry, 146, 152
For a Few Dollars More, 145,
force (political), 110, **114–15**
Ford, Gerald, 138
Ford, John, 90, 107–109, 111, 115, 194, 197, 199–201; *Fort Apache* (1948), 108; *The Man Who Shot Liberty Valance*, **107–16**, 197; *Rio Grande*, 108; *The Searchers*, 90, **194–202**; *She Wore a Yellow Ribbon* (1949), 108; *Stagecoach*, 107
Foreman, Carl, 22
Fort Apache (1948), 108

Foster, Jodie, 199
Francis II, 96
free market, 137
freedom, 28–29, **32–33**, **35–37**, 45, 56, 69, 128, 153; creative, 16; inner, 29; of speech, 58; universal, 175–76
Freeman, Morgan, 23, 26, 39
French, Leslie, 104
friendship vs. flattery, 136
Fukuyama, Francis, 156
Furneaux, Yvonne, 72
future, 14, 28–29, 78, 146, 151, 205

G

Gandhi, Mohandas, 21
Gangs of New York, 37
Garden of Eden, 15
Garden of Gethsemane, 92
Garibaldi, Giuseppe, 95–96, 97, 100, 101
Garibaldini, 95, 101
gay, 66–68; ambiguously, 83; see also: homosexual(s)
Geneva Convention, 19
Gestell, **35–37**, 38
Gibbons, Dave, 203
Glass, Philip, 117
globalism & globalists, 131, 139; globalization, 144
Gnosticism, 12
Goad, Jim, 198
God, 12, **65–66**, 80, 86, 88, 97, 132, 134, 140, **159–64**, 182, 215
Golden Age, 24, 26, 40
Golden Lion, 183
Gone with the Wind, 95
The Good, the Bad, & the Ugly, 145
Goode, Matthew, 217
goodness, 15, 16, 30, 48
Gordon-Leavitt, Joseph, 39
Gosha, Hideo, 124
Great Depression, 68, 123
Great War, 68; see also: World War One
Guénon, René, 26
guilt culture, 186–87
Guinness, Alec, 19, 21, 56, 81, 83

H

Hagakure, 125
happiness, 49, 57, 113
Hardy, Tom, 39
hate, 13, 16, 47
Hathaway, Anne, 39
Hauer, Rutger, 23
Hawkins, Jack, 21–22, 81, 88
Hayasaka, Fumio, 183
healthy vs. unhealthy, 167–68
hedonism, **164–66**, 169
Hegel, G. W. F., 19–20, 61–63, 124–25, 156, 169–70, 173–74, 175–76; *Phenomenology of Spirit*, 173
Herbert, Frank, 66
heredity vs. blank slate,

59–60
hierarchy (social), 66, 89; of values, 125
higher good, 84
Hildyard, Jack, 22
Hinduism, 12, 216
Hispanic Americans, 210
history, 19, 58, 61–63, **67–70**, 78, 82, 83, 93, 124, 125, 155, 156, 218; beginning of, 19, 61, 69–70, 182; cyclical theory of, 24, 26, 38, 40, 102; Traditionalist theory of, 24, 26, 38, 40; see also: Beginning of History; End of History
Hitchcock, Alfred, 81, 189; *Torn Curtain*, 189; *Vertigo*, 81
Hitler, Adolf, 126, 210
Hobbes, Thomas, 143, 154, 176, 182
Holden, William, 20, 21, 130, 131, 144
Holly, Buddy, 164
homosexuality, 10; homosexual(s), 8, 79, 91, 118, 122, 180, 217; see also: gay
honor, **19–21**, 32–33, 61–62, 101, 105, 111–12, 124–25, 128, 146–47, 151, **153–57**, 169, **172–82**, 189; duels over honor, 61, 112, 155, **173–74**, 190, 191; honor code, 151, 153; honor culture, 192; honor-driven man, 157, **171–73**, **177–80**
Hood, Gregory, 46
Hopper, Dennis, 1
Hosoe, Eikoh, 120
human nature, 15–16, 61, 175
human sacrifice, 197
humanistic ethic, 25, 28; see also: egalitarian-humanism
Hume, David, 176
Hunter, Jeffrey, 195, 199, 201
hypergamy, 15

I

idealism & idealists (moral or political), 19, 31, 48, 50, **57–58**, 111, 112, 115, 168, **176–77**, 211
identification, 167–68
ideologies, 55, 58, 87, 125, 122, 140–42
imagery, Christian, 12
imagination, 155; human, 168; poetic, 55
India, 20, 21
Indians (American), 33, 113–14, 153, 195, **196–200**
individualism, 69, 176; individuality, 141–42
Indo-European social "functions"/castes

(priestly, warrior, economic), 157
Inglourious Basterds, 181n2
initiation, 1, 29, 63–64, 68, 155; sexual, 8; spiritual, 41, **43–45**, 49
interracial couples, 181
Iraq, 93
irony, 63, **166–68**, 176, 214
Italy, 46, 95, 96, **103–104**

J

Jackson, Samuel L., 156, 162
Japan, 117, **120–25**, 183, 186
Japanese cinema, 183
Jarre, Maurice, 52, 55
Jefferson, Thomas, 175
Jehovah's Witnesses, 4
Jesus, 72, 151, 215; see also: Christ
Jewish dietary laws, 161
Jews, 144
Johnson, Brit, 199
Joker, **27–38**, 41–42, **45–48**, 128, 211; as agent of chaos, 33–37; as holding money in contempt, 27–33; 46–47; as exponent of dangerous truths, 37–38; as existentialist, 28–30, 41–42; as experimental psychologist, 30–32, 42, 48; as exponent of aristocratic morality, 32–33; as free from his past, 42, 45; as Nietzschean philosopher, 27–28, 38, 41; as unafraid of death, 28–29, 128
Jordan, 81, 93
Jutter, Sarah, 82

K

karmic records, 45
Keaton, Michael, 23
Keitel, Harvey, 160, 199
Kennedy, Arthur, 89
Kennedy, John F., 205, 211
Kill Bill movies, 163, 181n2
Kill Bill: Vol. 1, 181n2
Kilmer, Val, 23
Kinski, Klaus, 56
Kojève, Alexandre, 61, 125, 141–42, 156, 176; *Introduction to the Reading of Hegel*, 125, 156
Krishna, 216
Kurosawa, Akira, 183; *Rashomon*, 81, **183–93**

L

La Dolce Vita, **71–80**
Labour Party (UK), 21
Lampedusa, Giuseppe Tomasi di, 95, 96, 103, 105, 106; *The Leopard* (novel), 95–96, 99, 102–103, 105, 106
Lancaster, Burt, 96
The Last Emperor, 154
Last Man, 62, 142, 176; see

also: End of History
The Last Temptation of Christ, 117
Latin, 74
Latin America, 206, 211
Lawrence of Arabia, 17, 21, 52, 54, 58, **81–94**
Lawrence, T. E., 21, 58, 81–94; see also: *Lawrence of Arabia*
Le May, Alan, 199
League of Shadows, 24–25, 27, 29, 38, **39–41**, 43, 50
Lean, David, 17, 18, **20–22**, 52, 55–56, 60, 81, 85, 89, 90; *Doctor Zhivago*, **52–60**, 81; *Lawrence of Arabia*, 17, 21, 52, 54, 58, **81–94**; *The Bridge on the River Kwai*, **17–22**, 81, 89; *Ryan's Daughter*, 17
Ledger, Heath, 27, 37
Leftism & Leftists, 15, 50, 59, 66, 126, 143, 154, 203; '60s Left, 131
Lenin, V. I., 218
Leone, Sergio, 145, 147, 152–54; *A Fistful of Dollars*, 145; *For a Few Dollars More*, 145; *The Good, the Bad, & the Ugly*, 145; *Once Upon a Time in the West*, **145–55**
Lewis, C. S., 176

liberalism & liberals, 15, 21, 53, 66, 70, 95, 97, 107, 109, **114–16**, 129, **176–77**, 194, 198, 211, 213; anti-, 66, 108–109, **114–15**, 194, 198
lies, **49–50**, 54, 56, 114, 128, 187, **190–93**
life force, 11–12, 66, 168
Lincoln, Abraham, 3
Linkola, Pentti, 25
Locke, John, 154, 176, 182
love, 10, **13–14**, 16, 20, **28–30**, 56, 73, 77–78, 110, 112, 115, 123, 128, 184, 198, 199, **216–17**; tough, 28, 65
Lovecraftian plot devices, 208
loyalty, 18, 123, 126, 200
Lucas, George, 93, 201; *Attack of the Clones*, 201; *Star Wars*, 201
Lumet, Sydney, 130, 135, 144; *Network*, 61, **130–44**
Lynch, David, 1, 3, 5, 12, 15–16; *Blue Velvet*, **1–16**; *Dune*, 16; *The Elephant Man*, 16; *Eraserhead*, 9, 12, 16; *Twin Peaks*, 2, 3, 4, 5, 14; *Wild at Heart*, 8; *Mulholland Drive*, 5

M

MacLaughlin, Kyle, 1
A Man for All Seasons, 54

The Man Who Shot Liberty Valance, **107–16**, 197
Manicheanism, 4
mankind, 40, 57, 61, 141, 177, 215–16
manliness, 108, 111
Männerbünd(e), 62, **64–67**, 149, 152
Mao Tse-Tung, 218
marriage, 14, 72, 79, 100, 104
Martin, Strother, 107
Marvin, Lee, 109
Marx, Karl, 140, 175
Marxism & Marxists, 96, 126, 131, 140, 142–43, 154, 176, 206
masochism, 83, 91, 118, 120–21; female, 15; see also: sadomasochism
masses (the), 22, 57
master-slave dialectic, 20, 175
Mastroianni, Marcello, 72
materialism & materialists, 57, 122, 126, 159, 176; bourgeois, 105; values, 32–33
McKenna, Siobhán, 56
Mephistopheles, 139
mercy, 92, 212; see also: compassion
middle-class, 104; rising, 96, 98; upper, 118; see also: bourgeoisie
Midjord, Frodi, 145
Mifune, Toshiro, 183, 185

Miles, Vera, 109, 201
Miller, Frank, 215
Minutemen (1940s costumed vigilantes), 204–205, 209, 210; see also: Watchmen (1970s costumed vigilantes)
Minutemen, 204
miscegenation, 200
Mishima, Yukio, **117–29**; works: *Confessions of a Mask*, 120; *The Decay of the Angel*, 127; *Forbidden Colors*, 122; *Kyoko's House*, 118, 121–22, 127; *My Friend Hitler*, 126; *Patriotism*, 123–24; *Runaway Horses*, 118, 127; *Sun & Steel*, 125; *The Sea of Fertility*, 124; *The Temple of the Golden Pavilion*, 118–21, 127; *The Way of the Samurai*, 125; see also: *Mishima: A Life in Four Chapters*
Mishima: A Life in Four Chapters, **117–27**; see also: Mishima, Yukio
Miyagawa, Kazuo, 183
Modernism (architecture), 74
modernization, 126
modes of life, animal, 169; human, 169
money as contemptible, 27–33; 46–47, 61, 92,

101, 134, 136, 139, 142, 146–47, 149, 151, 153, 161, 171, 173, 177–78, 181, 195–96, 205
Monument Valley, 90, 194
Moore, Alan, 203, 215
moral absolutism, 213
moral order (objective), 183–84
moral principles, 16, 18
More, Sir Thomas, 58
Morelli, Rina, 96
Morita, Masakatsu, 126
Morricone, Ennio, 148, 152
mortality, 29, 65, 102; see also: death
Moses, 85, 88
The Mosquito Coast, 117
Muhammed, 85
Mulholland Drive, 5
multiculturalism, 121, 166–67, 169
murder videos, 131
Murphy, Cillian, 23, 39
Murray, General Sir Archibald James, 83
Mussolini, Benito, 126
My Friend Hitler, 125–26
myth(s), 163, 194, 198, 216
myth-making, 89–90

N

narcissism, 121, 127, 182; female, 15
national populism & populists, 96, **104–105**, 138; see also: national populism
National Socialism (German), 215; see also: Nazis
nationalism & nationalists, 82, 86–87, 89, 139, 141, 143; Arab, 89; Italian, 95, 97; Japanese, 126; see also: White Nationalism & Nationalists
nature, 15, 20, 24–25, 75, 80, 90, 110, 114–15, 119, 153, 155, 165, 173–75, 196; animal, 175; human, 15–16, 61, 167, 175; primal forces of, 139; see also: state of nature
Nazis, 66, 210, 211, 215, 218; see also: National Socialism
Neeson, Liam, 23, 24, 25, 40
Network, 61, 81, **130–44**
New York City, 204, 206, 208, 215
Ni Ni-Roku Incident, 123, 124
Nietzsche, Friedrich, 27, 61, 66, 69, 119
nigger (spiritual slave), 177–78, 181; see also: slavery, spiritual
nihilism & nihilists, 12, 50, 53, 78–79, 156, 181; comic, 156; youthful, 120

Ninchi, Annibale, 76
Nineteen Eighty-Four, 59
Nixon, Richard, 203, 204, 206
Nobel Prize for Literature, 53
Noël, Magale, 76
Nolan, Christopher, 23, 25, 27, 38, 50–51, 128–29; *Batman Begins*, **23–26**, 29, 38, 39–40, 43; *The Dark Knight Rises*, **38–50**; *The Dark Knight*, **26–38**, 39, 41–42, 44–46, 128
Norton, Edward, 62
nostalgia, 164, 214
nuclear war, 76, 78, 206, 208–209, 213, 218

O
O'Brien, Edmund, 111
O'Conner, Flannery, 80
O'Meara, James, 42
O'Toole, Peter, 55, 81, 83
Obama, Barack, 111
obedience, 18
Obsession, 117
Odysseus, 197
Oldman, Gary, 23, 39
oligarchy & oligarchs, 72, 96, 101, **104–105**
Once Upon a Time in the West, **145–55**
Ontario, 5
Orbison, Roy, 9, 15
Orwell, George, 59
Oscar (Academy Award), 17, 21–22, 52, 71, 130
Ottoman Empire, 81, 83

P
pacifists, 217, 218
paganism, 74, 102, 197
Palahniuk, Chuck, 66, 67
Palme d'Or, 71
A Passage to India (David Lean film), 17, 21
Pasternak, Boris, 52–54, 55
Patriotism, 123–24, 127
patriotism, 18, 141; "Patriotism" (story by Mishima), 123–24, 133
peace, 70, 87, 122, 124, 125, 141, 195–97, 202
Persian Empire, 87
Petrie, Flinders, 82
pettiness, 57, 92
Phaeton, 92
physiognomy, 118–19
piercing, 169–70
Pitt, Brad, 63
Planet of the Apes, 17
Plato, 61, 90, 96, 135, 156–57, 164, 182, 182; Allegory of the Cave, 90, 135; Platonism, 102; *The Republic*, 96, 156–57
playfulness, 166–68
plebiscites, 96, 98, 100
Plummer, Amanda, 157
Pointer, Priscilla, 3
political philosophy, 15, 82, 84, 141, 153
populism & populists, 66,

131, 139; see also: national populism
postmodernism, 164, 166, 168, 176, 181
Potlatch, 33
Powell, Michael, 55
pride, 18, 21, 111, 119, 147, 154, 171, **177–81**
Princeton University, 23
private life, 49, 57–58, 96, 213
progress, 24, 25, 38, 50, 78, 109, 114, 146–47
propaganda, 38, 130, 134, 142
psychology, 23–24, 183, 213
Pulp Fiction, 61, **156–82**

Q
quantity vs. quality, 218
Quinn, Anthony, 88

R
racism, 198–99
Raging Bull, 117
Rains, Claude, 81
Rameses II, 217
Rashomon, 81, **183–93**
rationalists, 165
Ravel, Maurice, 183
Ray, Man, 165
reaction (political), 72, 78, 103
The Red Shoes, 55
redemption, 21, 65
Reggiani, Serge, 99
relativism, 184, 193
Requiem for a Dream (film), 166
ressentiment, 212–13
Revolution (French), 15
Revolution (Russian), 54, 56–57
Rhames, Ving, 157
Richardson, Ralph, 56
Rightism, 60, 66, 154–55, 203; far-Right, 203; see also: conservatism
Right-wing, 203, 209, 213; archetypes, 206, 218; cinema, 109; ideas, 130–31; comic book, 218; politics, 122, 127, 210; students, 122, 124; superheroes, 210; right-wingers, 222, 213
Rilke, Rainer Maria, 169; "Archaic Bust of Apollo," 169
Rio Grande, 108
Risorgimento, 95, 97, 101
Robards, Jason, 148, 152
Röhm, Ernst, 126
Rome (19th century), 96, 101
Rome (ancient), 40
Rome (postwar), 72, 72, 74, 76, 77, 78
Rossellini, Isabella, 4
Rota, Nino, 71, 105
Roth, Tim, 157
Rousseau, Jean-Jacques, 16
rule of law, 84
Russia, 20, 52, 55, 57; see also: USSR
Ryan's Daughter, 17

S

Sade, Marquis de, 16
sadism, 10, 15, 91, 120, 121, 147, 150, 159, 180, 211; sadomasochism, 1, 11, 121, 179
Saint Sebastian, 120
Salina, 95; prince of, 96–99, 102, 103, 104
Samurai, 69, 118, 120, 123, **124–27**, 129, 180, 182; character in *Rashomon*, 184–90, 192
satire, 130, 203
Saudi Arabia, 138, 139, 141
Savitri Devi, 26, 129; *Impeachment of Man*, 129
scapegoat, 54, 86, 209, 216
Schmitt, Carl, 86, 108–109
Schrader, Paul, 117–18, 120–22, 124, 127, 199; *American Gigolo*, 117; *Auto Focus*, 117; *Bringing Out the Dead*, 117; *Cat People* (remake), 117; *The Last Temptation of Christ*, 117; *Mishima: A Life in Four Chapters*, **117–29**; *Taxi Driver*, 199
Scorsese, Martin, 117; *Gangs of New York*, 37; *Raging Bull*, 117; *Taxi Driver*, 37, 117; *The Last Temptation of Christ*, 117
Scorsese, Martin, 199
The Searchers (film), 90, **194–202**
The Searchers (novel), 199
Second World War, 17, 59, 104, 118, 123, 204, 215
self, 45; bourgeois, 64
self-determination (national), 87
self-esteem, 133
self-improvement, 64; self-destruction, 40, 64
self-indulgence, 115, 141, 165, 170
selfishness, 191–93
self-mythologizing, 82
seppuku, 126
seriousness, 156, 167–68
Sermon on the Mount, 119
Serrano, Miguel, 26
The Seven Pillars of Wisdom, 81, 93
sexual impotence, 8, 10, 214
sexuality, 1, 8, 91
Shakespeare, 18, 115
shame, 186–87, 188, 190, 192
Sharif, Omar, 55, 81, 83, 84
Shatner, William, 39
She Wore a Yellow Ribbon (1949), 108
Shōda, Michiko, 121
Sicily, 95, 100, 104
siddhis, 44
slave morality, 38, 119
slave(s), **19–21**, 56, 61, 63,

73, 119; morality, 38, 47; natural, 128, 174–77
slavery, 32, 56; spiritual, 128, 178; see also: nigger (spiritual slave)
Snyder, Zack, 27, 203–204, 214–15; 300, 215; *Watchmen*, 27, **203–18**
social climbing, 99
social contract, 114, 194
society, bourgeois, 21, 64; modern, 45, 64, 128
Sophocles, 18
soul, 1, 44, 50, 61, 70, 102, 141, 156, 162–63, 168–69, 174, 177, 180, 182
The Sound of Music, 52
Soviet Union (USSR), 53, 207, 208; see also: Russia
Sowell, Thomas, 136
spiritual types, 156–57; desire-driven man, 156, 157, **163–66**, 182; honor-driven man, 157, **171–73**, **177–80**, 182; spiritual man, 157, **158–63**, 182
spirituality, 1, 12, 24, 33, 43–45, 47, 94, 105, 162; aims, 47; aristocrat, 128; basis, 181; bourgeois, 147; enthusiasm, 179; initiation, 41; Islamic, 176; man, **158–63**, 182; modern, 181; path, 24, 157; slavery, 128, 175,

177; transformation, 47; values, 105, 119, 156; types, 156–57; quest, 162; void of postwar Japan, 122–23; war, 58; warrior, 47
SS (*Schutzstaffel*), 126
Stagecoach, 107
Star Wars, 201
state of nature, 110, 114–15, 153, 196; see also: nature
Steiger, Rod, 56
Stewart, James, 107, 108, 110
Stockwell, Dean, 8
Stolz, Eric, 163
Stoppa, Paolo, 98
Straight, Beatrice, 130
Strode, Woody, 107
subjectivity vs. objectivity, 183–84
Sugiyama, Yoko, 120
suicide, 19–20, 49, **122–27**, 191
Sun & Steel, 125
superhero movies, 27, 203
superheroes, 129, 204–205, 210, 211, 213, 214
superman (comic book character), 24–25, 214
superman (Nietzschean), 24–25, 41, 43–44, 45, 51, 205, 215, **217–18**
supernatural, 12, **15–16**
supervillains, 27, 207, 210
Switzerland, 138
Symbionese Liberation

Army, 142
symbols, 43, 216; status symbols, 177

T
Tarantino, Quentin, 156, 157, 160, 161, 163, 181, 182; *Django Unchained*, 181n2; *Inglourious Basterds*, 181n2; *Kill Bill: Vol. 1*, 163, 181n2; *Pulp Fiction*, 61, **156–82**
Tate-LaBianca murders, 15
Tatenokai (Shield Society), 126
tattooing, 170
Taxi Driver, 37, 117, 199
Taylor, Peter, 22
technology, 43, 46, 205, 214
Tenchu, 124
Terror (French), 15
Terror (political), 56, 110, 131, 142
Terror (Red), 54
Texas, 194, 196, 197, 201
Texas Rangers, 195, 196, 201
theocracy, 182
theory vs. practice, 57–58
Third Reich, 210, 215
Thomas, Lowell, 89
thumos, 61, 70
Thurman, Uma, 163
Tokugawa Shogunate, 124–25
Traditionalism & Traditionalists, 39, 44–45, 181, 218; Radical, 50–51; weaponized, 26, 38, 129; see also: history, Traditionalist theory of
Transcendental Meditation, 12
transvaluation, 27, 30–32, 119
Travolta, John, 156
tribalism, 86
Tristan und Isolde, 124
Triumph of the Will, 117
Trump, Donald, 132
Turks, 82, 86, 90, 91, 92
Twelve Step programs, 65; moment of clarity, 65, 161, 170
Twin Peaks, 2, 3, 4, 5, 14

U
Übermensch, 24, 41; see also: superman (Nietzschean)
Unabomber, 27, 66
unconscious, the, 1
underworld, 1, 3, 10, 23
US Constitution, 108
utilitarianism, 217

V
values, 27, 64, 125, 128; archaic, 103, 153; aristocratic, 119; bourgeois, 64; Christian, 119; Leftist, 50; materialist, 105,

156; origin of, 119; spiritual, 105, 119, 156
Van Cleef, Lee, 109
Vedanta, 44
Venice International Film Festival, 183
Vertigo, 81
Vinton, Bobby, 2
virtues, 18, 33, 90, 96, 98, 103, 106, 165
Visconti, Luchino, **95–98**, 102; *The Leopard*, **95–106**
Vishnu, 216
vitality, 30, 31, 47, 154; barbaric, 148; masculine, 66; vitalism, 66

W

Walken, Christopher, 171
Warfield, Marlene, 130
Watanabe, Ken, 23
Watchmen (1970s costumed vigilantes), 205–207; see also: Minutemen (1940s costumed vigilantes)
Watchmen (film), 27, **203–18**
Watchmen (graphic novel), **203–204**, 205, 206, **208–209**, **214–15**, 217
Wayne, John, 107, 109, 195
Weathermen, 15
Weir, Peter, 117; *Mosquito Coast*, 117

West (the), 108, 110, 113, 114, 146
West, Adam, 23
Western (genre), 153
White House, 138
White Nationalism & Nationalists, 50–51; see also: nationalism & nationalists
white people, 18
wholesomeness, 2
Wild at Heart, 8
Willis, Bruce, 156
will-to-power, 118–19, 168
Wilson, Michael, 22, 54, 81
Woolley, Leonard, 82
women, 21, 55, **67–68**, 73, 78, 111, 119, 147, 188, 189, 198, 204, 216; Oriental vs. Occidental, 75
worldview, 167–69; see also: culture(s)

X

Xenophon, 86–87

Y

Yamamoto, Tsunetomo, 125
Yatō, Tamotsu, 120
Young, Freddie, 52

Z

Zeitgeist, 36
Zen, 69
Zimmer, Hans, 39

About the Author

Trevor Lynch is a pen name of Greg Johnson, Ph.D., Editor-in-Chief of Counter-Currents Publishing and its webzine (http://www.counter-currents.com/).

He is the author of twenty-two books (all published by Counter-Currents, unless otherwise noted): *Confessions of a Reluctant Hater* (2010; 2016), *Trevor Lynch's White Nationalist Guide to the Movies* (2012), *New Right vs. Old Right* (2013), *Son of Trevor Lynch's White Nationalist Guide to the Movies* (2015), *Truth, Justice, & a Nice White Country* (2015), *In Defense of Prejudice* (2017), *You Asked for It: Selected Interviews*, vol. 1 (2017), *The White Nationalist Manifesto* (2018), *Toward a New Nationalism* (2019), *Return of the Son of Trevor Lynch's CENSORED Guide to the Movies* (2019), *From Plato to Postmodernism* (2019), *It's Okay to Be White: The Best of Greg Johnson* (Ministry of Truth, 2020), *Graduate School with Heidegger* (2020), *Here's the Thing: Selected Interviews*, vol. 2 (2020), *Trevor Lynch: Part Four of the Trilogy* (2020), *White Identity Politics* (2020), *The Year America Died* (2021), *Trevor Lynch's Classics of Right-Wing Cinema* (2022), *The Trial of Socrates* (2023), *Against Imperialism* (2023), *Novel Takes: Essays on Literature* (2024), and the present volume.

He is editor of *North American New Right*, vol. 1 (2012); *North American New Right*, vol. 2 (2017); *The Alternative Right* (2018); Francis Parkey Yockey's *Imperium* (Centennial Edition Publishing, 2024) and *The Enemy of Europe* (Centennial Edition Publishing, 2022); Julius Evola's *East & West* (with Collin Cleary, 2018); and other books by Alain de Benoist, Collin Cleary, Kerry Bolton, Jonathan Bowden, and Savitri Devi.

www.ingramcontent.com/pod-product-compliance
Lightning Source LLC
Chambersburg PA
CBHW022057160426
43198CB00008B/260